W9-BSX-195

Stock Cars

Stock Cars

By Dr. John Craft

Lowe & B. Hould
Publishers

This edition published in 2002 by Lowe & B. Hould Publishers, an imprint of Borders, Inc., 515 East Liberty, Ann Arbor, MI 48104. Lowe & B. Hould Publishers is a trademark of Borders Properties, Inc.

Previously published in 1997, 1999, and 2000 by MBI Publishing Company, Galtier Plaza, Suite 200, 380 Jackson Street, St. Paul, MN 55101-3885 USA

MBI Publishing Company books are also available at discounts in bulk quantity for industrial or sales-promotional use. For details write to Special Sales Manager at Motorbooks International Wholesalers & Distributors, Galtier Plaza, Suite 200, 380 Jackson Street, St. Paul, MN 55101-3885 USA. Library of Congress Cataloging-in-Publication Data Available

ISBN 0-681-87889-4

On the front cover: Dale Earnhardt's Chevy Lumina and Kyle Petty's Pontiac Grand Prix lead the pack around the turn at the 1993 Daytona 500.

On the back cover: *Top:* During the "Aero War" years of 1969 to 1971, the Chrysler Motor Company designed their Dodge Daytonas with high-banked, superspeedway action in mind. A bunch are seen here racing at Daytona in 1970.

Bottom: After spending two seasons in a Ford, Dale Earnhardt returned to the Chevy stable in a Monte Carlo. Here Earnhardt's number 3 does battle with Bill Elliott's Ford Thunderbird.

Printed in China

Contents

Chevy Stock Cars

Ford, Lincoln & Mercury Stock Cars

Chrysler, Plymouth & Dodge Stock Cars

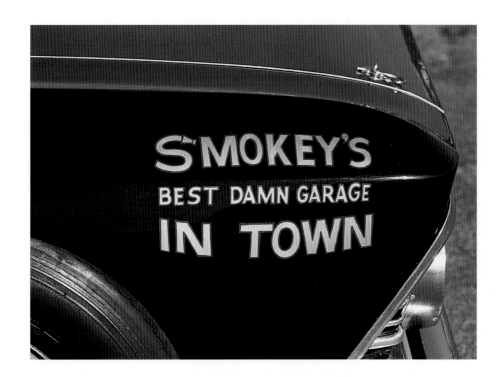

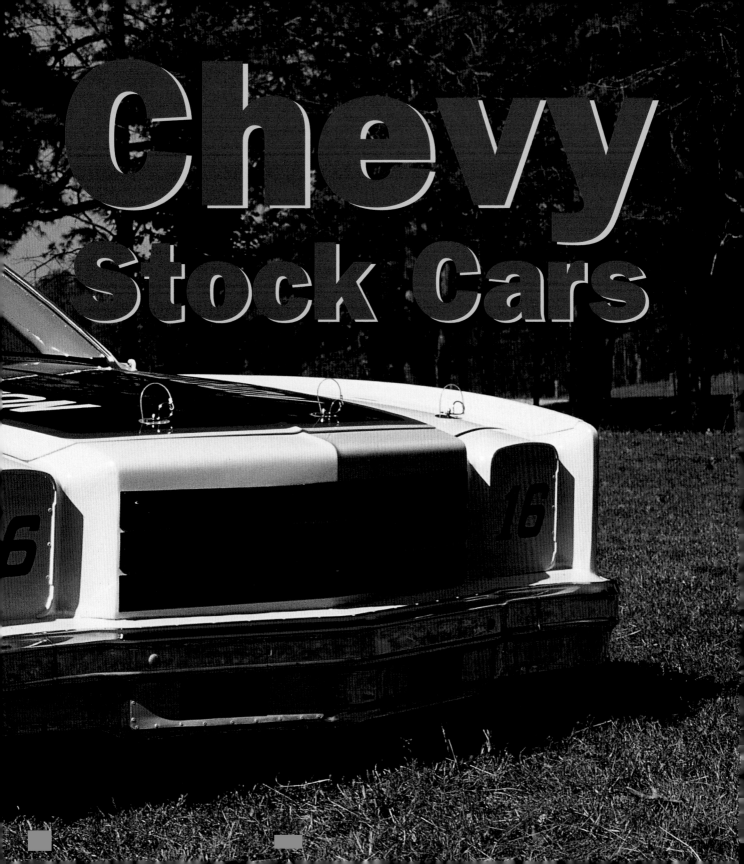

Chapter 1

THE 1950s
First Blood for the General

General Motors (GM) and Chevrolet have held a dominant position in stock car racing circles for so long that many think it has always been this way. And that's very easy to understand when one considers that since the very first season of Winston Cup (formerly Grand National) competition, the "General's" cars have visited victory lane more than 750 times. Competition cars of the Bow Tie persuasion have fared best of all over the first 50 years of National Association for Stock Car Auto Racing (NASCAR) fender-rubbin', accounting for more than 450 of those wins. Pontiac drivers have racked up more than 120 stock car trophies, and their Oldsmobile counterparts 116 more. Buick stockers round out the tally with 65 circle track triumphs. But GM drivers didn't always have a lock on stock car glory; in fact, it took Chevy drivers the best part of a decade to score their first Grand National (GN) win.

Look closely, this probably was your father's Oldsmobile. Especially if he happened to be a NASCAR race car driver in 1950. Rocket 88s like the one Buck Baker drove in the early 1950s were the cars to beat at the time. *Mike Slade*

1949 and 1950:
Rocket 88s Roar to Life

The racing world was a far different place in 1949 (when Big Bill France first cooked up the NASCAR series) than it is today. As originally conceived, for example, the series was based on American-built sedans that were required to be unchanged in any way from showroom trim. France, in fact, called NASCAR's top division the "Strictly stock series." And that name, and the restrictions it carried with it, was the reason for Chevrolet's initial lack of racing success. Though a 1948 Chevy had paced the Indy 500 the year before the NASCAR series was formed, in strictly stock trim a sleepy little 90-horsepower stovebolt six cylinder was anything but a race-ready powerplant. That probably explains the total absence of Chevrolets on the starting grid at the very first NASCAR race in Charlotte in June 1949.

But that didn't mean that General Motors drivers had to sit on the sidelines during that first season of competition. Not by a long shot. In fact, then, as now, some of the fastest cars on the starting grid at the old Charlotte fairgrounds had genuine GM pedigrees. In 1949 those cars were literally your father's

Big Bill France originally called his premier racing division the strictly stock series. And one look into the cockpit of Buck Baker's 1950 Rocket 88 Olds is all it takes to understand why. Things were disconcertingly stock.

The secret to the Rocket 88's success was a free-revving, 303-cubic-inch, overhead-valve, small-block engine. Though modest in performance by modern standards, a Rocket 88 engine struck fear into the hearts of all who had to race against it.

Oldsmobile. Olds ad flacks called the cars in question Rocket 88s, and, for once, Madison Avenue hype actually came pretty close to the truth. The cars truly were rocket ships.

The secret of the cars' speed was the all-new overhead valve-equipped (big news in the late Cretaceous), 303-cubic-inch V-8 engines that Olds introduced in 1949. Though rated at a mere 202 horsepower, the all-new engine had most of its late 1940s rivals covered in the "motorvation" department, even when installed in a not-so-svelte 3,455-pound Olds 88 with a full-frame chassis.

Race number one in NASCAR history featured no fewer than six Rocket 88 drivers. In that number were future series stars Tim Flock and Red Byron. Byron was an Atlanta-based mechanic who had built his reputation by souping up both 'shine cars and the revenuer pursuit vehicles that nightly played cat and mouse on the "thunder roads" of the rural Southland. Flock sprang from the driving side of the 'shine business having learned the finer points of nocturnal high-speed driving (that is, fleeing and attempting to elude) from his two older 'shine-hauling brothers, Bob and Fonty.

Though neither Byron nor Flock finished first that day in Charlotte (Byron came closest with a third-place berth), it didn't take long for a GM-badged comp car to visit victory lane. Not long at all, in fact. Oldsmobile/General Motors win number one came in the second race of the inaugural 1949 season in July. That particular race took place in a sleepy little Florida beach town called Daytona that would soon figure large in stock car racers' aspirations everywhere.

As longtime NASCAR fans recall, that first "Cup" race took place on a 4.15-mile-long beach and road course that incorporated equal stretches of paved portions of Highway A1A and white sandy (low tide!) beach straightaways connected by two fairly tight berm-flanked turns. Qualification in those days did not (as today) consist of hot laps around the track, but rather involved measured speed runs down the beach and back. When the sand had settled, Gober Sosbee's Rocket 88 qualified fastest overall with Red Byron's Olds just a few ticks of the stopwatch slower.

The race itself took 2 hours, 33 minutes to complete and turned out to be a Rocket 88 romp. Sosbee and Byron battled for the lead much of the event until Byron put him away for good on lap 34. Oldsmobile drivers Tim Flock, Frank "Rebel" Mundy, and Joe Littlejohn followed Byron's #22 across the line to make the finish a sweep for the Olds division. It wouldn't be the last time that a #22 General Motor's stocker crossed the finish line first at the race in Daytona.

All told, Oldsmobiles scored five wins in the eight-race 1949 Strictly Stock season. Byron's two victories and four top-five finishes earned him the modest sum of $5,800 and the season championship. Had there been a manufacturer's championship in 1949, Byron would have claimed that for the Olds division also.

The secret to the Rocket 88's success was a free-revving, 303-cubic-inch, overhead-valve, small-block engine. Though modest in performance by modern standards, a Rocket 88 engine struck fear into the hearts of all who had to race against it.

Bill Blair won the 1953 Daytona Beach race in a block-long Oldsmobile just like this one. He had the good fortune that day to be in the right place at the right time when race leader Fonty Flock's Rocket 88 ran out of gas on the last lap. Blair also had the good fortune to be driving a 135-horsepower Olds 88. A replica of Blair's car is currently on display at the North Carolina Auto Racing Hall of Fame in Mooresville.

Bill Rexford and two soon-to-be-famous fellows named Curtis Morton Turner and Glenn "Fireball" Roberts picked up the Oldsmobile banner and ran with it the very next season. Though Turner ultimately scored more 88 wins than Rexford, the NASCAR points system that, even then, rewarded consistency more than wins made Rexford the second series champ. Roberts also finished ahead of Turner in the points chase, though he only had one "X" in the win column. Both Roberts and Turner would go on to visit victory lane many more times in the upcoming Grand National seasons.

1951–1954: Other Manufacturers Meet the Challenge

The wins scored by Olds drivers in 1949 and 1950 on the NASCAR circuit did not go

unnoticed. Sportier lights in the buying public quickly recognized the performance potential of the Rocket 88 car line and began to show up in Olds showrooms in increasing numbers. That fact made an impact in Detroit. With an eye toward bolstering their own sales, sales types at Hudson decided to steal some of the glory being grabbed up by Rocket 88 drivers on the NASCAR tour. When it was determined that the flat head sixes under the hoods of race Hornets weren't up to the task of besting Olds' small-block overhead valve (OHV) V-8s, Hudson engineers were ordered to whip up some go-fast add-ons designed specifically for stock car competition. Hornet teams were able to skirt the NASCAR rules book by calling the performance hardware "export" equipment, causing tech inspectors to look the other way at teardown time. The end result was a much faster Hudson Hornet stock car that was able to battle with the best of the Olds 88 drivers.

Brothers Tim, Bob, and Fonty Flock joined forces to carry on Olds' winning ways, and as a result Rocket 88s visited victory lane circa 1951 many more times (20, in fact). But Herb Thomas' 7 wins and 15 top-five Hudson finishes (and the "export" bits and pieces under his hood) carried the day and the season championship. Fonty Flock finished up the year with 8 Oldsmobile-backed wins and was second in the points chase.

Hudson engineers redoubled their "export" engine component production for 1952. That act, coupled with the generous salaries offered to drivers by Hudson's now factory-backed racing effort, lured a number of top drivers (including Tim Flock) into the Hornet camp. As a result, the next four seasons were a struggle for General Motors drivers generally and Olds drivers in particular. One bright spot came in September of 1952 when Fonty Flock notched the first GM Southern 500 win in his Air Lift Special Rocket 88. Bill Blair bested all comers at the 1953 beach race in an Oldsmobile, and Buck Baker notched a second Southern 500 win for Olds at Darlington the same year. But those wins were the exception to the rule for the once all-conquering Rocket 88s. And things only got worse when Chrysler got into the NASCAR game.

1955: Overhead-Valve V-8s Save the Day

While Hudson and Chrysler teams were tearing up the Grand National tour during the mid-1950s, interesting things were going on behind the scenes at the various General Motors divisions. Buick engineers were hard at work making the straight eight a thing of the past. As it happens, Chevrolet engine and foundry folks were pursuing that same goal. And so, too, were their counterparts in the

The control cabin in Blair's Olds featured a bench seat (racing buckets were years away in 1953) and a not-so-sporty column shifter. The bus-sized wheel no doubt made navigating the sandy beach course at Daytona less of a chore.

Don't look for headers, four-barrel carburetors, or other modern go-fast goodies under the hood of Blair's 88. Nonetheless, the lumbering behemoth had what it took to win on Daytona's fabled beach course.

Mid-1950s Oldsmobiles were both fast and good looking, even when festooned with dirt-deflecting front screens like the one pictured here on driver Ed Negre's 1956 Rocket 88. *JDC Collection*

Pontiac division. As was the custom in the General's ranks in those days, engineers in the various divisions all worked from their own clean sheets. The days of the corporate small block were still—blissfully—decades in the future. As a result, by the end of the decade the tranquility of the Southland was regularly disrupted (on race days, that is) by the basso-profundo bark of four very different General Motors OHV V-8s. And before the nifty fifties and poodle skirts had both worn out their welcome, the world-changing Chevrolet small-block engine had exploded onto the motorsports scene.

In 1955, Chevrolet's "mouse" motor made its debut on both the showroom floor and starting grids all across the country. Work on the all-new engine commenced with the installation of Edward Nicholas Cole as manufacturing manager of the Chevrolet division. Cole's arrival on the scene coincided with the initial planning for the 1955 model year. A major part of the plan for the cars slated to take a bow that year was the development of an all-new OHV V-8 engine. Cole knew from the outset that if Chevrolet was going to have a shot at the new youth performance market, the division was going to have to develop an engine that would transform Chevy's reputation for building trustworthy but tepid transportation.

Cole tapped Ed Kelley and Harry Barr to design the new engine, and their basic design proved to be so successful that it is still in use today—both on and off the track. Working with a set of design parameters that included five main bearing journals and a desired displacement of 265 cubic inches, Kelley and Barr put pen to drafting paper and set to work. In final form the new engine was 30 percent more powerful than the sleepy little six cylinder it replaced while at the same time weighing a full 40 pounds less than the old stovebolt. PR flacks called the new 8.0:1 compression ratio mill the "Turbo-Fire" 265, and it boasted 162 horsepower when topped with a two-barrel carburetor. Kelley and Barr upped that figure to 180 before the end of the 1955 production year with the addition of a "Power Pack" option package consisting of dual exhausts and a single Carter WCFB four-barrel fuel mixer.

The new body style that the free-revving little small block was destined to serve duty in was also radically redesigned for 1955. There's little doubt today that Chevy's styling efforts that year rate right up there with the best designs of any car manufacturer anywhere at any time. But looks don't win races. Redesigned and greatly stiffened chassis, lighter ball-joint-equipped suspension components, and an 18 percent overall reduction in weight do. And

NASCAR tech inspectors circa 1955 hard at work. Unfortunately, their post-race labors after the 1955 beach race in Daytona took away Fireball Roberts' Buick win. Note the oh-so-racy white walls on Fireball's Fish Carburetor-backed car. *JDC Collection*

Buck Baker became Chevrolet's first National Driving Champion in 1957. He continued to campaign Bow Tie-based race cars like this #87 ragtop into the 1960s. *JDC Collection*

Chevy's new 150 and 210 sedans sported all those desirable traits. In due course, that translated into NASCAR victories.

Stock car win number one for Chevrolet and its all-new small-block engine came in March 1955 on a half-mile dirt track in Columbia, South Carolina. Fonty Flock was driving a #14 150 sedan for car owner Frank Christian that day and began the race from the back of the pack. Brother Tim started at the head of the field in his Kiekhaeffer-prepared Chrysler 300 and seemed destined to use his car's 300 horsepower to dominate the event. But, when the dust settled, it was older brother Fonty who got to kiss the pretty girl. That kiss and the $1,000 in prize money Fonty earned were the first sweet tastes of racing victory for Chevrolet drivers. Cars of the Bow Tie persuasion have been a regular fixture in winners' circles all across the country ever since.

Legendary mechanic and car builder Henry "Smokey" Yunick proved that Fonty Flock's first Chevrolet victory was no fluke seven months later in the Southern 500 at Darling-

ton. The fifth running of the Southern 500 had all the ingredients of a Hollywood thriller (and one decidedly better written than Tom Cruise's less-than-realistic *Days of Thunder*). The cast of players included crusty and conniving master mechanic Smokey Yunick. Driver Herb Thomas, who had nearly been killed in a racing accident four months earlier, played the sympathetic lead. Drama was provided by Thomas' hospital bed prediction that he would bounce back from his crash in Charlotte to win a third Southern 500. Outboard motor magnate Karl Kiekhaeffer and his all-conquering fleet of Chrysler 300s (cars that had been rolling over the competition like Hitler took France) played the heavy. The character actor role was filled by Indy champ Mauri Rose, who at Smokey's behest located a number of sets of special sports car tires that Firestone had created for road race work at LeMans. The underdog role was played by Yunick's brand-new little small-block-powered "Motoramic" 150 sedan. Down on power to Kiekhaeffer's great white fleet of 300-plus horsepower

The interior of Phil Reed's 1959 Impala.

Fonty Flock honed his driving skills in the north Georgia hills hauling liquid freight by moonlight. He scored Chevrolet's first win when he put his abilities to use in the Grand National ranks at Columbia, South Carolina. *Daytona Racing Archives*

Chryslers and unproven as the new kid on the block, Smokey's 1955 Chevy had to rely on brains rather than brawn to reach victory lane.

When race day dawned, Darlington was packed to the rafters with the Southern 500's first sell-out crowd of more than 50,000 spectators. As expected, when the green flag fell, Thomas' #92 Chevy was unable to claw its way to the front of the 69-car field on horsepower alone. In fact, Tim and Fonty Flock's Chrysler 300s dominated the first hundred-odd laps of the event. Until, that is, their heavier and faster cars started encountering tire trouble. By Smokey's count there were 680 blown tires during the running of the

1955 Southern 500, and most of those were suffered by cars other than Herb Thomas' little Chevy. By race's end, the special road race tires that Rose had salvaged from an Akron, Ohio, junkyard had proven to be worth their weight in gold. With Kiekhaeffer's cars far in arrears, the race was decided between Thomas' Chevy and "Little" Joe Weatherly's #9 Ford. When Little Joe's left front rim failed on lap 317, the resulting contact with the outside wall ended both a 129-lap stint in the lead and any chance of beating Thomas for the win. This would not be the last time that a Ford and a Chevrolet battled it out for stock car glory on the NASCAR tour.

In 1955 GM's Buick division also scored its first Grand National wins. The very first Buick triumph came (and went) at the Daytona Beach race in February. Rising star and hometown boy Glenn "Fireball" Roberts used his 255-horsepower Roadmaster to qualify fourth for the race and then went on to lead every lap of the 160-mile race to score what appeared to be Buick's first GN win. Unfortunately, a post-race teardown revealed pushrods that had been turned down 16/100ths of an inch. That discovery led to Fireball's disqualification 24 hours after he'd been declared the winner.

It was left to future champion Buck Baker to score Buick's first official win three months later at a 100-mile dirt track race at Charlotte Speedway. Herb Thomas claimed win number two for Buick in a Smokey Yunick car at Raleigh one month before his Southern 500 win at Darlington. As things turned out, those

Lee Petty started 17 convertible races in his "zipper" top Olds during the 1957 season. The cars (like other convertible comp cars of the day) were referred to as zipper tops because they'd race as ragtops one day and as hardtops the next. Rocket 88 Oldsmobiles were fast in both categories. *JDC Collection*

Buick drivers were around for the very first race of the all-new NASCAR series in 1949. By the mid-1950s, the Buicks were some of the fastest cars on the tour. Here, Buick pilot Pete Yow is seen dodging ruts in the 1956 beach race at Daytona. *Daytona Racing Archives*

Though Chevrolet introduced the 348-cubic-inch, big-block "W" engine in 1958, most Bow Tie racers chose to stick with their tried-and-true small-block 283s that year. It was a different story by 1960 when big blocks like the one in Junior Johnson's Kennel Club Special powered ahead and replaced the small block in Chevy racers' hearts.

two wins would be the last scored by a Buick racer in the Grand National division for 26 years. (But when Buick would eventually return to the winner's circle in 1981, it would do so with a vengeance.)

1956: Chrysler Rampage

Nineteen fifty-six dashed the hopes of GM racers everywhere (and just about everybody else too). Kiekhaeffer's Chryslers went on a tear that season and won nearly every race they entered. Surprisingly, at season's end, Kiekhaeffer suddenly closed up shop and left racing for good after winning two back-to-back Grand National championships.

Chevrolet got serious about stock car racing in the fall of 1956 by setting up the Southeastern Engineering Development Company (SEDCO) in Atlanta. SEDCO was devoted exclusively to running Bow Tie stock car operations. Once it was up and running, Chevy racers' fortunes began to improve.

When the 1957 season got under way, for the first time in two seasons all bets were off, and just about anybody had a chance to win.

1957: AMA Ban Silences Strong Ford Competition

Chevrolet took steps to make sure that more than a few of those "anybodys" were Bow Tie-mounted drivers by introducing a new and improved (read—bigger and more powerful) version of the small-block engine. Following the time-honored maxim that bigger is better, Chevy engineers broke out the boring bar and expanded their OHV engine's internals to 283 cubic inches. Better yet, they also cast up an all-new fuel-injected induction system that pushed horsepower figures to the magical 1-pony-per-cubic-inch level. When installed in the newly redesigned 1957 Chevy line, a formidable race car was created.

The only flies in the ointment were those pesky engineers over at Ford who had some induction tricks of their own up their sleeves. Like their Chevrolet counterparts, Ford folks had an all-new overhead valve V-8 to tinker with in the mid-1950s, and the quest for more grunt led them to bolt on a belt-driven McCulloch supercharger that put 1957 Fords out ahead of their "fuelie" competition both under the hood (300 horsepower to a 283's 283) and on the track.

Ford's factory-backed drivers (including a fellow named Ralph Moody) began the 1957 season with a string of victories that were sure to have thrown a wet blanket on Chevy's hope for headlines. Ford drivers won 15 of the first 21 events contested in the Grand National division in 1957. Chevy drivers, on the other hand, took the checker in just 5 races. The one bright spot in the statistics was the first Pontiac win in the NASCAR ranks, turned in by Cotton Owens at Daytona in February. Owens' win was convincing, as he led all but one of the race's 39 laps on the combination beach/road course. The power put out by the Ray Nichels-prepped Pontiac V-8 under Owens' hood proved that engineers in the Indian-head division were on the right track with their own engine development program. But, as mentioned, any promise displayed in Owens' beach race triumph was overshadowed by Ford's overall dominance on the track. Something would have to be done—and quickly!

The man with the plan turned out to be GM exec Harlow "Red" Curtice. Ford's dominance at the track in early 1957 put both Chevrolet and General Motors in a tough spot. Though the Bow Tie division had engineers like Zora Duntov who were literally chomping at the bit to go racing in a big way, Curtice felt constrained in giving them their head. The reason was the corporation's fear that highly publicized factory-backed

GM racing might draw too much attention to the fact that the General's market share in those days came perilously close to deserving Justice Department scrutiny for antitrust violations. Curtice decided if he couldn't defeat his Blue Oval rivals on the track, he would just have to outsmart them in the boardroom. Lucky for him that Ford's top executive at the time was an exceedingly gullible fellow named Robert McNamara.

Curtice sealed Ford's racing fate far from the tracks by convincing McNamara to sign on to the American Motorsports Association (AMA) ban on factory-backed motorsports competition that Curtice himself had cooked up. McNamara swallowed the bait—hook, line, and sinker— and totally shut down Ford's factory-backed racing teams at mid-season. The record book reflects that from that point on, Chevrolet's racing fortunes took a dramatic turn for the better. Though Bow Tie teams had won just 5 Grand National events during the first part of 1957, Chevy drivers finished first in 14 of the 32 NASCAR races that took place after the ban. In that number was a win by

Buck Baker (#87) scored Chevrolet's first Grand National driving championship in 1957 with the help of a fuel-injected, 283-powered "Black Widow." With Bud Moore turning the wrenches, Baker won 10 races and finished in the top five at 20 other events. Speedy Thompson can be seen bringing up the rear in another "Black Widow."
JDC Collection

Bill France opened the gates to his palace of speed in Daytona in 1959. Its 33-degree banking initially took the breath away from most drivers on the tour when they first saw the track—but not for long. Soon hotshoes like Richard Petty (pictured here in a blue #43 Olds convertible) were tearing around the 2.5-mile track with reckless abandon. *JDC Collection*

Speedy Thompson in the 1957 running of the always-important Southern 500 at Darlington.

At season's end, Chevy driver Buck Baker had secured both his second and Chevrolet's first Grand National driving title. The fuel-injected 1957 "Black Widows" that team mechanic Bud Moore built for Baker produced 10 wins, 30 top-five finishes, and more than $30,000 in prize money.

While Chevrolet drivers like Baker, Jack Smith, Bob Wellborn, and Speedy Thompson were adding check marks to the Chevrolet win column, a fellow named Lee Petty from tiny Level Cross, North Carolina, made the

switch from Chrysler to Oldsmobile. In his entourage was a gangly lad named Richard who helped turn wrenches on dad's 277-horsepower Super 88s. Father and sons' (the elder Petty's other son Maurice also helped out with pit chores) efforts produced four Oldsmobile wins in 1957. These weren't destined to be the last GM wins scored by a member of the Petty family.

1958: Petty Power

With archrival Ford Motor Company (Fomoco) snoozing on the sidelines and the General's R&D engineers still hard at work producing new and improved go-fast parts for Chevrolet, Oldsmobile, and Pontiac NASCAR teams, 1958 promised to be a good year for GM teams on the circuit. And indeed it was.

Future champion Rex White began the competition year with a win for Chevrolet in the first race of the calendar, and Paul Goldsmith piloted Smokey Yunick's Pontiac to a convincing win from the pole at the beach race in Daytona. Smokey's black-and-gold Poncho carried #3 racing livery and was powered by Pontiac's 370-cubic-inch answer to Chevrolet's newly introduced 348-cubic-inch "big-block" engine. Though both divisions were supposedly out of the racing business and officially honoring the AMA ban that Red Curtice had engineered, race-oriented engineers were burning the midnight oil in a not-so-clandestine quest for more and more speed.

Interestingly, though Bow Tie teams had access to the newly introduced Impala car line and its 348 "W" engine, most opted to re-up their enlistment with the tried and proven 1957 vehicles they'd raced the season before. It turned out to be a wise move. Fireball Roberts, for one, went on a tear in his 1957 car, winning the Southern 500 and five other races. Chevy pilots like Buck Baker, Speedy Thompson, and Jim Reed helped bring Chevrolet's season total to an impressive 23 wins. In addition, Pontiac drivers brought home three more wins for the GM banner that year.

Even so, these numbers were not good enough to keep Lee Petty from winning a third Grand National championship for Oldsmobile. Using the same formula that would later serve son Richard so well, Petty ran just about every one of the 51 events that made up the 1958 season and won 7 of them. Twenty-one other top-five finishes added up to Petty's second national title and $26,565 in winnings.

1959: The Debut Daytona 500

In 1959, Big Bill France opened his high-banked palace of speed in Daytona. Once he

During the 1950s many future stars got their start in NASCAR's convertible division, including a lanky lad named Richard Petty. He is seen here at Daytona in 1959 literally driving his dad's Oldsmobile (#43). He soon graduated to mounts with roof panels and Grand National stardom. *JDC Collection*

did, the face of Grand National stock car racing was forever changed. Gone was the treacherous old part-sand and part-pavement beach course, and in its place was a speedway so big and so tall that drivers were struck dumb in wonder (read—fear) the first time they pulled into the infield.

The very first Daytona 500 was run on February 22, 1959. Bob Wellborn was fastest during qualifying, and he set the first fast lap around the Big D at a then-blistering speed of 140.121 miles per hour. Unfortunately, the engine under the hood of Wellborn's 1959 Impala only lasted until lap 75 of the 200 that made up the race. The late stages of the race

Following pages
Junior Johnson won the 1960 Daytona 500 in a Ray Fox-prepped Impala just like this one. Apparently, his race car was a completely stock street car until just one week before the February 14, 1960, event. Floridian Don Rhuff built this replica of Johnson's 1959 race winner.

Chevrolet Impalas sprouted wings for 1959. And that's perhaps part of the reason they flew around NASCAR's superspeedways that season. The 305-horsepower, 348-cubic-inch "W" engines under their hoods probably helped a little bit too. Here Bob Wellborn is seen battling it out with a couple of Fords in the 1959 Daytona 500. Some things never change. *JDC Collection*

saw Chevrolet drivers take a back seat to T-Bird-mounted Johnny Beauchamp and Oldsmobile pilot Lee Petty. Though Petty's block-long (and finned!) Olds 88 didn't look the part of a race car, from lap 148 forward it was the only car in the 59-car field that was able to give Beauchamp a run for his money—even after the checkered flag fell. And that's because the final dash across the stripe that Beauchamp and Petty made was so exceedingly close that at first NASCAR officials declared Beauchamp the winner by a hair. It wasn't until 61 hours later that a photo analysis of the finish revealed it had been Petty's land-yacht-sized 88 that had actually edged Beauchamp out for the win. And so it was that the first Daytona 500—the Super Bowl of stock car racing——was won by your father's (or at least Richard's father's) Oldsmobile.

Chevrolet drivers had another good year on the tour and snagged 14 Grand National trophies in the process. Jim Reed drove a "bat-winged" 1959 Impala to glory in the Southern 500, and Rex White drove a similarly winged #4 Chevrolet to 5 short-track wins. That having been said, it was Lee Petty who once again snagged the national driving title. And though he'd opened the year in an Olds, the elder Petty jumped ship and returned to Chrysler shortly after the 500, so his GN crown provided little reason to celebrate back in Detroit.

As the 1950s ended, Ford was still securely on sabbatical. The dawning of a new decade held more than a little promise for General Motors racers.

Chapter 2

THE 1960s
BANNED IN BOSTON

The kick-off of the new decade had to have been an optimistic affair for GM racers in general and Chevrolet drivers in particular. The Ford Motor Company (Fomoco) was still securely on the sidelines, and Chrysler's racing efforts were primarily concentrated on the two teams fielded by Lee Petty. The odds were clearly in favor of continued GM dominance in stock car circles for the length of the new decade, or so it seemed.

The 1960s began exactly as anticipated, but they would not end that way. Few who gathered in the garage area in advance of the 1960 running of the Daytona 500 would have guessed that the 1960s would turn out to be a decade filled with lost opportunities for drivers in every one of the General's divisions. But at least that "winter of discontent" didn't

Though this man may be unfamiliar to many modern NASCAR fans, he was well known and feared on the circuit in the late 1950s and early 1960s. His name is Rex White, and during his time on the tour he finished in the top-10 at an incredible 70 percent of the races he started. And most of those events found him at the helm of a Chevrolet race car. In 1960 he won both the fans' hearts (Most Popular Driver) and the season points race (Grand National Champion). *JDC Collection*

descend on GM until 1963. And 1960 was a particularly good year for Chevrolet drivers in the GN ranks.

1960: Chevy Success Continues

Junior Johnson started the ball rolling by winning the 1960 Daytona 500 in a Ray Fox-prepped Impala. Interestingly, ace mechanic Fox originally had planned to sit out the 500. All that changed just nine days before the race when a group of backers proposed that he build a car for the second running of the 500. Working around the clock, Fox was able to transform a showroom 1959 Impala into a race-winning Grand National stock car in just seven short days. Legendary driver Junior Johnson translated a ninth-place start into a first-place finish with the help of the 320 ponies cranked out by the 348 big-block engine under the hood of his bat-winged Chevrolet. Johnson's win was made more dramatic by what track announcers perceived as a series of near rear-end collisions in which he was involved. To them it appeared that Johnson's Chevrolet nearly ran into the back of a number of cars at different points in the race. What was really happening was Johnson's discovery of superspeedway drafting, and the near collisions were simply Johnson

Bubble-top Catalinas were some of the prettiest cars on and off the track in 1961. Here's a trio of them being driven at Daytona that year by (left to right) Junior Johnson, Cotton Owens, and David Pearson. *JDC Collection*

setting up the cars he nearly "crashed" into for slipstream passes. Nose-to-tail racing at Daytona is now a common sight, all because of Junior's 1960 discovery at the helm of a bat-wing Impala.

Joe Lee Johnson backed up Junior Johnson's superspeedway win with a victory in the inaugural World 600 at the newly opened Charlotte Motor Speedway, but Rex White was the most successful GM driver that season. His 6 Impala wins and 25 top-five finishes were what it took to secure the first Grand National driving title of the 1960s. His winnings for the 1960 title topped $57,000.

Pontiac drivers also proved to be a force on the 1960 tour and ultimately scored just 2 fewer wins than the 15 turned in by the Bow Tie brigade. Fireball Roberts drove Smokey Yunick's #22 to a popular win in the Dixie 300 at the new superspeedway in Atlanta, and Buck Baker notched his second Southern 500 win in a block-long Poncho of his own.

If Chevrolet drivers were concerned by the success of their Pontiac brethren, they had good reason, as they would find out just one season later.

1961–1962: Super-Duty Pontiac Power

Chevrolet's Grand National victories made quite an impact on both the buying public and a couple of fellows named Knudsen and Wangers. Both just happened to work in Chevrolet's rival Pontiac division, and both were inveterate racers. Best of all for Pontiac fans, both occupied positions in Pontiac's food chain that permitted just about every one of their high-performance whims to become actual corporate fact in a very short time (bureaucratically speaking, that is).

Semon "Bunkie" Knudsen had taken control of Pontiac's leadership in 1958, and Jim Wangers served Knudsen as the division's chief ad man. Both were dedicated to the idea that Sunday wins on the track translated

Chevrolet driver Johnny Beauchamp made headlines during Speedweeks 1961 at Daytona when he and MoPar-driver Lee Petty took a little excursion off the track during a qualifying race. Fortunately, neither driver was killed. *JDC Collection*

into Monday traffic on the showroom floor. To that end both (like their Bow tie counterparts) had made sure that the back door at Pontiac's R&D division remained wide open to racers, even though the division was officially adhering to Curtice's AMA ban on factory-backed racing.

Knudsen and Wangers' "racy" outlook, coupled with Pontiac's styling decision to downsize the Catalina line for 1961, helped make 1961 and 1962 standout seasons for drivers in the "Indian Head" division. Marvin Panch fired the first shot in Pontiac's battle to defeat archrival Chevrolet by winning the 1961 running of the Daytona 500 in a Smokey Yunick-prepared Pontiac. When Panch's gold-and-black #20 Ponch crossed the stripe, the only other cars on the same lap were Joe Weatherly's Bud Moore-built Pontiac and Paul Goldsmith's Ray Nichels-built Catalina.

Adding insult to injury was the fact that Pontiac drivers had also swept both of the twin qualifiers that preceded the 500. Fireball

Roberts used his #22 Yunick-prepped Catalina to lead Jim Paschal and Jack Smith's Catalina to the checker in race one, and Fireball's black-and-gold car cinched the 500 pole with a 155.709-mile-per-hour lap on pole day. Qualifier two ended with a Pontiac train made up of Joe Weatherly, Marvin Panch, and Cotton Owens arriving at the line before everyone

Fireball Roberts took in the rapidly passing 1962 scenery from this perch. Note the essentially stock nature of Grand National stock car control cabins in 1962 as well as car builder Yunick's total lack of color coordination.

Previous pages
Fireball Roberts won the Daytona 500 in 1962 with the help of this 421 Super Duty Catalina. Smokey Yunick built the #22 car in his Daytona Beach "Best Damn Garage in Town" shop, and hometown hero Roberts went on to score the popular win. More recently, the black-and-gold car has been on display at the International Motorsports Hall of Fame in Talladega, Alabama.

else. As you can see, Daytona Speedweeks in 1961 were most definitely an all-Pontiac affair.

And that's pretty much the same way that the rest of the season went too. Pontiac drivers like Junior Johnson, David Pearson, and Jack Smith captured almost the entire slate of headline-producing big track events in 1961. The only "big one" that got away was the Southern 500 that Nelson Stacey claimed in a Holman & Moody-equipped Ford Starliner. Even so, the rules book's favoritism (in points) for drivers that started most of the races on the tour resulted in yet another Grand National driving title for Chevrolet, this time scored by Ned Jarrett in his #11 Impala. Though the soft-spoken Jarrett won but a single race during the 50-race season (compared to 9 for Joe Weatherly and 7 for Junior Johnson), he started 46 races and scored top fives in 23 of them. And that was enough to take the title and $41,055.90 in winnings.

The big news for 1962 was the addition of a punched-out version of the Super Duty (SD) 389 to the Pontiac arsenal. First introduced in late 1961 as an over-the-counter, drag race-oriented powerplant, the new 421-cubic-inch SD Poncho motor made the Catalinas captained by Fireball Roberts, Joe Weatherly, Cotton Owens, and Jack Smith even more intimidating than they had been the year before.

Driving to Daytona for Speedweeks 1962 must have been like a condemned man's stroll toward the electric chair for Chevy drivers that year. After all, if their 409 engines hadn't been able to best Pontiac drivers powered by SD 348s the year before, how were they going to be able to beat those same drivers and their bigger and better 421 SD motors in 1962? The answer: they weren't.

Fireball Roberts made this clear during qualifying by capturing the pole with a speed of 156.999 miles per hour and then going on to convincingly win the first of Daytona's two traditional qualifying races.

Chevrolet engineers introduced a new motor at Daytona in 1963 that featured poly-angled valves, a beefy four-bolt bottom end, and generously proportioned, equally spaced ports. Developed under a veil of secrecy even within GM ranks, the new engine quickly became known as the "Mystery Motor."

Joe Weatherly completed the qualifying trifecta for Pontiac by winning his qualifier in Bud Moore's #8 Poncho. Roberts went on to dominate the race proper on his way to his first Daytona 500 win. It was an incredible and impressive performance for Pontiac for the second straight year, and Chevrolet drivers were distraught.

Fireball Roberts became the King of Daytona that year, winning the Firecracker 250 on July 4th in a Banjo Matthews-prepped Catalina (having split with Smokey shortly after Speedweeks). Joe Weatherly took his first Grand National driving title in Bud Moore's red-and-black Catalina by winning 9 events and finishing in the top five at 30 others. All told, Pontiac drivers had won an incredible 52 of 105 races contested during the 1961 and 1962 seasons.

1963: Factory Ban Backfires/ Mystery Motor Unveiled

Unfortunately, Pontiac drivers were collectively destined to win just four more times in 1963 and then remain absent from NASCAR victory lanes for the next 17 straight seasons.

There are several reasons for the dramatic reversal of racing fortune that awaited Pontiac (and GM) drivers during the balance of the 1960s. Part of the problem was Henry Ford II's decision in early 1962 to formally invalidate the 1957 AMA ban on factory-backed racing that Red Curtice had snookered Robert McNamara into. (By then McNamara was long since gone from the "Glasshouse" in Dearborn,

Junior Johnson navigated superspeedway traffic with this not-so-ergonomic steering wheel in 1963. Note the production-based bucket seat and instrument panel. Chevrolet stock cars were mostly just that in 1963.

Though Roger Penske has long been associated with motorsports as a winning Indy car and NASCAR team owner, it might come as a surprise to some that during the 1960s he was one of the best sports car drivers in the country. When not at the helm of a usually Chevrolet-powered sporty car, he, on occasion, tried his luck in the stock car ranks. His #02 Pontiac is pictured here at Riverside in 1963. *JDC Collection*

having joined the Kennedy administration as secretary of defense.) Pontiac's total domination of the NASCAR (not to mention NHRA) series in 1961 and 1962 finally convinced the powers-that-be at Ford that GM wasn't honoring the AMA ban after all. That coupled with the clock cleaning that Ford dealers were getting in the race for sales convinced Henry Ford to ditch the ban and go racing. A revitalized Holman & Moody quickly set about taking wins away from both Pontiac and Chevrolet drivers shortly thereafter. Chrysler's decision to get more involved in factory-backed NASCAR racing didn't help either.

But the big reason for the hard times the GM drivers fell upon after the 1963 season was the very same AMA ban on factory-backed motorsports that had hamstrung Ford

drivers since 1957. You see, Pontiac's total domination on the track had also captured the attention of GM's top brass. Their concern about possible monopoly litigation being initiated by trust busting U.S. attorneys was, if anything, greater in 1962 than it had been five years before. As a result, they decided that a little profile lowering was called for, and the best way to achieve that goal was to actually honor the AMA ban that Red Curtice had engineered in 1957. Go figure.

As a result, the funding pins were knocked out from under both Pontiac's and Chevrolet's clandestine racing programs just before the beginning of the 1963 NASCAR season. So serious was GM about shutting down its racing efforts that "repossession" orders went out to race teams just before the

Daytona 500 that were designed to reclaim any high-performance parts (and cars) that had already gone out to racers through GM's now-closed (welded shut, actually) back door. And it goes without saying that all factory-subsidized R&D work on new racing-destined components also came to a crashing halt.

It's easy to imagine the disarray that GM's decision left Pontiac and Chevrolet camps in on the eve of the most important race of the season. Even so, there were still some bright points for GM drivers in the 1963 season before the lights went out in their race shops altogether.

Chevrolet's racing program for the 1963 Grand National season was particularly promising in the days just before the Daytona 500. Stung by Pontiac's domination of the high banks (and the low ones too) in 1961 and 1962, Bow Tie engine and foundry types set out to build a race-specific big-block engine that was better able to handle the competition than the not-so-fine 409 had been.

Starting with a clean sheet of paper, they began by inking a rock-solid bottom-end design that featured a unique four-bolt main journal design consisting of conventional two-bolt caps that were then surrounded by an additional double-bolted reinforcing girdle. A battleship-strength-forged reciprocating assembly came off the drawing board next, followed by a set of free-flowing head castings that carried a poly-angle valve layout and equally spaced intake and exhaust ports. Bits and pieces of the package also included a trick cowl induction "Ram Air" setup and a pair of cast-iron exhaust manifolds that flowed just about as well as a matching pair of still-outlawed tubular headers could.

A veil of mystery surrounded the all-new engines. So much so, in fact, that people began to call them "Mystery Motors." A handful were assembled for pre-season testing, and both Pontiac and Chevrolet drivers were invited to Pontiac's southwestern proving grounds (in Mesa, Arizona) for a head-to-head comparison of the new motor with Pontiac's SD 421 engine of the season before.

In that number was North Carolinian and Pontiac racer Junior Johnson. When it became apparent that the new 427-cubic-inch Chevy motor was more than a match for the SD 421, Johnson and others (such as Smokey Yunick) elected to switch to Impalas for 1963.

Though the NASCAR series has always been the dominant stock car racing series, it wasn't always the only one. During the early days, a number of other sanctioning bodies gave Big Bill France's series a run for its money. The United States Auto Club (USAC) was in that number, and for a while in the early 1960s, stock car races were sanctioned by that body across the Midwest. Here is a shot of Roger Penske (#02) in his Ray Nichels-prepped Pontiac chasing Parnelli Jones (#15) in a USAC race at Indianapolis Raceway Park in 1963. *JDC Collection*

Following pages
Junior Johnson switched to Chevrolet for 1963 when a pre-season comparison proved that the all-new Mystery Motor that Chevrolet introduced that season was more than a match for the 421 Super Duty Pontiac motor he had campaigned the year before. Unfortunately, GM pulled the rug out from under all General Motors drivers by dropping its factory backing just before the Daytona 500 that year. *Daytona Racing Archives*

Joe Weatherly won a second straight Grand National drivers' title in 1963 driving a string of different race cars. When his factory-backed Pontiac ride (pictured here) ran out of steam shortly after Atlanta in the spring of the season, he jumped from car owner to car owner piloting Pontiacs, Plymouths, Dodges, and even Mercurys on his way to the points title. *JDC Collection*

As mentioned, GM's decision to finally honor the AMA ban was a very belated one, and one that didn't take place until race teams were well into their preparations for Speedweeks 1963 at Daytona. As you might have guessed, GM's attempt to "repossess" every one of the 48 new MkII 427 motors (as they were officially called) that had been cast up to that date was met with little enthusiasm by the teams that had received them. Ultimately, Chevy execs decided (probably wisely) against driving to the hills of Carolina (and elsewhere) to actually try and physically take back the engines.

Even so, GM shut down all development of the engine and stopped all production of Mystery Motor engine parts cold. Though racers like Johnson and Yunick would be campaigning MkII 427-powered Impalas in 1963, they'd have to get by on only the spare parts they'd amassed before GM shut down the program.

Bobby Johns campaigned a series of #7 Chevrolets during the mid-1960s. His colorful blue-and-white cars were often the only Bow Tie-badged competition cars in the garage area. One wonders how much better he and the other independent GM drivers could have run with the same level of factory backing their Brand X rivals enjoyed. *JDC Collection*

Who said that the new Taurus race car is the first four-door racer to compete in the NASCAR series? Anyone who makes that claim surely has forgotten the #6 four-door 1964 Olds that Ed Brown drove in the 1965 Motor Trend 500 at Riverside. He finished 14th—ahead of such series hotshoes as Fred Lorenzen, Ned Jarrett, Parnelli Jones, and Dick Hutcherson. *JDC Collection*

When the NASCAR tour rolled into Daytona for 1963, all eyes were on the Chevrolet teams. Word of their new engine's power had leaked to the press, and even before Johnson's Ray Fox-prepped Impala rumbled out onto the track, Fomoco drivers were raising a ruckus about the car's legality. And, of course, they had a point. No one was contending that the new Mystery Motor was a regular production option. But even the "crate motor," over-the-counter exemption that Pontiac 421 engines had enjoyed didn't really provide much homologation cover for an engine line that consisted of fewer than 50 castings.

Ford execs decided to press the point by having John Holman (one half of Ford's Holman & Moody race factory) drop by his local Chevy dealership to order up a Mystery Motor of his own for testing. Caught between a rock and a hard place and hoping at all costs to

avoid any publicity that might bring out the legal eagles, Chevy execs actually sold Holman a copy. And that's probably the only Mystery Motor that ever got delivered to someone not named Fox, Yunick, or Johnson.

Junior Johnson proved the validity of Ford racers' concerns by quickly destroying the track lap record at Daytona during testing. His white #3 Impala tripped the clocks at an incredible 165.183 miles per hour during second-round qualifying, a speed nearly 10 miles per hour faster than Fireball Roberts' pole-winning speed of just one year before. Junior backed up his fast lap with 40 more to win the first qualifying race for the 500. Indy ace Johnny Rutherford drove Smokey Yunick's #13 Mystery-Motored Impala to an equally impressive rookie win in the second pre-500 qualifier, and his black-and-gold car was followed closely across the stripe by Rex White's

The number on Nat Reeders' Impala is symbolic of both the amount of factory backing and the number of wins that Chevrolet drivers racked up in 1965 (the season he campaigned the car in the Grand National ranks). It would take five more years for Bow Tie drivers to begin visiting victory lane again with any regularity. *JDC Collection*

#4 MkII 427-motivated Chevy. Rutherford's victory was both the only win ever scored by a NASCAR driver in his first Grand National event and Rutherford's sole NASCAR triumph.

Unfortunately, new engine teething problems hobbled the Mystery Motor drivers during the race proper. Johnson's rocket retired on lap 26 with distributor problems while Rutherford and White finished laps down to the winner Tiny Lund in a Wood Brothers-prepped Ford.

And that's pretty much the way the season played out for the now non-factory-backed Chevy teams—great qualifying speed followed by mechanical gremlins during the race itself. Johnson ultimately recorded super-speedway wins at Atlanta and Charlotte (along with a handful of short-track victories). But by the end of the season, his Holly Farms team was so short on replacement parts that he had to go to Holman & Moody and buy back the spare Mystery Motor that Chevrolet had sold the legendary Ford race shop at the beginning of the season.

Joe Weatherly was another "de-factory-backed" racer who struggled on during the 1963 season. Though he started out in Bud Moore's #8 Catalina, when Moore's funds dried up, Little Joe hopped rides wherever he could find them until Moore signed on with Mercury at season's end. The two Pontiac wins that Weatherly scored (one in the Rebel 300 at Darlington) helped him win a second straight Grand National driving title. Sadly, it was to be the well-liked Weatherly's last, as he was killed in a racing shunt at Riverside Raceway in early 1964.

1964–1969: Independents Carry the Banner

In a strange way, Weatherly's death paralleled the death of GM drivers' Grand National aspirations for the balance of the decade. Though independents like Smokey Yunick and Bobby Allison soldiered on with GM mounts at selected races, not one Oldsmobile, Pontiac, or Buick win was recorded between 1964 and the late 1970s.

Chevrolet drivers managed only a paltry eight wins between 1964 and 1971 themselves. Still, Bow Tie-equipped NASCAR race cars did make some news during the remainder of the 1960s.

Wendell Scott's Chevrolet

Wendell Scott, the series' first black driver, scored his first Grand National win in a 1962 Chevrolet at a 100-lap race in Jacksonville, Florida, in December 1963. The journeyman racer from Danville, Virginia, personified the term "independent driver," and his victory at Jacksonville over the likes of Buck Baker, Jack Smith, Richard Petty, and Joe Weatherly, though not confirmed until after the event due to a scoring mix-up, was still a historic one. As things turned out, it was Scott's only full series victory. His Chevy win was also the

Once upon a time back when the Earth was still cooling, each of the General's divisions relied on engines of their own individual design—both on and off the track. This is what a racing Oldsmobile power plant looked like around 1965. All of that changed in 1978 when the sanctioning body recognized the Chevrolet small-block engine as the corporate engine for all GM race cars. *JDC Collection*

NASCAR stockers had lost a good deal of their "stockness" by the mid-1960s, as can be seen in this shot of a Smokey Yunick-prepared 1966 Chevelle. Then again, it's been said that Smokey's cars were always significantly less "stock" than those of his competitors. Lowered over a handmade frame and riding on handmade suspension components, Smokey's Chevelles were sleek, fast, and probably all "illegal."

only visit paid to victory lane by a GM driver until 1966.

Bobby Allison's Chevelle

Bobby Allison provided the next race victories for the Chevrolet division in 1966 with his home-built 1965 Chevelle. As longtime NASCAR fans will recall, Bobby Allison was one of the founding members of the "Alabama gang" and as independent minded a racer as there was in the mid-1960s. Allison's career had gotten off to a start on the hard scrabble modified tour while he and brothers Donnie and Eddie were still growing up in Miami, Florida.

By the mid-1960s, Allison had moved up to the Grand National ranks and had served as a journeyman driver for a number of teams. Though he'd piloted many different brands of race cars for others, Bobby's personal competition machine at the time had Bow Ties all over it. When not campaigning someone else's car, Allison's mount for 1966 was a diminutive #2 Chevelle that he had built in his two-car garage on Berry Drive in Hueytown, Alabama.

It was nothing short of heresy for Allison to expect to win on the Grand National division with a "Brand X" car. After all, Ford and Chrysler were the big dogs on the tour, and their factory-backed racing efforts were spending money by the bushel basket full, all in an attempt to win on Sunday. It just wasn't possible for an unfunded independent like Allison to presume he had a shot at victory—let alone while he was driving a home-built Chevrolet of all things.

While that may have been the conventional wisdom in those days, it seems that nobody bothered to tell Allison that chances for a Grand National victory were remote. And it probably wouldn't have mattered if they did.

You see, Allison had an ace in the hole. Actually, it was an ace under his hood. And that was the 327 engine that his tiny Chevelle relied on for power. NASCAR rules of the day linked weight to displacement. Specifically, Grand National (GN) cars in 1966 had to weigh 9.36 pounds for every cubic inch they displaced. Factory Fords and Dodges running 427- and 426-cubic-inch engines had to weigh in at just short of 2 tons as a result. Allison's 327-powered Chevelle got to diet down to a racier 3,060.72 pounds, by dint of the "mouse" motor under its hood. And that lighter weight paid big dividends at the track.

Allison's other advantage was the "front steer" suspension setup that Chevelles came factory equipped with. He felt that it offered better "feel" than the "rear steer" system that Ralph Moody had perfected on his Holman & Moody-built Galaxies.

Allison put those ingredients together at Oxford, Maine, in July 1966 to score the first

Chevrolet GN win in nearly three years. After the race Allison said of his lightweight little Chevelle: "I think a new wrinkle has started. We're pleased in two ways. It [the Chevelle] handled well right off the trailer. And secondly, it blew right by all the hot dogs."

Allison blew right by hot dogs like Ned Jarrett, David Pearson, Richard Petty, and Buddy Baker a second time four days later at a 60-mile event at Islip Speedway and yet again in August 1966 at Beltsville in the Maryland 200. Though those short-track wins weren't the headline producers that a Daytona 500 victory might have been, they were cause for Chevrolet fans in the stands to take heart.

When the factories took note of Allison's under-funded performance, they immediately elected to remove the Chevelle-sized thorn in their paw by giving him a full ride in a factory-backed car. First in line was Fomoco, who offered him a seat in Bud Moore's Mercury. When that relationship soured in 1967, Allison dusted off the Chevelle and then dusted off the competition at GN races in Winston-Salem and Savannah. Next came the chance to drive a Cotton Owens Dodge, but Allison's stint as a factory driver came to an end after he won a third race in his Chevelle (at Oxford, Maine) at a race that Owens had elected to sit out. Chrysler execs were less than enthusiastic about a Chevrolet win scored by their "Dodge" driver, and so Allison was an independent once again. That lasted until late 1967 when Allison was offered a full Holman & Moody ride with former champ Fred Lorenzen as team manager. Allison scored one more win in his Chevelle in July 1968 back at Islip Speedway just after he quit his factory ride (again!) that season. It was to be the last GN win scored by a GM driver that decade. But things would get dramatically better once the 1960s were over.

Smokey Yunick's Chevelles

Smokey Yunick also provided some encouraging moments for Chevy fans in the 1960s. As independent a thinker as Allison,

Smokey Yunick's legendary mid-1960s Chevelles all relied on various versions of the Chevrolet big-block engine for power. One of Smokey's speed secrets in those days was to destroke a rat motor to less than the legal 427 cubic inches the rules book allowed in order to secure a few extra rpm down the back stretch.

Smokey believed that if the rules book didn't specifically prohibit a particular piece of mechanical equipment, then it must be legal. And that very liberal interpretation of the sanctioning body's edicts led directly to a string of truly memorable Chevy stock cars.

The years 1965 and 1966 offered independents like Smokey more of a chance at victory as Chrysler and Ford (in turn) boycotted the Grand National tour during these seasons. The two automotive giants took issue with Big Bill France's always-confusing rulings about factory-backed Hemi race engines. Taking advantage of the situation, Smokey cooked up the first of his black-and-gold Chevelle groundbreakers for the August 1966 running of the Dixie 400 at Atlanta.

The absence of big-named Ford Motor Company (Fomoco) drivers and the dominance by factory cars of just one stripe (while the other carmaker sat on the sidelines) had a predictably negative impact on gate receipts.

Without factory backing, Pontiac drivers like Ken Spikes had little real hope of winning races on the NASCAR tour during the mid-1960s. But that didn't stop the cars they campaigned from looking good. *JDC Collection*

Promoters were howling for France's head by the summer of 1966, and he was desperate to do something to create at least the appearance of multi-make competition out on the track. Since Dodge and Plymouth drivers were winning just about everything that year while Fomoco types stewed, word from on high leaked out that tech inspection wouldn't be all that rigorous for any independent Ford or Chevrolet teams that decided to show up at Atlanta. Both Junior Johnson and Smokey heeded the call, and the end result was two cars that will forever live in NASCAR lore.

Johnson's entry was yellow and had, at least at one point in the past, started out as a 1966 Galaxy. In Atlanta trim the car looked anything but stock. The top was chopped, the

nose looked squashed, and the bustle rose toward the sky in a most un-stock-like way. Wags around the garage area took to calling the car the "yellow banana" due to its very suspect configuration. But NASCAR tech officials deemed the car legal to race.

Smokey's approach was subtler but just as direct. His efforts to reduce aerodynamic drag focused on making his Chevelle smaller in just about every dimension. According to those who actually got to appreciate his handicraft, the car looked normal until someone actually compared it to an, ahem, full-sized stock Chevelle. Fellow Chevelle racer Bobby Johns for one, took notice of the car's shrunken silhouette, and soon people were calling Smokey's #13 car the 15/16th Chevelle. It, too, was deemed legal to race.

Unfortunately for both Johnson and Yunick, race victory was not in the future for either car. Lorenzen hit the wall hard in Johnson's banana on lap 139 just after Curtis Turner had retired Smokey's car with a broken distributor. Neither car was allowed to run again, and shortly thereafter NASCAR instituted the first body template rules.

Smokey's next headline-producing Chevelle was built for duty in the 1967 Daytona 500. Smokey made a dramatic entry to the garage area on pole qualifying day with his #13 Chevelle shrouded in mystery under a car cover on the trailer. Once unloaded and in its stall, Smokey, driver Turner, and the rest of the crew left the car alone until the last possible moment for a shot at the pole. Turner then climbed in,

fired the car up, and took it out on the track for its run at the pole. Two laps later he'd set a new lap record of 180.831 miles per hour— more than 5 miles per hour faster than Richard Petty's 1966 pole-winning speed. It was an incredible performance, to say the least, and factory teams were furious. To say that Smokey had stolen their thunder was an understatement. And

Following pages
Rex White drove a "bubble-top" Chevrolet much like this one during the 1961 season. Though a much better looking machine than it's GM and Brand X rivals, it unfortunately was down on power when compared to them. Florida's Harold Doherty built this replica of White's Impala. *JDC Collection*

Though Olds drivers dominated the first few years of the NASCAR series in the late 1940s and early 1950s, by the mid-1960s, the few hearty souls who ventured out onto a Grand National track under Oldsmobile power had little chance of victory. Had drivers like this unknown 1969 independent enjoyed the same factory backing that their Fomoco and Chrysler rivals did, they probably could have invested in the components (not to mention trailers) necessary to win. *JDC Collection*

yet, to hear Smokey tell the story today, his only speed secret was destroking the displacement of his Chevelle's 427 big block down to 410 cubic inches.

Whatever the basis for the car's speed was, Turner was only able to make 25 circuits of the track during the race before the engine blew. Smokey rebuilt the motor and turned up with Turner at Atlanta in April. The #13 Chevelle was once again the fastest thing at the track during testing. That is until Turner demolished the car in practice in the most dramatically airborne way possible. Following the shunt, nervous Chevy execs who had been slipping Smokey parts on the QT tried to "repossess" the remains of the Chevelle. So Smokey sent the car back to Michigan. But not until he'd crushed the car into a cube. It doesn't pay to make Smokey Yunick mad.

The third and final Chevelle that Smokey created was built for duty in the 1968 Daytona 500. Like the others, it started life as a 1966 model, but by the time it rolled off the truck in the garage area, it was anything but. Smokey was an early student and advocate of aerodynamics, and he also knew how important optimum weight distribution was for on-track handling. His last little Chevelle was built with an eye toward both of those variables.

Construction of the car commenced with the fabrication of what was probably the first purpose-built tube frame chassis in NASCAR history. Smokey then installed the car's body over the car as far to the rear as possible for improved weight distribution. He also biased the body as far to the left as possible for the same

reason. The car's floorboard was lowered to both serve as an aerodynamic belly pan and to keep planned driver Gordon Johncock's weight as low as possible in the car. Sectioning the front bumper and adding an extra inch and a half strip of metal before re-chroming further enhanced aerodynamics and handling. The end result was a rudimentary front airfoil that worked in concert with a vortex-generating channel in the roof panel to keep the car glued to the ground at speed.

Glenn "Fireball" Roberts was arguably the first superstar in the NASCAR series. He was college educated, articulate, and photogenic. He also happened to go fast as stink while at the wheel of a stock car (such as the Smokey Yunick-built Poncho he won the 1962 Daytona 500 with). *JDC Collection*

Unfortunately, when Smokey tried to get the car through tech at Daytona, he was handed a long list of things he'd have to change to make it legal to run. First on that list was "remove frame and replace with stock." Smokey responded to that list by firing the car up and driving it through traffic across town to his Daytona Beach garage. Bill France announced to the press the next day that Smokey had made that five-mile trip without the benefit of having a gas tank in the car. The car was never allowed to turn even one lap on a NASCAR track, but it still became a racing legend.

The 1960s, though brimful with promise at the dawn of the decade, turned out to be an unmitigated failure for the "General's" stock car racing efforts. When the 1960s ended, few GM fans would have guessed that better days for Chevrolet drivers were just around the corner. But indeed they were.

Chapter

THE 1970s
THE BOW TIE RETURNS

Though Fomoco and Chrysler cars had dominated the Grand National series during the 1960s, by 1970 their collective interest in motorsports was on the wane. The federal government had begun making increasing demands on the major automotive manufacturers in the areas of air pollution and occupant safety. That fact, coupled with the escalating price of fossil fuels, caused executives like Lee Iacocca to reconsider their corporations' commitment to factory-backed auto racing. Iacocca cut Ford's racing budget by 75 percent upon his ascension to Ford's top spot in late 1969, for example, and by 1970 Ford was out of racing altogether. Chrysler continued to fund factory-backed teams for just one more season, and then they too pulled up stakes and went home.

Sterling Marlin is a second-generation NASCAR driver. His father, Coo Coo Marlin, was a journeyman driver and Chevrolet partisan during the 1970s. The senior Marlin is pictured here in his 1970 Monte Carlo. The highlight of Coo Coo's career was his surprise win in one of the twin 125 qualifiers for the 1973 Daytona 500 in the Monte Carlo pictured above. *JDC Collection*

The sudden departure of factory funding left both the sanctioning body and racers in disarray. Winston would ultimately step in to fund the series in 1972, but the loss of factory R&D and subsidized high-performance parts made it tough for teams to field competitive cars. Those teams (like Petty Engineering) that had stockpiled the largest inventory of racing exotica initially fared the best, but ultimately the supply of those high-dollar, race-only components began to wane.

Luckily for racers like Junior Johnson, though Chevrolet had been on the racing sidelines during the balance of the 1960s, the corporation had never ceased the production of high-performance engine and drivetrain parts. Better yet was the plentiful and economical nature of those parts. You see, unlike Chrysler and Ford, who had focused on exotic engines like the Boss 429 and the 426 Hemi Chevrolet's focus on more common engines like the 427 "rat" motor and the 327-350 "mouse" motor not only created an abundant supply of factory-cast parts, it also resulted in a huge support network of aftermarket suppliers who were already making Chevy go-fast goodies for the legions of Bow Tie fans and their street cars.

Cale Yarborough enjoyed great success as a Chevrolet driver during the mid-1970s. One of the secrets of that success was the drooped snout on his Laguna S-3 Chevelle race cars. *Mike Slade*

1971–1972: Junior Johnson Leads the Comeback

As a result, when Ford factory support for Junior Johnson's Torino Talladega team dried up in early 1971, it was a no-brainer for him to return to his General Motors roots and switch back to a Chevrolet-based team. Johnson combined forces with Charlotte Motor Speedway's Richard Howard and placed an order with Chevrolet for a handful of its new-for-1970 Monte Carlo bodies and a sufficient number of 427 crate motors to last a full season. Key personnel on the new team included

driver "Chargin'" Charlie Glotzbach, legendary crew chief Herb Nab, and a young Holman & Moody line mechanic named Robert Yates.

It took several months out of the first part of the 1971 season for Johnson to get his new team up and running. In race trim his new Monte Carlos sported the same white #3 racing livery that Junior's Mystery Motor Impalas had in 1963, right down to the red-and-blue stripes that ran from hood to trunk lid. Race number one for the new Chevy team took place at Charlotte in the Memorial Day running of the World 600. Charlie Glotzbach made sure that everyone knew of the team's arrival on the Grand National scene by ripping off a pole-winning lap of 157.788 miles per hour during qualifying.

During the race itself Glotzbach battled with Bobby Allison's Holman & Moody Mercury for the lead until a late-race crash removed the Monte Carlo from contention. Win number one for the team was not long coming, however, and was scored at Bristol in the Volunteer 500 in July 1971. Though that triumph turned out to be the team's only win of the season, it signaled the end of Chevrolet's long drought on the NASCAR circuit.

In 1972 the team added Bobby Allison as team driver and the Coca-Cola sponsorship package that he brought with him. The new combination was successful right out of the box. Win number one for Allison's "Coke Machine" came at Daytona in the second of the traditional Twin 125 qualifiers that precede

Following pages
Cale Yarborough's Olds Cutlass was quite the aerowarrior. Though its Busch livery was arguably not as fetching as the Holly Farms Chevelles Yarborough had campaigned before, there's no doubt that it was just as fast. *Mike Slade*

Junior Johnson supplied Holly Farms-backed (among other sponsors) Chevelles and Monte Carlos for South Carolina native Cale Yarborough during the 1970s. Yarborough returned the favor by winning the Winston Cup championship three times in a row for Johnson's team. *Mike Slade*

Though the big-fendered 1973–1977 Monte Carlo line might at first glance seem to be aerodynamically challenged, it actually turned out to be a pretty stout comp car. This particular car, for example, played an integral part in Dale Earnhardt's first Winston Cup championship.

Earnhardt's front office looked something like this in 1980. Note the Dodge A-100 van seat that Ironhead still prefers today. Try to find a stock component somewhere in this photo.

the 500. The team's first win in a full-scale superspeedway event came one month later when Allison edged A. J. Foyt's Wood Brothers Mercury in the Atlanta 500. When Allison won again at Bristol in the Southeastern 500, Chrysler and Ford teams began to grouse about the rules book's preference for wedge motors like his 427 (1972-era restricter plates were more generously proportioned for wedge motors than for Hemis). It was a sure sign that the Coke team was hitting them where it hurt. Allison kept up that pummeling through to the end of the season.

All told, Allison and his #12 Monte Carlo scored 10 wins in 1972, including a stop at victory lane in the all-important Southern 500 at Darlington. Those wins and 15 other top-five finishes earned Allison a second-place berth in the seasonal points chase and $348,405 in winnings. The results of the first season in what is now called NASCAR's "modern era" foretold Chevrolet fortunes in the balance of the decade. Chevrolet was back—in a very big way.

1973–1974: Loading up the Chevy Bandwagon

It didn't take long for other Grand National teams to sit up and take notice of the success enjoyed by Junior Johnson's Chevrolet-based team. As supplies of Chrysler and Fomoco exotica began to disappear, more and more teams made the switch to GM. Since Johnson had been there "firstest with the mostest," it will come as no surprise that his Chevy-based team continued to enjoy the most success with Bow Tie-based comp cars. Cale Yarborough signed on as team driver in 1973, and for the next six seasons his Junior Johnson-equipped GM stockers were the class of every racing grid they graced.

Adding to Chevy's success in 1973 was Benny Parsons who earned the first Grand National (now Winston Cup) driving championship of the modern era at the helm of L. G. DeWitt's Monte Carlos and Chevelles. And he

Earnhardt's first quality ride on the Winston Cup tour was provided by Rod Osterlund in 1980. Short-track duty was handled by big-fendered Monte Carlos like this one currently on display at the International Motorsports Hall of Fame in Talladega.

did it the old fashioned way—by running consistently in every race he entered. In fact, Parsons scored just one race win (at Bristol in the Volunteer 500) during the entire season, but though not often in first place, he wasn't far from it. By season's end Parsons had notched 15 top-five finishes and 21 top tens on his way to the title and $128,321 in winnings.

The last gasp for Chrysler drivers on the Winston Cup tour came in 1974. Richard Petty won his final non-GM national title that year, but the Chevrolet writing was already on the wall of his Randleman shop by the end of the season. And much of it was written by "graffitists" Junior Johnson and Cale Yarborough. Cale's #11 Carling Chevelle graced the winner's circle in Darlington at the Southern 500 that year as well as at nine other tracks.

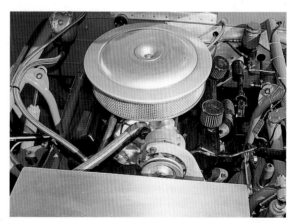

The venerable Chevrolet small block has been winning races since its introduction in 1955. Dale Earnhardt relied heavily on his small blocks to provide the "motorvation" for his first Winston Cup championship in 1980.

Richard Petty jumped ship for General Motors in late 1978. His trademark red-and-blue colors first showed up (in the modern era) on Chevy sheet metal at Michigan in August of that year. *Mike Slade*

Chevrolet wins for the first four years of the new decade totaled 32, and the future was looking bright. But truly the best was yet to come.

1975: Small-Blocks Invade the Scene

By 1975 the big-block NASCAR race engine had become a thing of the past. And that included the by-then venerable Chevrolet "rat" motor. First introduced in Mystery Motor form in 1963, the Chevy poly-angle-valved, big-block wedge motor was never as exotic as, say, a Boss 429, 426 Hemi, or 427 single overhead cam (SOHC) motor, but on balance, it was probably a more effective overall performer. Though deprived of racing glory during the 1960s when it was first homologated in 396 form, Chevy's rat at least got a brief moment in victory lane during the first few years of the modern era. Interestingly, its competition replacement was an engine even older than the Mystery Motor. And that, of course, was the incredible Chevrolet small-block race engine, which by 1974 had evolved into a full 358 cubic inches.

Cale Yarborough and Junior Johnson would erase all doubts about the small-block Chevrolet engine's potential as a championship contender during the 1976, 1977, and 1978 Winston Cup seasons. By the mid-1970s the 350-cubic-inch "mouse" motor had been massaged to produce more than 450 horsepower. When coupled with the slope-nosed shape of a slippery Chevelle Laguna S-3 body, speeds in excess of 200 miles per hour were just a stab of the throttle away. And that potential was quickly translated into superspeedway wins by Yarborough and the Holly Farms team.

65

Darrell Waltrip used the slippery shape of this Oldsmobile Cutlass to score a big superspeedway win in the 1979 running of the Talladega 500. The "corporate" Chevrolet small-block engine under the Gatorade car's sloping hood probably played a role in that victory too. *JDC Collection*

1976–1977: Championship Seasons for Chevy and Yarborough

When not rocketing around the high banks, Johnson's team relied on boxier Monte Carlo chassis for short-track duty. Though not nearly as sleek as the Laguna S-3, a 1973–1977-style Monte Carlo's more generously proportioned flanks allowed for plenty of fender rubbing on the shorter bull-ring circuits. The car's long snout and short trunk also provided better weight distribution (due to engine setback), which in turn enhanced handling. Yarborough and company relied on both body styles to rack up 9 wins and 22 top-five finishes on the way to his first Winston Cup championship in 1976. Chevrolet wins totaled 13 that year and grew to 21 the following season.

Yarborough and his swoopy S-3 were back at Daytona for 1977, though probably not greeted with much enthusiasm by the other teams in the garage area. He used what he'd learned during his win in the 1976 Firecracker (also held at Daytona) to win his second Daytona 500 that year. He and Johnson then steamrolled the competition in 8 more events, winning 2 more superspeedway races and 6 out of the 10 short-track events he entered. By season's end he'd secured his second Winston Cup championship.

Yarborough's only real competition that season was a brash young Kentuckian named Darrell Waltrip, who campaigned Chevrolets for the Di-Gard team. Collectively, Waltrip and Yarborough won 15 of the 30 races that made up the 1977 season and finished in the top five at 26 others. Along the way, Waltrip's knack for self-promotion inspired Yarborough to saddle him with the nickname "Jaws" and

Like most Chevrolet teams on the tour, Dale Earnhardt and Rod Osterlund elected to campaign the Olds Cutlass chassis at superspeedway events during the late 1970s and early 1980s. The car's slippery shape coupled with tried-and-true small-block Chevy power helped Earnhardt win his first Winston Cup crown in 1980.

The small-block Chevrolet has become a familiar sight in the Winston Cup garage area. Dale Earnhardt relied on a "mouse" motor for every one of his seven Winston Cup titles. Though limited to just 358 cubic inches, a modern small-block motor can churn out more (700-plus) horsepower than one of its big-block brothers from the early 1970s.

North Carolina's Alex Beam has recently restored one of Dale Earnhardt's championship-winning 1977 Olds Cutlasses. Its angled snout and fastback roofline made the car plenty quick on the big tracks.

the rivalry (if not the affection) between them only intensified.

1978: Oldsmobile Takes the Baton

The ever-changing NASCAR rules book struck Chevrolet fans a blow during the 1978 season. The sanctioning body decided during the off-season that the Laguna S-3's drooping snout gave Chevy drivers a bit too much of an aerodynamic edge over their boxier competition and so, with a wave of the rules-book pen, banned the body style from competition.

Fortunately for GM partisans, sister division Oldsmobile had already built a 442 Cutlass body style (in 1977) that featured an angled beak that was nearly as aerodynamically efficient as the S-3's snout, and the NASCAR rules book said nothing about banning it. Best of all, the sanctioning body decided to recognize the

Richard Petty jumped the Chrysler ship for General Motors in late 1978. It proved to be a wise move when, in 1979, Petty and a fleet of Monte Carlos and Cutlasses won the King's seventh Winston Cup title. Petty drove this car to victory in the 1979 Daytona 500. *Mike Slade*

Mid-seventies Monte Carlos were boxy and seemingly ungainly. Nonetheless, they made superb race cars. Their long hood lines and short rear deck allowed big time engine rear set, for example, and that helped weight distribution a bunch. *Mike Slade*

Chevrolet small block as a "corporate" engine that same year. That meant that Chevrolet racers interested in swapping to Olds sheet metal in search of an aerodynamic edge could still rely on their race proven "mouse" motors.

So that's just what Cale Yarborough and Junior Johnson did for the 1978 season. Cale scored the Oldsmobile division's first NASCAR win in 18 years in January of that year when he came home first in the Winston Western 500 at Riverside. In May he put his new Olds' slippery shape to good use by winning the Winston 500 at Talladega from the pole (191.904-mile-per-hour pole speed). Big-track wins at Michigan in June and Darlington in the Southern 500 followed in short order. Those wins, coupled with 6 other visits to victory lane and 23 top-five finishes, added up to Yarborough's third straight Winston Cup title.

Olds wins that year came in at 11, while Chevrolet victories (scored mostly on short tracks where generously fendered Monte Carlos still ruled) fell to 10.

The other big news in the GM ranks for 1978 was Richard Petty's decision to jump ship from Chrysler Company cars and return to the GM fold. King Richard made the change late in the season at Michigan, where he debuted a #43 Monte Carlo at the August 400-mile race. Though Petty's mechanical change of allegiance did not bear fruit in 1978, things came up roses for him the following season.

1979: The King and His Cutlass Reign

As Petty adherents are sure to recall, the King's first competitive outings in the NASCAR ranks came at the wheel of one of his dad's Oldsmobile stockers. And it was in a #43 Olds Cutlass that Petty snapped a 45-race winless streak by winning the 1979 Daytona 500. Petty's win was made all the more spectacular by the fact that he'd had a large portion of his stomach removed during the off-season (due to ulcers) and was supposed to be sitting at home recuperating instead of averaging 143 miles per hour on his way to a sixth win in the 500.

Petty followed up on that auspicious start to the season by adding four more wins to his even then-impressive total. Twenty-three top-five finishes gave Petty an unprecedented seventh national driving title. Olds wins totaled five for 1979, and all came at superspeedway events. Petty and most other GM drivers continued to rely on their bulbous-fendered Monte Carlos for the bulk of their on-track time in 1979. And those unlovely, if effective, cars visited the winner's circle 18 times as a result.

Dale Earnhardt was a first-time winner on the Winston Cup tour that year in his #2 Monte Carlo at Bristol in the Southeastern 500, and Darrell Waltrip added seven Chevy wins to his

Chevrolet Monte Carlos (like Bobby Allison's "Coke Machine" pictured here) were winners right out of the box. In fact, the car line has racked up more NASCAR wins than any other GM body style. *JDC Collection*

The secret of the Laguna S-3's success was its sloped front facia. It cut through the car much better than cars that carried more upright grilles. And that meant faster speeds on the track. *JDC Collection*

tally with the help of a #88 Monte Carlo that same season. Bigger things were just around the corner for Waltrip as 1979 drew to a close.

It is clear now that the 1970s truly belonged to Chevrolet and General Motors in NASCAR competition. Though few would have predicted it when the decade dawned, Chevrolet teams scored 90 Winston Cup wins between 1971 and 1980 and added 5 Winston Cup titles to that total for good measure. Though the 1970s were kind to GM drivers, the best was truly yet to come.

Though boxy and squared off, Bobby Allison's 1971 Monte Carlo was still plenty fast on the super speedways. It's likely the full Race Rat motor under the car's hood had a little something to do with that. *Daytona Racing Archives*

Chapter 4

THE 1980s
COMPETITION HEIGHTENS

With Ford forces reduced to combing junkyards for "racing" gear, the 1980s were destined to be the golden decade for GM drivers.

The cars became faster and smaller with improvements throughout the decade. New models Buick Regal, Monte Carlo SS, and Lumina took center stage when aerodynamic improvements, creating a second Aero War in 1986 and 1987, changed the role of aerodynamics in the racing world.

The era also featured GM cars taking the Winston Cup for 9 of the 10 years. Legendary drivers such as Dale Earnhardt, Darrell Waltrip, Bobby Allison, Rusty Wallace, and Terry Labonte made such a feat possible. Allison, Wallace, and Waltrip won their titles only during this decade.

1980: Last Year for "Big" Cars

The 1980 season was to be the last for cars rolling on 115-inch wheelbased chassis.

The colorful Buicks that Darrell Waltrip used to pummel the competition during the 1981 and 1982 seasons owed much of their speed to the drooping hoodline and angled grille that were part of the Regal styling package those years. *JDC Collection*

Grand National and Winston Cup cars had rolled into battle over chassis of that length for what seemed like forever. But that all had to change for 1981 as the days of the "full-sized" car had come and gone on the NASCAR tour. The days of the block-long Galaxies, Impalas, and Marauders that had originally set the 115-inch wheelbase limit were long since over, and after that season so too would be descendants of those cars like the mid-1970s-style Monte Carlos, Cutlasses, and Thunderbirds.

But before those lumbering throwbacks were relegated to the boneyard, they were allowed to have one last season in the sun. Buddy Baker kicked off that last year of the behemoths with an Olds Cutlass win in the Daytona 500. Darrell Waltrip and Junior Johnson continued their winning ways for their respective Chevrolet teams, and newcomers like "Texas" Terry Labonte scored first wins in their Chevrolets. But the year belonged to an up-and-coming second-generation stock car driver named Dale Earnhardt.

As is well known now, "Ironhead" is modified champ Ralph Earnhardt's son. And in the Earnhardt family, blood does really tell when it comes to driving skill. Dale Earnhardt's first stab at the Winston Cup ranks had come back

Waltrip's Buicks looked good from just about any angle—except perhaps from the rear. Unfortunately, that's about the only view that D.W.'s competition got to check out during the 1981 and 1982 Winston Cup seasons.

in 1975, and for the next few seasons he skipped around the series in search of a quality ride. By 1979 Earnhardt was a seasoned driver and had hooked up with Rod Osterlund's Chevrolet-based team. It proved to be a winning combination. Earnhardt accomplished the nearly impossible by winning a race in his first full year on the tour and taking Rookie of the Year honors. The very next season (1980), however, he managed to do the completely impossible by winning the Winston Cup championship in only his second full year on the tour. A big part of that title, of course, can be attributed to the yellow-and-blue #2 Chevrolet Monte Carlo that Osterland set up for Earnhardt every week. He recorded 5 wins that season and finished in the top five in 14 other races on his way to Winston Cup title number one. It wasn't to be his last.

1981–1982: Buicks Return to Victory Lane

As mentioned, 1981 was the first year for NASCAR's new downsizing rule. Overnight, the 115-inch wheelbase cars that had been

the standard for nearly two decades became out of date, and teams were forced to build (or cut down) chassis based on a 110-inch wheelbase. All bets were off for every manufacturer, and each team had to essentially start fresh in learning how to make the new, shorter cars handle.

The first team to learn how to do just that belonged to—not surprisingly—wily old veteran Junior Johnson. Never one to be afraid to try something new if it seemed to hold mechanical promise, Johnson was one of the first to abandon the Monte Carlo line in favor of the Buick Regal body style, the reason being aerodynamics. Unlike its Chevrolet and Pontiac siblings, the Buick Regal featured a forward-sloping grille and tapered hood line that was very efficient at cutting through the air at superspeedway velocities.

Power for Johnson's Mountain Dew-backed team that season was provided by a pumped-up 358-cubic-inch small block. The soda maker's green-and-white racing livery graced the #11 car, making it one of the best-looking Cup cars on any starting grid. Darrell Waltrip's driving skill also made it one of the fastest.

Waltrip slipped behind the wheel of Johnson's Dew-mobile for the season opener at Riverside after having to buy himself out of his old DiGard contract. It turned out to be a bargain at twice the price. Win number one for the new combination came at Rockingham in March, and from there on, Waltrip never looked back. By season's end, the flashy green-and-white Buick had won 12 races and notched 21 top-five finishes. The 4,880 points Waltrip accumulated were enough for him to win his first Winston Cup crown.

Fellow Buick drivers Richard Petty, Bobby Allison, and Cale Yarborough did their part to bring Buick's win total to a whopping 22, and those were the first marks in Buick's win column since Fireball Roberts' victories way back in 1955. Morgan Shepherd's win at Martinsville in the Virginia 500 was the first scored by a Pontiac driver in nearly as long (since 1963). Chevy drivers did not fare well, recording only a single win in the first year of the 110-inch wheelbase rule.

The Dew Crew had another big year on the Winston Cup tour in 1982. But they didn't begin their 1982 "tear" until after Bobby Allison had scored a popular victory in the Daytona 500 with his #88 DiGard Buick. It was the first "Super Bowl" win for that manufacturer and foretold the year that Buick drivers would enjoy on the tour. Waltrip's win total for 1982 came in again at 12. And as in 1981, fellow Buick driver Bobby Allison came in second behind the Dew car in the seasonal points race.

All told, Buick drivers scored 25 Winston Cup wins. Pontiac drivers were shut out that season, but Monte Carlo drivers managed 4 wins.

1983: GM Divisions Divvy Wins

Cale Yarborough began 1983 on an auspicious note for Bow Tie fans by winning the Daytona 500 with a new Monte Carlo SS. Tired of taking a back seat to the Buick Regal in aerodynamic prowess, Chevrolet engineers cooked up a bolt-on beak for the 1983 Monte Carlo line that replaced the car's former upright grille. The new nose featured a flexible fascia that offered a more angled attack to the wall of wind encountered at 200 miles per hour. Allison stood his ground with his Buick and scored win number one for 1983 at Richmond. Richard Petty also returned to the winner's circle in his Pontiac at Rockingham.

Overall the new-and-improved Monte Carlo proved to be the best car on the tour in 1983, winning 15 races. Buick pilots like Allison came in second with 6 wins, and Pontiac drivers scored 5.

Coming out on top of the points race was Bobby Allison, who finally stepped out of the Dew Crew's shadow to crown his spectacular career with a championship finish. Allison accomplished the victory with 6 wins and 18

That's Morgan Shepherd's #98 Buick getting sandwiched between Bobby Allison's Regal and Richard Petty's Grand Prix. The scene was a typical one on the superspeedways of the early 1980s: no Fords in sight. *JDC Collection*

top-five finishes. Ironically, Darrell Waltrip was second to Allison for a change in his Chevrolet Pepsi Challenger.

1984: Labonte Brings Home the Bacon

Cale Yarborough broke the double ton during qualifying for the 1984 Daytona 500 in his #28 Chevrolet. With a qualifying speed of 201.848 miles per hour, it was the first time that a driver had officially qualified for a Winston Cup race with a speed equal to or in excess of 200 miles per hour. It was an encouraging performance in the face of the aerodynamic prowess displayed by the newly returned to racing Ford Thunderbird line. After sitting on the sidelines since 1971, the Ford Motor Company had decided to return to racing (at least on a limited basis—the days of

Following pages
Though the late 1980s Buick Regal wasn't as aesthetically pleasing as it had been in the early 1980s, it was still a formidable competitor when decked out in NASCAR trim. *Mike Slade*

All four of the General's performance-oriented divisions were well represented in the NASCAR ranks during the mid-1980s. They collectively dominated the series. Unfortunately, today only Chevrolet and Pontiac are still in the game.

unlimited factory racing budgets are never to return), and for the first time since the mid-1970s, GM drivers had to seriously contend with someone other than fellow GM drivers for wins on the tour.

That having been said, the revitalized forces at Ford still weren't enough to prevent "Texas" Terry Labonte from scoring his first Winston Cup crown in a Billy Hagen–prepared Monte Carlo. Two wins and 17 top-five finishes were enough for the title in 1984. Darrell Waltrip was the most frequent visitor to victory lane in his Budweiser-backed Monte Carlo (7 times), but that total wasn't enough to cinch his third national title. That would come soon enough.

"Texas" Terry Labonte was an Olds pilot in the late 1980s. Though his Piedmont-backed Cutlass enjoyed jet sponsorship, the boxy little car's configuration was less than aerodynamic. Comparing Labonte's car with Richard Petty's swoopy Grand Prix 2+2 will dispel any doubts about that. *Mike Slade*

Harry Gant scored the last NASCAR wins for the Oldsmobile division (to date) during the 1992 season in a #33 Cutlass. The very next season, Olds and Buick decided to drop their backing of the Winston Cup series. One of Gant's Cutlasses has been returned to race duty on the vintage race circuit.

Richard Petty's Pontiac was arguably the prettiest of the long-nosed 2+2s that ran during the 1987 and 1988 seasons. Unfortunately, it never found its way to Victory Lane, but boy it sure looked fast!

1985: More Glory for GM

As you might have guessed, 1985 was another standout year for Chevrolet drivers on the tour. Cale Yarborough notched his second straight Daytona 500 win in his #28 Monte Carlo, and Darrell Waltrip visited victory lane for the first time that year at Bristol. Yarborough took the first Talladega race to under-

Pontiac's answer to the aero-Thunderbird threat during the late 1980s was the Pontiac Grand Prix 2+2. Richard Petty's 2+2 is pictured here. Interestingly, though the cars were built for optimum superspeedway velocity, Rusty Wallace scored the only 2+2 wins on road courses.

The droopy nose and special front fascia of the Grand Prix 2+2 looked fast sitting still. This particular Grand Prix was last raced by Indy ace Al Unser Jr. during 1987–1988 at the now defunct Riverside raceway in California. It is still cutting hot laps today on the vintage race circuit.

score the top-speed potential of his slope-nosed Chevy, and Bobby Allison proved that Buick Regals still had what it took for super-speedway wins by besting all comers in the grueling World 600. In addition, Richard Petty scored career wins 199 and 200 that season aboard a Pontiac. The latter triumph came in storybook fashion at the Firecracker 400 as President Ronald Reagan looked on. His record will, of course, never be topped.

Dale Earnhardt had returned to Richard Childress' team for 1984 after two years as a Ford driver, and his big-track wins (two wins that season and four in 1985) gave a hint of the success the team would enjoy in the near future. But it was Waltrip who stood on top of

No matter what the sheet metal might have suggested, Pontiac racers in the mid- to late 1980s (as today) all relied on "corporate" Chevrolet small-block engines for motivation.

the NASCAR hill at the end of 1985, securing his third Winston Cup crown (and car owner Junior Johnson's sixth).

Together, Buick, Pontiac, and Olds drivers went 29 and 0 in 1985.

1986–1987: Aero Wars

Speeds continued to rise at Daytona and Talladega during the mid-1980s. Much of that increased velocity could be traced to the efforts of Chevrolet aerodynamacists. When Ford's sleek Thunderbirds began to get uncomfortably close, GM engineers elected to smooth out the Monte Carlo's formal roofline by grafting on a "bubble-back" rear window and abbreviated trunk lid. The end result was a fastback roofline that more efficiently directed air toward the rear deck spoiler. The new car was dubbed the Monte Carlo SS Aero Coupe, and it was destined to be both one of the best looking and most successful Chevrolet race cars of all time.

Bill Elliott created quite a stir by rocketing around the Big D at more than 205 miles per

One of the reasons for the Monte Carlo Aero Coupe's high-speed prowess was the grafted-on bubble-back rear window that engineers cooked up to create a fastback roof line. It worked.

Previous page
The 1987 and 1988 seasons were the high point of the modern-day factory-backed aero wars. Speeds those seasons regularly topped the 200-mile-per-hour mark. Chevrolet's entry in that competition was the Monte Carlo Aero Coupe—and aerodynamic it was.

Dale Earnhardt became the man in black in 1988 when the Childress team picked up Goodwrench sponsorship. Earnhardt's been bad in black ever since. One of his team cars from the 1988 season is on display at Richard Childress' team museum in Welcome, North Carolina.

hour during pole qualifying for the 1986 Daytona 500. That impressive speed notwithstanding, it was Geoff Bodine's #5 Monte Carlo SS that graced the winner's circle at race end. It was the first of 18 such post-race trips taken by Bow Tie drivers that year. Tim Richmond was the most frequent visitor to victory lane that year; his Chevy victories included road course (Riverside), superspeedway (Darlington Southern 500), and short-track (Richmond) triumphs.

While the always-flashy Richmond was living large in victory lane, Dale Earnhardt was methodically working his way toward a second Winston Cup Championship. His 5 victories that season included triumphs at Atlanta, Charlotte, and Darlington. Sixteen top-5 and 23 top-10 finishes earned Earnhardt 288 more points than fellow Chevrolet driver Darrell Waltrip, and won him the 1986 NASCAR crown.

Earnhardt's second championship season was the same year that Pontiac, Olds, and

Buick drivers all returned to victory lane. Terry Labonte scored the first win for a down-sized Olds Cutlass at Rockingham in the Goodwrench 500. Pontiac's all-new "bubble-backed" aero warrior, the Grand Prix 2+2, got its first trip to victory lane at Bristol with the help of Rusty Wallace, and Bobby Allison used his #22 Buick to take the Winston 500 at Talladega. As in years past, each of the non-Chevrolet GM victories was achieved with the grunt of corporate Chevrolet small-block, 358-cubic-inch engines.

The high point of the modern era's factory-backed aero wars came in 1987. When GM and Fomoco drivers filed into Daytona for 500 testing that year, all knew that really big speeds would be in the offing. Monte Carlo Aero Coupe and Grand Prix 2+2 teams had had a whole season to refine the performance of their special aero-variant race cars, and Ford troops came packing an all-new and even swoopier version of the Thunderbird.

Ford drivers came out on top in the first test of aerodynamic superiority that season by winning the Daytona 500. Bill Elliott lived up to his awesome appellation at Daytona with a pole-winning lap of 210.364 miles per hour and

The control cabin of Waltrip's Aero Coupe featured an all-encompassing roll cage, a single form-fitting alloy bucket seat, and a brace of analog gauges to monitor engine function.

Darrell Waltrip's last Junior Johnson-built race car was a Budweiser-backed Monte Carlo Aero Coupe. Alex Beam of Davidson, North Carolina, has restored one of those cars to race trim. D.W.'s teammate, the late Neil Bonnett, drove a nearly identical #12 Budweiser Monte Carlo. Between them, they scored 4 wins and 27 top-5 finishes.

a convincing win in the 500 proper. Talladega was also a Ford tour de force as Elliott once again set fast lap time with a blistering 212.809-mile-per-hour circuit, and Davey Allison won the event from a third-place starting position.

Ford's prowess on the superspeedways that season led directly to the reintroduction of the carburetor restrictor plate for the second time in NASCAR history. And those flow-restricting, horsepower-robbing "safety" components are still bunching up cars and causing spectacular wrecks to this very day.

As fast as Ford drivers were on the big tracks, their wins there weren't enough to prevent Dale Earnhardt from scoring his third straight Winston Cup title. His 11 wins bettered Elliott's total by 5, and those triumphs coupled with an incredible 21 top-5 finishes added up to Winston Cup crown number 3 for both Earnhardt and his Monte Carlo.

Pontiac drivers recorded 1987 wins at Riverside and Watkins Glen, while Bobby Allison won the Firecracker 400 in a downsized Buick. Olds drivers did not fare so well, scoring no wins that year.

1988: An Off Year

In many ways, 1988 was the best season and the worst season for longtime GM driver Bobby Allison. Without a doubt one of the season's highlights came in the Daytona 500 when Bobby edged out his son Davey's Thunderbird to claim his second Daytona 500 victory. But that win turned out to be Bobby's last on the tour, due to the near-fatal shunt he would suffer at Pocono in June. Today Bobby is tied with Darrell Waltrip for third on the all-time NASCAR wins list at 84 victories (though his total should be 85 thanks to a Grand American victory that Bobby Allison scored with a Holman & Moody Mustang at a combined Grand American and Grand National event in 1971; a win that the sanctioning body refuses to recognize). Richard Petty suffered a potentially career- (and life-) ending wreck of his own in the Daytona 500. Although his #43 Pontiac was totally demolished, Petty was lucky enough to walk away to race another day.

Chevrolet drivers scored fewer wins than their archrival Ford foes for the first time in seven years during the 1988 season. Bill Elliott accounted for six of the nine Thunderbird wins recorded that year; those wins, combined with the nine other top-five berths he recorded, resulted in his first Winston Cup driving title. That title was the first for a Ford driver since the corporation had withdrawn from racing after the 1969 Grand National season, and it was the beginning of the heightened competition between Fomoco and GM drivers that has characterized the Winston Cup series ever since.

Pontiac driver Rusty Wallace scored six wins for the Indian-head division in 1988 to come in second behind Elliott in the points race. All told, Chevy drivers won eight times, with Pontiac drivers tallying the same, and Buick and Olds drivers each scored two.

1989: Luminas Take the Torch

Rusty Wallace used his second-place finish in the 1988 points race as a springboard to the 1989 title. But before he got to walk across the stage in New York as the new Winston Cup champ, Darrell Waltrip crowned a stellar career with a win in the 1989 Daytona 500. His #17 Tide Monte Carlo SS crossed the stripe first in his 17th trip to Daytona.

En route to the championship, Wallace scored all 6 of the wins in the Pontiac column in 1989, while Chevrolet pilots Dale Earnhardt, Waltrip, Geoff Bodine, and Ken Schrader conspired to score 18 wins for Chevrolet. The most notable of those (Daytona 500 aside) was the Southern 500 cinched by Dale Earnhardt in the Goodwrench Monte Carlo. Ricky Rudd recorded a win for Buick at Sears Point, while Olds driver Harry Gant performed similar honors for that marque at the spring Darlington race.

Chevrolet drivers reluctantly had to surrender the "keys" to their tried-and-true Monte Carlos late in 1989 due to GM's decision to retire the marque in favor of the new

NASCAR abandoned all semblance of "stockness" in 1989 when it allowed GM to campaign the Lumina body style. Though never UAW equipped with either a V-8 or rear wheel drive, that's just how the new Luminas raced—and won!—that year. *John Craft*

and slipperier-shaped Lumina line. There was just one problem with that plan: Chevrolet wasn't building any V-8-powered, rear-wheel-drive Luminas. And that drivetrain configuration had been the rules-required standard since the beginning of NASCAR in 1949. But, of course, the NASCAR rules book has always been subject to change—at a minute's notice——when the sanctioning body is so inclined. And that's just what happened in 1989.

In many ways, the last links with the old Grand National days and the Strictly stock series that preceded it were severed when the Chevrolet Lumina was legalized for Cup competition. Certainly all pretense that NASCAR racing was in any way associated with "stock" production American sedans was forever ended in 1990.

That having been said, Chevrolet drivers wasted little time in proving that their new Luminas were every bit the race cars that Monte Carlo SSes had been.

So the on-track battles continue into a new decade.

Chapter 5

THE 1990s
A GLIMPSE OF THE FUTURE

The last decade of the century was destined to be a winning one for GM adherents. New and evermore aerodynamic body styles, new ponies squeezed old small block motor, and a string of Chevrolet biased rule book concessions all added up to NASCAR wins—a lot of them.

1990–1991: Luminas Power into the New Decade

The first full season for the all-new Lumina was in 1990, and Derrike Cope was the first to score a Lumina win in the Daytona 500. Dale Earnhardt was snake bit as usual in the 500 that year. He seemed destined for certain victory until he blew a right front tire on the last lap of the event. Ironhead went on to overcome that disappointment during the rest of the season, and by year's end he secured his fourth Winston Cup crown. His 9 wins (including a third Southern 500 triumph) helped Lumina drivers visit victory lane a grand total of 13 times. Pontiac drivers turned in 3 wins, while Olds and Buick drivers scored 1 each. Brett Bodine's win at North Wilkesboro in the spring race proved to be the last earned by a Buick driver in the Winston Cup series to date. Perhaps the marque will one day return to the starting grid on the NASCAR tour, but until it does, Buick's total of 56 series wins and 2 Winston Cup championships will remain unchanged.

California native Ernie Irvan burst onto the scene with his first Cup win in 1990 and backed it up by joining the very exclusive club of Daytona 500 winners in 1991. His Lumina win was the first of 11 scored by Chevy teams that season. Earnhardt accounted for 4 of those, and though others accounted for more, Ironhead's consistency (and 21 total top-10 finishes) earned him a fifth national driving title. He again missed out on a win in the Daytona 500 that year but made up for it with a superspeedway win at Talladega. Harry Gant put Olds out in front in the Southern 500 at Darlington. Four other Cutlass victories made 1991 the best year for Olds drivers on

When Chevrolet elected to retire the Monte Carlo marque (temporarily) in late 1989, Bow Tie teams had to switch over to Lumina-based comp cars. Though based on staid little front-drive, six-cylinder street cars, the rear-wheel drive, small-block-powered Luminas made fine race mounts for drivers like Ernie Irvan, Dale Earnhardt, and Darrell Waltrip.

the tour since 1979. Pontiac drivers recorded three wins of their own.

1992: Oldsmobile Signs Off

In retrospect, Davey Allison's win in the 1992 Daytona 500 (with a Robert Yates-prepped Ford) was probably an omen. And that's because 1992 was to become only the second year in the modern era (to that date) when a non-GM-based team was able to win the prestigious Winston Cup driving championship. Alan Kulwicki was the man to beat in the points race that season and his "Underbird" independent team overcame incredible odds to cinch the title for Ford.

Dale Earnhardt provided some reason to cheer with a win in the World 600 at Charlotte, and Ernie Irvan drove his Kodak Lumina across the stripe first at Daytona in the Firecracker 400 and at Talladega in the Talladega 500. In addition, Darrell Waltrip scored a popular Chevrolet win in the Southern 500 that season. Pontiac drivers also won at Richmond and Rockingham. Unfortunately, King Richard Petty scored none of those wins during his final season on the tour. It's a fair prediction to say that his record of 200 wins will never be bettered. It's just too bad that he couldn't have added an additional victory or two during his 1992 "Fan Appreciation Farewell Tour."

The two Oldsmobile wins scored by Harry Gant at Dover and Michigan turned out to be the last recorded by Cutlass drivers in the century. Like Buick, Olds elected to drop its racing funding following the 1992 season,

Richard Petty's last full season on the Winston Cup tour was spent behind the wheel of a svelte little Grand Prix like this one.

Though Richard Petty's driving days are in the past, his familiar #43 Pontiac is still a regular fixture on the Winston Cup tour. His most recent driver is John Andretti.

so GM teams for 1993 had to select between either Chevy or Pontiac sheet metal (for in reality, modern NASCAR "stock" cars are identical beneath the skin).

1993: Pontiacs Push Ahead

Dale Jarrett got 1993 off to an auspicious start for Bow Tie drivers by putting Joe Gibbs' Lumina in the winner's circle at the Daytona 500. Jarrett, one of a growing number of second-generation NASCAR drivers, did what his dad (Ned Jarrett) never got a chance to do during his own standout Grand National career—win the Daytona 500. Earnhardt reprised his now familiar role of bridesmaid in the 500 by finishing second to Jarrett, a mere 0.16 seconds behind him on the track.

Rusty Wallace gave an early indication of the strength that Pontiac drivers would display during the season by winning the second race on the 1993 tour at Rockingham in his Penske-prepped Grand Prix. All told, Pontiac drivers visited victory lane 11 times that year. And that was more than both Chevrolet and Ford drivers could say at the end of the 30-race season. Chevy drivers did make headlines with wins on big tracks like Talladega in the Winston 500 (Ernie Irvan), Darlington in the Rebel 500 (Earnhardt), Charlotte in the World 600 (Earnhardt), Daytona in the Firecracker 400 (Earnhardt), and back at Talladega in the fall race there (Earnhardt).

Although the Southern 500 was claimed by Mark Martin in a Ford and Ernie Irvan defected

Ernie Irvan drove one of the flashiest Grand Prixes on the circuit. His candy sponsorship is an example of the increasing number of non-automotive sponsors that have made an investment in Winston Cup racing.

mid-season to replace Davey Allison (tragically killed in a helicopter accident) in Robert Yates' T-Bird, on balance both Pontiac and Chevrolet drivers had a good year in 1993, which included winning the series title. Earnhardt claimed his sixth seasonal title with 6 wins and 17 top-five finishes, bringing him one notch closer to King Richard Petty's record 7 Winston Cup titles. Ironhead got to pocket $3,353,789 in compensation for those labors in addition to adding yet another trophy to his Lake Norman, North Carolina mantel.

1994–1999: Gordon Takes Center Stage

It might have been easy in 1994 to think that things would follow pretty much the same pattern for the rest of the 1990s: Earnhardt and Wallace dividing up wins, leaving the leftovers to hapless Ford pilots like Mark Martin. But that's not how things were destined to turn out. And the first evidence of that fact made itself known in 1994. For that was the year that a young lad from Indiana first got a chance to visit a stock car victory lane. Jeff Gordon was the youth in question, and his first Winston Cup win came on May 29, 1994, in the always-grueling World 600 at Charlotte. He soon became a regular fixture in victory lane.

Sterling Marlin scored yet another Chevrolet win in the Daytona 500 in his Kodak yellow #4 Lumina. Unfortunately for Chevy fans, Ford drivers won the next three races on the tour. It wasn't until Darlington that a Bow Tie driver (Earnhardt) was able to best the newly resurgent Fomoco forces. The new-found speed that GM defector Rusty Wallace and the rest of his T-Bird stablemates displayed in 1994 made

Dale Earnhardt won his fourth, fifth, sixth, and seventh Winston Cup championships with the assistance of Chevrolet Lumina race cars.

Earnhardt's chances of winning his record-tying seventh Winston Cup title more than a little problematic. This was especially so since by season's end Thunderbird drivers had scored nearly twice as many wins (20) as their Chevrolet rivals (11). Pontiac drivers fared even worse with hotshoe Rusty Wallace off at Ford and were shut out of the winner's circle completely. But despite all the obstacles, Earnhardt's consistency and the NASCAR rules book's preference for total top fives over total wins produced yet another Winston Cup crown for Earnhardt and team owner Richard Childress.

Change was the theme for 1995. First and foremost for Chevy drivers was the reintroduction of the Monte Carlo nameplate to the starting grid. Like the Luminas it replaced, the new-for-1995 Monte Carlo was based on a street-going version that sported front-wheel drive and a V-6 motor. The sanctioning body deemed the chassis "legal" for competition and even permitted Chevrolet aerodynamicists more than a little dramatic license with the new race car's hindquarters in order to create "parity" with Ford drivers out on the track. And that turned out to be a good thing for Chevy drivers.

Parity as defined by the sanctioning body that season translated into a Chevrolet sweep in the Daytona 500 (led by Sterling Marlin) and the next 6 races on the tour. It wasn't until April that a non-Bow Tie-badged race car got to grace victory lane. And even then, that win turned out to be the exception for 1995 rather than the rule. All told, Chevrolet

Though Jeff Gordon's boy-next-door looks might get him carded at a nightclub, he's been "The Man" on the NASCAR tour almost since his first Winston Cup race. His rainbow-hued Monte Carlo is easy to pick out as it effortlessly slices through the pack during the last laps of a race.

Slight of build and high pitched in voice, Jeff Gordon is the very antithesis of the burly man's-man drivers who piloted GM race cars during NASCAR's earliest days. Be that as it may, the lad has left all of those two-fisted types in the dust on his tear-through the record books. *John Craft*

Previous pages
Derrike Cope in his Lumina was the surprise winner of the 1990 Daytona 500 when Dale Earnhardt's Lumina blew a tire coming out of turn four on the last lap of the race.

Monte Carlo drivers recorded 21 wins that season (to Ford's 8). Parity indeed! Jeff Gordon added 7 wins to the 2 he'd scored in 1994. Those triumphs earned him the nickname "Boy Wonder" and his very first Winston Cup driving title.

Slight of build and diminutive in stature, the youthful Gordon seemed to be an unlikely candidate for NASCAR stardom—especially when compared to "man's man" types like Curtis Turner, Fireball Roberts, Buddy Baker, and Dale Earnhardt.

But that's just what he became—seemingly overnight—a NASCAR star. And so much so that the Winston Cup tour has become the Hoosier's playground during the second half of the 1990s.

As the new millenium dawns, young Gordon has won a grand total of three national driving titles (1995, 1997, and 1998) and in just six short seasons has recorded an incredible 47 victories (as of July 1999)—a figure that ranks him 11th on the all-time wins list.

In 1998 alone Gordon scored so many wins (13) that race promoters began to worry about a fan backlash similar to the one that occurred during the 1955 and 1956 series when Karl Kiekhaeffer's all-conquering Chryslers won just about everything in sight. So dominant has Gordon become that Ford and Chevrolet partisans alike howl in glee on those rare occasions when his pretty rainbow-hued race cars fall out of an event short of the winner's circle. Fellow Monte Carlo driver and Hendricks teammate Terry Labonte turned out to be the only match for Gordon during the last half of the 1990s, and Texas Terry proved that point by winning his second Winston Cup crown in 1996.

In the two seasons since, it's been all Gordon and just about all Chevrolet. Even the introduction of new jellybean-shaped (four door!) Ford Taurus race cars in 1998 wasn't enough to slow the Chevrolet juggernaut. As this book is being written, Chevrolet engineers have an all-new and even sleeker Monte Carlo racer just waiting in the wings to start racking up NASCAR wins.

Regardless of what Ford's sales literature might say, it's Chevrolet racers who are truly racing into the future! GM drivers have been around the NASCAR scene since the early days of NASCAR back in 1949. And they've been winning ever since. Don't look for that to change any time soon.

"Texas" Terry Labonte won his second Winston Cup championship with his Monte Carlo in 1996. But despite Labonte's win that year, most of the last half of the 1990s belonged to Jeff Gordon, who drove his Monte Carlos to championships in 1995, 1997, and 1998.

Ford, Lincoln & Mercury
Stock Cars

Davey Allison and Bill Elliott were the fastest men in NASCAR in 1987. Both drivers regularly qualified their Thunderbirds at speeds in excess of the double ton, and between them they won eight races.

Introduction
First On Race Day

It's been said that Ford stands for First On Race Day. Without a doubt, few automobile manufacturers—either foreign or domestic—can match the Ford Motor Company's motorsports accomplishments. Indy, LeMans, F-1, NHR—Ford drivers have been there and done that—many times. Ford's dominance in four-wheeled competition has vexed rivals from "Il Commendatore" Enzo Ferrari to Bill "Grumpy" Jenkins, and the Blue Oval has graced world champions in just about every form of organized competition.

Nowhere has Ford (and sister division Lincoln Mercury) motorsports muscle been more strongly felt than in the stock car ranks. Though not major players during the first few seasons of Big Bill France's Grand National division, Fomoco-badged competition cars soon began to make their mark. By the middle of the first full decade of stock car competition, factory-backed Fomoco teams had so thoroughly flummoxed their General Motors rival that GM execs opted to slow the Blue Oval juggernaut through behind-the-scenes intrigue rather than on-the-track confrontation.

After being sidelined for a handful of seasons, Ford and Mercury teams returned to the fray and soon regained their preeminent position. Ralph Moody and John Holman served as the focus of Fomoco's 1960s racing endeavors, and their collective contributions shaped both the sport then and the series today. Competition cars and racing R&D that came out of the Holman & Moody shop led directly to the success enjoyed by such legendary drivers and mechanics as David Pearson, Robert Yates, Cale Yarborough, LeeRoy Yarbrough, Junior Johnson, Bud Moore, Fred Lorenzen, Ned Jarrett, Banjo Matthews, Leonard and Glenn Wood, Fireball Roberts, Joe Weatherly, and a host of others.

Fomoco drivers made the 427 FE, Boss 429, and 351 C engines both famous and feared in stock car circles, and the corporation's early emphasis on aerodynamics led to the focus on low coefficient of drag numbers that still holds sway today both on and off the track.

After a bleak decade-long absence from the series during the "Fuelish" 1970s, Ford racers reclaimed their places at the head of the pack and have remained there ever since "Awesome Bill" Elliott broke Bow Tie fans' hearts during the early 1980s.

As the dawn of the next century approaches, Ford is still a strong force in the NASCAR series. To date, Ford and Mercury drivers have scored more Grand National/Winston Cup wins than any other automotive manufacturer, and it's doubtful that things will be any different in the foreseeable future.

Though late 1940s, Lincolns were anything but svelte, they actually made fairly respectable race cars. It was a Lincoln, after all, that Jim Roper piloted to victory in the very first NASCAR race. Tim Flock (shown here on the Daytona Beach course) and a number of other drivers also drove hot-rod Lincolns during the first few seasons of what later came to be called Grand National racing. *Daytona Racing Archives*

1

NASCAR's First Years Through the AMA Factory Ban

NASCAR's Beginnings: Pre-1950

It's not exactly clear what Jim Roper expected that day in June of 1949 when he pulled his 1949 Lincoln up to the starting line. But it's pretty much a certainty that he had no idea what he was getting the Ford Motor Company (Fomoco) into. After all, as far as he knew, that day's race at the Charlotte Speedway was just one more of the increasingly popular sedan races that were beginning to be held across the Southland during the late 1940s. And though a charismatic giant of a fellow named Bill France was behind this particular bull-ring affair, there was really nothing to distinguish Big Bill's newly-formed National Association for Stock Car Automobile Racing (NASCAR) from the other fledgling sanctioning organizations of the day— at least at the time, that is.

The race in question was the first ever organized by NASCAR for its new "Strictly Stock Division," and Roper, along with 33 other drivers, was on hand for the 200-lap affair that Sunday afternoon in North Carolina. When the starter gave the command, Roper floored his Mecklenburg Motors-backed Lincoln with all the rest.

Like many of his competitors in the field, Roper had driven his "race" car to the track that day. Making that feat even more remarkable today is the fact that he'd driven the same car more than a thousand miles cross-country to the event (after having read about the race in a newspaper comic strip of all places!). It seems that purpose-built race cars and block-long team transporters were still more than a few years in the future back in 1949.

But that didn't mean that the on-track competition was in any way deficient. Future stars

1949-1960

like Frank "Rebel" Mundy, Fonty Flock, Lee Petty, Buck Baker, Tim Flock, Red Byron, Herb Thomas, and Curtis Turner took the green flag at the same time that Roper did, and their collective presence in the field was a virtual guarantee that the race action would be fast and furious. Lee Petty totaled his Buick in the first ever NASCAR wreck (in a car that he borrowed from a neighbor for the event);

a number of other drivers also came to grief while challenging for the lead.

When the last circuit around that dusty, rutted dirt track was complete, Glenn Dunnaway had brought his 1947 Ford home three full laps ahead of Roper's second-place Lincoln. But a post-race inspection of the winning car turned up a set of non-stock leaf springs. As a result, Roper was

Ford executives paid Bill France's NASCAR series little attention until the mid-1950s. It was then that folks in the Dearborn "Glass House" finally decided to get into factory-backed stock car competition in a big way. The first step in that process was securing the services of Indy 500 ace Pete DePaolo (right) to head up the effort. One of DePaolo's first acts was to sign up promising young driver Ralph Moody. *Daytona Racing Archives*

When Pete DePaolo stepped aside as the leader of Ford's factory stock car effort, Ralph Moody (center, checkered shirt) and John Holman (in car) stepped in to fill the void. Holman & Moody are joined here by early team drivers (from left) Curtis Turner, Joe Weatherly, Marvin Panch, and Bill Amick. *Daytona Racing Archives*

credited with the win as twilight settled over the track. First place paid a handsome $2,000 for NASCAR race number one, and Roper used some of the purse to buy a new refrigerator. As things turned out, it was the lanky Kansan's first and last NASCAR triumph. But it was not to be the last time that a Fomoco-powered race car visited a Grand National (later to become Winston Cup) winner's circle—not by a long shot.

The cars that Henry Ford built became associated with racing and organized competition right from the very start of the Ford Motor Company's operations. In fact, Ol' Henry built his first competition car as far back as 1901, when the company was but little removed from the basement shop where the very first Fomoco car (the Quadracycle) had been built in 1896. The now famous #999 Ford racer made its initial appearance in 1904, and H. F. hired legendary driver Barney Oldfield to pilot it to a number of speed records. That particular Ford was the first automobile to exceed 90 miles per hour—a phenomenal velocity for its day.

It didn't take long for Ford to begin to appreciate the positive effect on sales that racing headlines produced.

Ford's corporate interest in motorsports, quite naturally, rubbed off on a certain percentage of the buying public. Soon Ford Model Ts were being stripped down for organized competition at tracks all across the country. Fenderless Ford-backed race cars soon began appearing at the Brickyard in Indianapolis. Ford's association with speed was heightened by the exploits of the flathead V-8 during the 1930s, and soon both racers and bank robbers (such as Clyde Barrow) were making fast getaways in Ford-powered cars.

Postwar Fords continued to find favor with the buying (and hot rodding) public due to their enviable combination of low price and high horsepower. As a result, Ford race cars played a large role in the early rough-and-tumble days of modified "jalopy" racing that directly preceded the advent of the NASCAR tour. And when Big Bill France's genius led to the very first "Strictly Stock" NASCAR race, cars of the Fomoco persuasion constituted nearly half of the starting field (in addition to Roper's car, there were 2 other Lincolns, 10 Fords, and 1 Mercury on the grid when the green flag fell).

As Roper's pre-race commute from Kansas suggests, NASCAR racing was a whole lot different in

Hard charging Curtis Turner won the 1956 Southern 500 in a car just like this. "Pops" qualified his "Purple Hog" 11th that day before going on to best the field at the "Lady in Black."

Fomoco stock cars circa 1956 were motorvated by a beefed-up version of the factory Y-block overhead valve engine. Though not as stout as, say, a Chrysler FirePower Hemi, a full boogie Y-block could still be counted on for in excess of 230 ponies.

the days when Harry Truman was still giving them hell in Foggy Bottom. "Stock" meant stock in 1949, and Roper's car sported just about every piece of sheet metal and brightwork that it had when it rolled off of the assembly line. The same could be said for the 336-cubic-inch straight eight under the car's hood. Chances are that not many more than the engine's original complement of 152 ponies were on hand to propel Roper to victory that day in 1949.

That having been said, it was yet another sleepy straight eight that provided the oomph for Fomoco's second NASCAR win just four months later. That particular race took place on a half-mile dirt oval in Hamburg, New York, in September. Jack White came home in first place after 200 dusty

Stock ergonomics characterized the control cabin of mid-1950's Ford race cars. Stock bench seats and column shifters were part of the program, as were stock dash panels and roll-up windows. Note the wispy roll cage that was all the rules book required in 1956.

109

circuits of the track in his Moyer Company-sponsored 1949 Lincoln.

When that eight-race inaugural season was over, Oldsmobile driver Red Byron had cinched the very first NASCAR Driver's Championship. He and his fellow Olds drivers won five of the races contested, with Lee Petty's Plymouth accounting for the lone event not won by a GM or Lincoln car. Things would change dramatically in 1950, and the first wins scored by Ford- and Mercury-badged stock cars were just around the corner in the first full decade of what soon came to be called the Grand National series.

Though the first fledgling NASCAR season had consisted of but a handful of short track events, it had attracted more than a little attention from racing fans. Things were definitely looking up for Bill France's new series when cars began filing into Daytona for the 1950 season opener on the famed beach course there. Though steep banking and asphalt pavement were years in the future at Daytona, the 4.17-mile beach and road course just south of town was still a pretty impressive track. It consisted of equal parts surface street and hard-packed sand straights that were connected by treacherously rutted sand and dirt corners. Forty-one cars qualified for the 200-mile, 48-lap event in Daytona that year. In that number were nine Lincolns and seven Fords. Former tank corps driver Harold Kite qualified his #21 Lincoln third on the grid. With a "capacity" crowd of 9,500 spectators looking on, Kite muscled and manhandled his pregnant-looking 4,600-pound "race car" into the lead on lap 1 and went on to win the race by a 53-second margin over Red Byron's Olds. Kite averaged a not-so-blistering 89.894 miles per hour on his way to winning the $1,500 race purse that day.

Tim Flock, who was soon to become a legend on the tour, backed up Kite's Daytona win with a second Lincoln triumph at race number two of 1950 in Charlotte. Though no one knew it at the time, Flock's victory in the Edmund's Motors 1949 Lincoln would prove to be the last Grand National

win for the marque in history. But other Fomoco car lines were waiting in the wings to continue the Blue Oval winning tradition.

In fact, Ford win number three took place that same season at Dayton, Ohio. The race in question was a 100-mile event contested on the dirt-covered Dayton Speedway. The green flag fell on 25 cars that day in the Buckeye State, and in that number was the #27 1950 Ford driven by Jimmy Florian for Euclid Motors. Like its assembly line mate the Lincoln, Florian's Ford was powered by a 239.4-cubic-inch flathead V-8 that churned out just 100 horses. Even so, Florian (who in a novel twist raced bare-chested that day to beat the heat!) was able to put each and every one of those ponies to good use during the race. Florian's Ford ran near the front all day and led on two occasions for a total of 40 laps. He took the lead for the final and most important time on lap 168 (of 200 total), when he slipped past the always-hard-to-pass Curtis "Pops" Turner. The Cleveland mechanic kept his Ford out in front for the balance of the race and got to kiss the pretty girl at race's end. He also got to pocket the $1,000 first-place purse.

Florian's win turned out to be the start of the most successful string of wins yet to be recorded by any manufacturer on the NASCAR tour. Over the years that followed, Ford drivers continued to taste victory on the Grand National/Winston Cup circuit. To date, cars carrying the Blue Oval have visited a NASCAR victory lane no fewer than 450 times—more than any other marque. That winning total continues to grow each and every racing season.

Nineteen fifty was also the first year that a car from Ford's sister division, Mercury, visited the winner's circle. That inaugural triumph took place at a 100-mile event held on dirt in Vernon, New York. North Carolinian Bill Blair scored win number one for the Mercury car division on June 18th before a crowd of 15,000 spectators. Lloyd Moore notched a second Mercury victory at the

Ford upped the horsepower ante for 1957 by homologating a special supercharged version of the 312-cubic-inch Y-block engine. Ford engineers rated the engine at 300 ponies in street trim that year. It's a safe bet that ace tuners like Ralph Moody coaxed even higher figures from the littler huffer on race day.

next-to-last race of the 1950 season in Winchester, Indiana. Two more Mercury Man division wins were on tap for 1952.

Racing Dearth for Ford: 1951–1954

Though all three of Fomoco's car divisions had enjoyed some success during the first two seasons of Grand National stock car racing, as things turned out it would be nearly five long years before the next Blue Oval-powered stock car would visit a NASCAR victory lane. Unfortunately, when the factory horsepower wars broke out during the early

1950s, Ford's sleepy little flathead V-8 was found to be lacking in "ammunition." Corporate disinterest in organized motorsports also played a role in keeping Ford cars out of the win column. Other more progressive carmakers like Hudson began to build special factory high-performance components specifically for stock car competition with predictable results—fabulous Hudson Hornets began to win with regularity. Olds drivers found their own advantage with that car line's all-new high-horsepower, overhead-valve V-8s, and they too scored more than a few Grand National victories. Chrysler

Motor Company (Chryco) drivers picked up Hemi power in 1951, and soon they, too, started to show up in the winner's circle. All Fomoco racers could do was stew while General Motors, Mopar, and Hudson were winning in the early 1950s.

The mid-1950s saw the NASCAR tour mature from a marginally organized series consisting of just a handful of races to a mature tour made up of 33 different events. Purses grew with each passing season and so, too, did attendance at tracks along the circuit. Master promoter Bill France staged a Grand National race in Dearborn that was heavily attended by Big Three execs in 1951, and the Southern 500 quickly became a national headline generator.

The increasing public interest (as indicated by burgeoning gate receipts) was not lost on car makers in Detroit (or Dearborn). When Chevrolet's public relations bandwagon began to play up the wins scored by Chevy stock car drivers in 1954, Ford execs simply could not continue to ignore the importance of winning races on Sunday. The General's Chevrolet division had long been Ford's arch rival for the mid-priced car-buying public. While wins scored by high-line Chrysler letter cars and econo-Hudsons could be ignored, when Chevrolet began to rack up high publicity wins in NASCAR circles, the powers that be at Ford just couldn't look the other way. And so it was that Ford decided to venture into factory-backed motorsports in 1955.

It was an event that took place in 1953, however, that brought Ford into victory lane. That was the introduction of the all-new, overhead-valve (OHV) Y-block engine family. The Ford Motor Company began its 51st year of production in 1954 by

While Holman & Moody were working their mechanical magic on the East Coast, Bill Stroppe was turning out trick race cars on the opposite coast. Tim Flock, whose ride is pictured here, drove both convertible and hardtop Mercurys for Stroppe in the 1950s. The cars looked sharp and were plenty fast. *Mike Slade*

"M" Power Mercurys came factory equipped with 335 horsepower versions of the corporate Y-block. Two four-barrel carbs, alloy valve covers, and cast-iron exhaust manifolds were all regular parts of the under-hood scenery.

pulling the wraps off of an all-new 130-horse OHV engine. Though displacing nearly the same 239 cubic inches of its predecessor "flatty" V-8, the all-new engine possessed loads of potential and soon grew to 272, then 292, and finally 312 cubic inches (by 1956). The new engine line would soon turn out to be just the solution to the Ford horsepower deficit and to the Blue Oval slump on the track.

Ford Gets Serious About Racing: 1955–1957

For the 1955 season, Ford tapped open-wheel ace Buddy Schuman to supervise their effort, and series hotshoes Curtis Turner and Little Joe Weatherly got the nod for driving chores.

The 1955 Southern 500 was the targeted debut of the Ford-backed, two-car team, and work

got under way for that race with the construction of two Fairlane-based race cars at Ford's experimental garage in Dearborn. In accordance with the rules book of the day, extra shocks were added at all four corners and reinforced rims were installed. A rudimentary single-hoop roll bar (yes, bar, not cage) was installed at about the same time that most of the cars' interior accouterments were removed. Power was provided by a highly-tuned 292 Y-block that was rated at 230 horsepower. A three-on-the-tree manual tranny was all that Ford had in its torque reduction arsenal for 1955, so that's what backed up the willing little small block. When construction was complete, the cars were dressed in a coat of purple Schwam Motors (a Charlotte Ford dealer) racing livery.

During qualifying for the race, Weatherly rocketed around the "Lady in Black" at an average speed of 109.006 miles per hour with Turner a couple of ticks behind at 106. Though not fast enough to capture the pole (which future Ford driver Glenn "Fireball" Roberts snared with a 110-mile-per-hour lap in his Buick), both Weatherly and Turner started towards the front of the pack, and both ultimately spent more than a little time in the lead. Unfortunately, a shunt sidelined Little Joe at mid-race, and a tie rod end put an equally unceremonious end to Turner's day. Herb Thomas' win in Smokey Yunick's 1955 factory-backed Chevrolet

must have stung a bit, but Ford wins were just around the corner, specifically around the corner of the Memphis-Arkansas dirt track in LeHi, Arkansas just one month later.

Interestingly, Ford's second win on the Grand National tour was served up not by the Schuman team but rather by Chrysler 300 team owner Karl Kiekhaefer! In addition to sponsoring his usual fleet of all-conquering Chryslers at the LeHi event, Kiekhaefer also backed Speedy Thompson's 1955 Fairlane, and at race's end it was Speedy who took the trophy home. Marvin Panch backed that Ford performance up with a second-place finish in his own #98 Ford.

Like their Ford counterparts, Stroppe-prepped Mercs were basically stock in the control cabin department. And that included a factory-based bench seat (with passenger seat back removed), a stock dash, and factory-installed door panels. Note the air corp gun camera that was one of the first attempts at capturing in-car footage during a race.

Curtis Turner was one of the earliest stars on the NASCAR tour. He earned that fame with the help of a fleet of fast Ford race cars. Here he is at the helm of a supercharged 1957 Fairlane on the beach at Daytona. *Daytona Racing Archives*

Late in the 1955 season, Indy ace Pete DePaolo was lured to the NASCAR ranks to head up Ford's factory effort. He set up shop in Long Beach, California (of all places), and scored one late-season win with the help of driver Buck Baker at Martinsville in October of 1955. When the season finished, Kiekhaefer's Chrysler teams had won just about all of the NASCAR marbles, but Ford drivers had snared two wins and garnered more than a little ink with strong performances in several other events. Things would be even better in 1956.

Preparation for Ford's second official factory-backed season on the Grand National tour got under way with the construction of four Y-block powered

Fairlanes in the Ford "EX" garage at Dearborn. Assembly-line chassis formed the basis for NASCAR stockers in 1956, so the first order of business was removing the various and sundry street-related components that served no purpose in oval-track racing. Chassis reinforcement came next. That included rewelding all the original UAW seams, adding extra metal in high-flex areas, and fabricating extra reinforced shock mounts for the quartet of jounce controllers that were destined for use fore and aft. The final step taken to improve the cars' cornering resolve was the installation of a single loop roll cage.

The 1956 rules book permitted the use of any stock-style brake lining, which, of course, meant that standard drum brakes were fitted to each corner of the chassis. Reinforced rims carrying slender-period bias-ply rubber made the whole package a "roller." Body modifications were almost nonexistent by today's totally fabricated standards. Running lights were removed and their openings were covered; the driver's door was bolted shut and some chrome trim was removed. Beyond that, the team's Ford Fairlanes looked pretty much the same as they had when rolling down the assembly line. Stock was pretty much the theme in the four cars' control cabins, too. Rear seat removal was permitted by the exceedingly thin 1956 rules

book, as was 86ing the passenger's seat back on the stock bench seat. Aircraft surplus seat belts were also part of the program, but beyond their addition and that of the rudimentary roll cage, the rest of the cars' ergonomics were unchanged from showroom condition.

Ford stock cars circa 1956 were powered by a newly enlarged and enlivened 312-cubic-inch version of the corporate OHV V-8. In race tune, the 3.80x3.44 bore and stroke engines could be relied on for something in the vicinity of 230 horsepower—barely enough to keep one of the cars up on Daytona's banking today.

When Robert McNamara pulled Ford's racing irons out of the fire in 1957, the newly formed Holman & Moody team elected to soldier on without factory backing. Team efforts were first centered around Y-block-powered Fairlane 500s like this 1958 that Curtis "Pops" Turner campaigned at Charlotte. Note the stock brightwork that Turner carried into battle in the late 1950s. *Daytona Racing Archives*

But by the 1950s' standards, a race-prepped 312's power output made for formidable competition, especially when presided over by Joe Weatherly and Curtis Turner, who reprised their roles as Ford team drivers for the new season. Rising star Fireball Roberts also signed on to drive for DePaolo in 1956, as did New England ace Ralph Moody. All four drivers would become legends in their own right by the end of Ford's Total Performance era (an era that took its name from Ford's performance advertising program). In many ways, that unparalleled period of Blue Oval domination began with their pairing in the 1956 season. DePaolo also assembled a first-rate support staff to keep his fleet of four Fairlanes properly prepared for each race entered by the team. In that number was a husky fellow named John Holman, who had served variously as a mechanic for Bill Stroppe's West Coast-based Mercury team and as team truck driver for Lincoln's legendary Carrera Pan Americana Mexican Road Race team. Ford fans will, of course, immediately understand how significant that first pairing of John Holman and Ralph Moody (not to mention Turner, Weatherly, and Roberts) ultimately turned out to be since the now fabled Holman & Moody car-building team was a direct result.

Ford's first victory of the official 1956 season had come in the waning months of 1955, when AAA champ Chuck Stevenson clinched the road course event on the as-yet-unpaved Willow Springs Speedway in California (the Triple A served as a competing sanctioning body to France's

Holman & Moody began to build customer cars in 1958 and 1959 out of bare "Square Bird" chassis that had been "discarded." The wins scored by those Thunderbirds were the first in a long line of victories that continue today. Pictured here at speed in Daytona in 1959 are drivers Tom Pistone, Bob Welborn, and Curtis Turner. *JDC Collection*

NASCAR organization in the 1950s). That win was a portent of the success waiting for Blue Oval and Mercury drivers in the season ahead.

The first race of the 1956 calendar year—the beach race in Daytona—took place in February, and during the straight-line speed runs that constituted qualifying for that event, the new Ford contingent made its presence known. Moody translated a 22-second starting berth into a more than competitive third place finish during the 160-mile beach race at the not yet "Big" D—just behind Billy Meyers' second in a Stroppe-prepped Mercury. On his way to the flag, Moody completely flipped his #12 Ford but pressed on undaunted when he landed on his wheels in the soft sand!

One month later, Meyers parked his 312 motorvated Merc in the winners' circle at West Palm Beach to score the first Fomoco win of the calendar year. Moody scored his first victory for the DePaolo team in June at LeHi, Arkansas, and that victory ended the incredible string of 16 straight wins for Kiekhaefer's Chrysler teams. Fireball Roberts notched the next team win in a 250-miler at Raleigh in July and then again in a 100-mile event at Chicago two weeks later. Curtis Turner scored arguably the team's most significant win of the season at Darlington in September, when he outpaced a 70-car field to claim the Southern 500. Moody and Roberts conspired to produce a total of 9 team wins in addition to Turner's triumph at the "Lady in Black." Weatherly's 6 top-five finishes helped add to a team total of 40 in that category—not too shabby for the team's first full season of competitive effort.

All told, when factoring in the victories scored by Bill Stroppe's West Coast Mercury team and the wins recorded by independently-backed Ford and Mercury drivers, Fomoco's 1956 tally was 19 wins in 56 events. Kiekhaefer's 300Cs, which dominated the season with a total of 22 trips to the winner's circle, were the only cars to visit that hallowed spot more frequently than the Ford and Mercury contingent.

All in all, things looked quite rosy for Fomoco's prospects in 1957.

Ford racers were also enjoying more than a little success in NASCAR's sister "convertible" division during the 1956 season. Turner (serving double duty in both the convertible and Grand National divisions) won the beach race that served as the "undercard" event at Daytona in 1956. Weatherly and Roberts also double-dipped in the convertible division that season, and all three of them found that some of their stiffest "zipper top" (as convertible stockers were referred to because they were Grand National cars with their tops unbolted) competition was meted out by a young fellow from Virginia named Glenn Wood, whose #22 Ford was prepared by his younger brother Leonard. The 1956 convertible series produced a total of 26 Ford wins (of 45 events contested) and provided the impetus for the now legendary Wood Brothers Grand National team that still competes on the NASCAR tour today.

It's a pretty safe bet that folks in the Dearborn "Glass House" were pleased with the results of their first full season of NASCAR stock car competition. Money and midnight oil soon began to be expended in pursuit of even more stock car success in the coming season. Soon, special power-train pieces ostensibly designed for export and police work began to pop out of Blue Oval casting boxes. Their intended destination was, of course, the NASCAR circuit. And so, too, was the special Thunderbird and Fairlane McCulloch supercharger engine package that Ford rolled out for the 1957 model year. Rated at 300 horsepower (340 in race trim), the new force-fed induction system was the last word in high tech for 1957 and more than trumped Chevrolet's 1-horsepower-per-cubic-inch, fuel-injected 283 small block.

On the personnel side, Ford extended offers of employment to ace mechanic Smokey Yunick and up-and-coming driver Marvin Panch. Yunick's previous relationship with hotshot driver Paul Goldsmith

Nineteen fifty-eight was the year that Ford rolled out its all new big-block FE engine family. Displacements that year were modest but still good enough to produce 350 horsepower. By 1963, Ford engineers had perfected the 427 FE engine that went on to dominate the 1960s' scene both on and off the track.

ensured that he, too, would be making an appearance behind the wheel of a Fomoco car in 1957.

As was the custom in those days, the 1957 Grand National season got under way in late 1956, with race one running at Willow Springs in California. New DePaolo driver Marvin Panch left the field in his dust (literally, as the road course there was still dirt) and won the race from the pole position. Fireball Roberts came home second that day to further darken Chevrolet's prospects for the coming season. Panch, Roberts, Moody, and Goldsmith then went on a tear through the Grand National ranks, winning 13 of the next 19 events. Making matters even worse for Chevrolet and Mopar drivers were

the 3 additional Ford wins scored by independent drivers along the way.

John Holman's promotion to the directorship of DePaolo's team just into the season undoubtedly had a positive effect on Ford's winning streak. His natural leadership ability gave a focus to Ford's efforts that some had felt was lacking when DePaolo alone had been charting the course.

AMA Ban/Holman & Moody Set Up Shop: 1957–1960

Unfortunately, trouble was just around the corner for the Ford juggernaut. That trouble came in the form of a ban on factory-backed motorsports competition that was enacted by the Automobile Manufacturer's Association (AMA) in June of 1957. In reality, the ban had been engineered behind the scenes by GM exec Harlow "Red" Curtice. Realizing that Ford's continued high-profile rout of the GM teams was bound to have a deleterious effect on The General's market share (and perhaps aware of just how gullible Ford General Manager Robert McNamara really was), Curtice got the AMA to ban all factory-backed racing efforts. When, as expected, McNamara took the edict seriously and shut down all Fomoco racing efforts, Chevrolet teams (who were still clandestinely receiving factory support) were able to reverse the tide of Blue Oval wins. Whereas before the ban Ford drivers had won 15 of 21 events contested, they were only able to capture 12 of 32 after it went into effect.

As history records, the faucet of Ford funding dollars remained turned off until McNamara left to become the Kennedy Administration's secretary of defense, searching for light at the end of the Vietnam tunnel. If any good did come out of the AMA ban for Ford fans, it was the resulting pairing of Ralph Moody and John Holman in Charlotte, North Carolina. When McNamara closed down DePaolo's operation, then-racing-chief Jacque Passino pulled the strings that made it possible for Holman & Moody to set up shop with the leftover parts already in the funding pipeline. Joe Weatherly fielded the very first H&M-sponsored car in July 1957 at the Raleigh 250 in Raleigh, North Carolina, where he started 10th and finished 3rd.

With Ford officially on the sidelines, the 1950s ended with a fizzle for Ford fans of Grand National stock car racing. But Holman & Moody soldiered on and, in a visionary move, began to build "customer" turn-key race cars. In an era when drivers normally built their own competition mounts (save for the lucky few with factory backing), it was indeed novel for Holman & Moody to begin building competition cars for the bucks-up buying public. Some of those first customer cars were built out of "scrapped" Thunderbird unit body chassis that Holman had been able to back-door out of Dearborn for a pittance. When fitted with a race spec version of the all-new FE (Ford Engine) big-block engine introduced in 1958, the lightweight little "Squarebirds" were indeed formidable mounts—factory-backed or not.

The NASCAR record book shows that Holman & Moody team win number one came at Champion Speedway in Fayetteville, North Carolina, in March 1958. Curtis Turner had stayed on as an H&M driver even after McNamara had packed Ford's racing tent, and his unparalleled skill as a short-track driver no doubt played a role in the 50-mile feature victory. It was to be but the first of many Ford and Mercury wins scored by a Holman & Moody-prepped racing car. Turner added 2 more wins to the H&M victory column later that season. Other Ford wins came courtesy of Junior Johnson (6, in fact), Parnelli Jones, Joe Weatherly, Jim Reed, and Shorty Rollins, but Chevrolet drivers carried the day (and the season) with 23 Grand National victories.

Unfortunately, things were destined to get worse before they would get better for Fomoco drivers and fans along the NASCAR circuit. Nineteen fifty-nine produced a new low in the number of Blue Oval visits to victory lane, and, all told, just 10 Ford (and no Mercury) wins were recorded that year.

Though an off-year for Ford teams, things were afoot behind the scenes (and on the surface streets of America) that would soon return factory drivers to the position of total domination they'd enjoyed just before the 1957 AMA ban went into effect. And those forces were driven in large part by the buying public. Though Ford had retreated from racing, it had not lost track of what the automotive buying public wanted in the way of performance—and that was horsepower. Ford answered that demand by quickly increasing the size of its corporate big block from 332 to 352 cubic inches. Each pass with the boring bar produced even more horsepower, and quite naturally, independent drivers quickly put those ponies to work in the NASCAR ranks.

Aiding in their quest for victory was the slippery, fast-backed shape of the all-new Galaxie Starliner line that was introduced in 1960. In race trim, a 360-horse 1960 Starliner was good for speeds in excess of 145 miles per hour on big tracks like Daytona. The car's swoopy shape helped out at lesser tracks, too, and as a result, Ford drivers scored 15 wins that season. Joe Weatherly is credited with 3 of those triumphs for the Holman & Moody team, and the Wood Brothers scored their first ever Grand National wins (including the National 500 at Charlotte) that season. Another

future Fomoco champion, Ned Jarrett, also recorded Ford wins in 1960.

Nonetheless, with Ford still officially out of racing and its GM rivals still very much in it, Chevrolet and Pontiac drivers pretty much ran away with the 44-race series (20 total wins, plus 1 for Oldsmobile).

At season's end, Lee Iacocca was elevated to the general manager post at Ford (in place of the not-so-dearly-departed McNamara), and Ralph Moody signed a promising young Midwestern driver named Fred Lorenzen to an H&M contract for the upcoming season. Better yet, Ford announced that it was breaking out the boring bar once again, and for 1961, the FE block would displace a full 390 cubic inches. Things were looking up!

A boxy Thunderbird just like this one took the checkered flag first (or so it seemed) at the inaugural Daytona 500 in 1959. T-Bird driver Johnny Beauchamp was initially declared the winner of that event and got to kiss the pretty girl in victory lane. Unfortunately, photo analysis of the finish four days later ultimately revealed that Lee Petty's Oldsmobile actually had inched Beauchamp's car out at the line. Curtis Turner scored the first of many Thunderbird wins one month later at Hillsboro, North Carolina.

Nineteen sixty-nine was the first season of the aero wars. Fomoco combatants rolled into battle at the helm of stretch-nosed Mercury Cyclone Spoiler IIs and Torino Talladegas. By season's end, drivers like LeeRoy Yarbrough (#98) and Richard Petty (#43) had pummeled their winged and wingless rivals into submission with their superior aerodynamics. *Courtesy Ford Motor Company*

2

Ford Returns with Total Performance

Iacocca Takes the Helm: 1961

Lee Iacocca's ascension to "Glass House" heights was a breath of fresh air for performance-oriented Ford engineers. Rising as he did from the sales ranks, Iacocca was well aware of the effect that Sunday wins had on Monday sales floor traffic. And so it was that the doors that McNamara had closed to Ford racers in 1957 began to open up just a bit.

Fast Freddie Lorenzen scored his first Holman & Moody win at Martinsville in the 1961 Virginia 500. His trademark white and blue #28 Galaxie had started second on the grid before going on to lead the event from lap 118 to its conclusion on lap 149. Lorenzen's next win came at Darlington in the Rebel 300, where his 375-horse, 390-powered Starliner started on the pole. Lorenzen also won at Atlanta for H&M.

However, the biggest Holman (and Fomoco) win scored in 1961 was, without doubt, the triumph recorded by Nelson Stacy in the headline-producing Southern 500. The pugnacious Cincinnati native scored the upset victory by passing Plymouth driver Marvin Panch with just seven laps to go before a crowd of 80,000 cheering fans.

Ford Resumes Factory Backing: 1962

Nineteen sixty-two was the season that Ford dispensed with the AMA ban altogether and announced its return to fully factory-backed sponsorship of motorsports competition. Interestingly, that move was sparked in part by poor aerodynamics. Though 1960 and 1961 Galaxies could be bought with smooth-flowing Starliner roof panels, for 1962 the squared-off look was in,

1961–1970

and Galaxies sported an upright, drag-producing back light. It was a step backwards in aerodynamics that the extra cubic inches carried by the new 406-cubic-inch engine couldn't overcome. When Fireball Roberts swept Speedweeks in Daytona that year with his convertible rooflined (and 421 Super Duty-powered) Catalina, Ford racers looked to Dearborn for help.

Their requests were answered just before the Atlanta race with a new factory Ford "option" called the Starlift roof. Basically a removable version of the previous Starliner top panel, the new option supposedly was intended to bolt onto a Galaxie convertible in street application. Problem was, when that was attempted, the windows wouldn't close all the way (you see, there was no Starlift window option). It was obvious to all that the new lid was intended specifically for the NASCAR circuit. And that placed Bill France and his sanctioning body in a bit of a bind. After all, they'd

Why is this man smiling? It could be because he is Ralph Moody, and he knows just how dominant the race cars he builds will be throughout the 1960s. The Starliner he's leaning on is an early example of Ford aerodynamics. Like the Talladegas, Spoiler IIs, and Thunderbirds that would follow it onto the track, a 1960/1961 Starliner owed much of its speed to its slippery shape. *Daytona Racing Archives*

Nelson Stacy was an early Holman & Moody team driver. He piloted his #29 H&M-prepped race cars with the same tenacity he'd displayed as a tank driver in World War II. *Daytona Racing Archives*

been quietly looking the other way when Chevrolet and Pontiac offered up over-the-counter "stock" options (like the crate Super Duty 421s that Poncho drivers had been whipping the competition with), so how could they nay-say Ford's new roof?

So at first they didn't. As a result, Lorenzen and Stacy turned up at the Atlanta 500 with Holman & Moody-prepped Starlift Galaxies and stole the show. Fast Freddie took what turned out to be the body style's only NASCAR win. In a move dripping with more than a little hypocrisy, NASCAR banned the new roof panel just after the race. That act prompted Henry Ford II (the Deuce) to announce shortly thereafter that the Ford Motor Company would no longer be honoring the AMA

ban on factory-backed motorsports competition. Holman & Moody was put back on the company payroll in short order, and big plans were laid for the future. Not the least among those was a proposed version of the tried and true FE engine that had been punched out to an estimable 427 cubic inches. Though 1962 produced just six Grand National wins (in that number a Southern 500 triumph by Larry Frank), things would be quite different the very next season.

A Phenomenal Season: 1963

During the off season, Ford stylists cooked up an all-new Galaxie body that was much better at cutting through the wind than its predecessors had been.

Though different in just about every regard than the boxy 1962s it replaced, the new 1963 was most changed in the roofline area. Instead of the upright back light of the year before, the new full-sized cars featured a sporty looking "convertible" roofline that was the next best thing to the Starlift panels of yore. Power for the slippery new chassis was provided by a new and improved version of the FE that boasted 427 cubic inches and 410 horsepower. Blessed with a race-proved, cross-bolted bottom end and free-flowing "Low Riser" heads, the new oversquare big block was both reliable and powerful at high rpm. Dan Gurney proved just that at Riverside in a Holman & Moody-prepped Ford when he won the Riverside 500 in January of 1963.

Daytona was next on the schedule, and Ford drivers had high hopes as they pulled into the garage area at the Big D. Until, that is, Junior Johnson and his Bow Tie stablemates fired up their all-new and decidedly non-production 427 Mystery Motor engines for the very first time. Though Big Bill France had made a show of banning the 1962 Starlift option for being a non-production item, he suddenly decided to look the other way when Chevrolet drivers showed up with an all-new non-production polyangle-valved 427 big block (of which ultimately only 48 or so were ever cast up).

Fomoco forces were very unhappy with the situation until reliability problems sidelined the new porcupine-powered Chevrolets. Ford fans' anger at the sanctioning body's duplicity was more than a little assuaged when Iowa native Tiny Lund scored the very first Daytona 500 win for the Blue Oval in

Glenn "Fireball" Roberts was one of the first Holman & Moody team drivers in 1956. Unfortunately, Ford's competition pull-out forced him to switch to GM cars in 1957. Fireball finally returned to the Ford fold in 1963 to campaign this Passino Purple "Pontiac Eater" built by Holman & Moody. He proved he still knew how to pilot a fast Ford by winning his very first Galaxie outing that season. *Mike Slade*

West Coast racer Bill Stroppe built some of the best-looking race cars to ever grace a Grand National racing grid. Stroppe was fond of red, white, and blue and painted his team Mercurys in those hues in the 1950s and 1960s. Darel Dieringer drove this #16 Marauder for Stroppe in 1964.

storybook fashion. Lund had saved Marvin Panch's life by yanking him bodily from a burning sports car wreck just days before the 500 (Tiny was a small man in name alone). Panch had rewarded that brave act by nominating Tiny for the Wood Brothers Galaxie ride he'd have to give up while recuperating. As mentioned, Tiny crossed the finish line first, followed by Fast Freddie, Ned Jarrett, Nelson Stacy, and Dan Gurney who were also all mounted in 427 Low Riser-powered Galaxies.

Lorenzen's performance during the 1963 season was particularly memorable. He backed up his second-place finish at Daytona with wins in the Atlanta 500, the World 600 (at Charlotte), the Volunteer 500 (at Bristol), the Western Carolina 500 (at Weaverville), the Mountaineer 500 (at Huntington),

and the Old Dominion 500 (at Martinsville). Lorenzen's success earned him $122,587.28 in winnings. It was the first time that any Grand National driver had broken the six-figure mark.

Ford fans will also fondly remember that 1963 was the year that Fireball Roberts returned to the Ford fold in a "Passino Purple" #22 H&M Galaxie. Fireball won his first 1963 Ford event at Bristol in the Southeastern 500. He went on to score three more Ford wins that season, the most important of which was a victory in the 1963 Southern 500, which ran unimpeded without a single caution. It was a convincing win to say the least, as Fireball had set the fastest lap in qualifying (at 133.648) before going on to win at an average speed of 129.784 miles per hour. Making the win even sweeter for Fomoco fans was the fact that Marvin Panch (Ford), Fred Lorenzen (Ford), Nelson Stacy (Ford), Darel Dieringer (Mercury), Rex White (Mercury), Joe Weatherly (Mercury), and Tiny Lund (Ford) had freight trained across the Darlington finish line in Fireball's wake. Total Performance indeed!

Ford drivers won 23 events in 1963. And that was more than any other manufacturer. Nineteen sixty-three was also the year that Mercury returned to the win column after a six-year hiatus. Darel Dieringer served up those honors at the last race of the season, the Golden State 400 at Riverside, where he piloted his Bill Stroppe-prepped red, white, and blue Marauder to victory lane. That particular Riverside event also marked the arrival of Bud Moore to the Fomoco fold. It was the beginning of the association between Moore's Spartanburg-based team and cars of the Fomoco persuasion that continues today.

Ford and Chrysler Battle It Out (Hemi Supremacy): 1964–1965

There's no doubt about it, 1963 was a phenomenal season for Ford's Total Performance team. As a result, it's pretty likely that Ford and Mercury teams were looking forward to more of the same for 1964. Especially so, since GM had pulled up stakes and withdrawn from racing during the 1963 season for fear that its continued clandestine (in the face of the AMA ban) racing activities would result in antitrust litigation from the feds.

But things don't always turn out as planned. Fomoco drivers began to understand that fact (in spades) the very first time that Richard Petty fired up his all-new 426 Chrysler Hemi engine in the Daytona garage area during Speedweeks 1964. Like the year before, Ford forces found themselves confronted by an all-new, not-in-the-least-production engine that the sanctioning body had deemed legal for Grand National competition.

Nineteen sixty-three Marauders shared the same convertible-style roofline that their Galaxie counterparts carried. It was as much a concession to styling concerns as to speed. One thing is for sure, the swoopy new roof worked a whole lot better than the vertical-back-light, formal roof panels of 1962 ever had. *Courtesy Bill Holder*

Though Ford's top brass howled about the fact that no regular production Hemi cars were slated for production (and indeed wouldn't be for two full years) NASCAR officials turned a deaf ear and gave the purpose-built racing engine their stamp of approval. And unlike the previous year, the formidable new foe would not be plagued by the same type of teething problems that had hamstrung the Chevrolet Mystery Motor.

Proof of that fact became all too clear at Daytona during qualifying where Petty and his Mopar minions ran away with both qualifying and the race. When the checkered flag fell, it was Petty first, followed by two other Plymouths. Adding to

Fred Lorenzen was a midwesterner who caught Ralph Moody's eye during the 1960 NASCAR season. He signed on as an H&M team driver the next year, and the rest is history. During the 1960s, Lorenzen became NASCAR's Golden Boy. He won 26 Grand National events and was the first driver to win more than $100,000 in a single season. Fast Freddie is posing inside the Holman & Moody shop with his new "fastback" 1963 Galaxie stocker. That's legendary mechanic Herb Nab leaning on the car's windscreen. *Daytona Racing Archives*

the funk that Ford drivers found themselves in was the pall that had fallen over the series ever since Joe Weatherly had been killed in the Motor Trend 500 while at the wheel of a Bud Moore Mercury. Even NASCAR's decision to allow all Fomoco cars to run special High Riser head castings atop their 427 engines had not been enough to brighten the Ford Teams' outlook—especially after Daytona.

Things got even worse at the World 600 in May when Fireball Roberts became involved in a shunt with fellow Ford drivers Ned Jarrett and Junior Johnson. Tragically, the still evolving NASCAR rules book did not require fuel cells (nor truth be known, did any working examples yet exist at the time). As a result, when Fireball's purple Galaxie got turned upside down and burst into flames on the backstretch, Fireball was doomed. Horribly burned before he could be pulled from the wreck, he lingered until just days before the Firecracker 400 in July.

Though Ford and Mercury drivers notched a total of 35 victories in 1964 (including triumphs at Atlanta, Wilkesboro, Martinsville, Darlington, Charlotte, Bristol, and Watkins Glen), the 1964 season was not generally a happy one for Ford teams. Petty's 1964 driving championship suggested that something would have to be done—and fast—if Ford was to have any chance of recapturing the Grand National spotlight.

Chrysler Boycotts: 1965

Ford responded with the 427 single overhead cam (SOHC) engine. When Petty drove home (literally) the supremacy of the hemispherical combustion chamber, Fomoco engine and foundry engineers wasted little time in coming up with a Hemi design of their own. But not just any Hemi, you understand. Their version featured a free-revving head casting that sported one overhead-mounted cam per cylinder and sewer-pipe-sized passages leading in and out of the chambers. Horsepower was predicted to be in the 650 range.

Ford's 427-cubic-inch big block came on line during the 1963 season and saw service well into the 1970s. Though not graced with hemispherical combustion chambers, the high-revving FE was still able to crank out more than 600 horsepower with ease. Here John Holman oversees a 427 dyno run. That's an incredibly young Waddell Wilson working on the front damper. *Daytona Racing Archives*

Following pages
Though not as sleek as the Galaxies they replaced, the restyled Ford full-sized line in 1964 was still more than a little fetching. The race cars that sprang from that production run were fast to boot. Tiny Lund drove an independently-backed 1964 during that period, which has been recently returned to racing trim.

133

The NASCAR rules book in 1964 was far less stringent than the one in use today. Note, for example, the single driver's side roll cage bar that was all the sanctioning body required. Production-based bucket seats like the one installed in this Bill Stroppe Marauder were also part of the program that season.

Stock cars were still pretty stock circa 1964. Note the factory dash panel, the production-based bucket, and the full roll-up windows in Tiny Lund's 1964 Galaxie.

Chrysler got wind of the new SOHC motor and fired back its response in the form of a dual overhead cam version of the 426 that had the potential to produce more than 900 ponies in race trim.

Bill France took in the fracas from the sidelines, and as the 1965 season approached, he decided to act. Shortly before the new year, France announced that safety (and not lack of regular production status) required the outlawing of both the 426 Hemi engine and the concessionary Ford High Riser head castings. Chryco teams promptly announced a boycott of the series that no amount of counternegotiation could undo.

As you might have guessed, 1965 became the year that Fomoco drivers won just about everything there was to win on the Grand National circuit. Fred Lorenzen started that successful season with a rain-shortened triumph at the Daytona 500, and then he and his Blue Oval buddies went on to win an incredible 48 of 55 events contested—including every single superspeedway race on the schedule.

Marvin Panch backed up Lorenzen's win at Daytona by leading a five-car Ford sweep across the stripe in the Atlanta 500 in April. Junior Johnson, just a handful of races away from hanging up his driving gloves, proved he still knew the way to the winner's circle at the Rebel 300 at Darlington in May. Lorenzen took the checkered flag first in the grueling World 600 on Memorial Day. Panch and the Wood Brothers put their name on a deed of ownership at Atlanta by winning the Dixie 500 in June, and the Woods tasted victory again at Daytona when a car they set up for A. J. Foyt bested all comers in the Firecracker 400. Ned Jarrett proved he could win more than just short-track events at Darlington in the Southern 500 where the soon to be two-time NASCAR champ cruised to a whopping 14-lap margin of victory.

Fast Freddie put a Holman & Moody lock on victory lane at Charlotte when he won the National 400 in October, and Curtis Turner rounded out Ford's (and the Wood Brothers') stellar superspeedway season with a triumph at Rockingham in the American 500. All in all, the only way to get a look at the checkered flag in 1965 was from behind the wheel of a Grand National Galaxie. Ford short-track winners that season included Junior Johnson, Tiny Lund, Dan Gurney, Marvin Panch, Dick Hutcherson, Cale Yarborough, A. J. Foyt, and the eventual season champ, Ned Jarrett. Darel Dieringer gave Mercury fans something to cheer about when he won one of the Daytona qualifiers in a Bud Moore-built 1964 Marauder. Though Dodge and Plymouth drivers did trickle back to the series in the waning days of the

season, it was too late for them to undo what has to be the most successful season ever enjoyed by a car manufacturer on the NASCAR tour.

Perhaps as important as the string of victories scored by Fords in 1965 was Ralph Moody's perfection of the Grand National chassis that took place that same year. Though the cars that rolled out of the H&M shop that season had all begun as UAW assembly-line stockers, the chassis mods that mechanical genius Moody outfitted them with turned out to be the industry standard for the next decade and a half—for all cars, regardless of make or manufacturer. Starting with a stock coil-spring

When the sanctioning body permitted Chryco racers to field non-production Hemi engines in 1964, they threw Ford racers a bone in the form of equally non-production High Riser (HR) heads. Though legalizing the HR castings helped a bit, it didn't balance the books entirely. As a result, 1964 was an off year for Ford teams on the tour.

Fred Lorenzen was the class of the 1965 field in his #28 Holman & Moody-prepped Galaxie. Twenty-two years later, Davey Allison was able to make that same boast with the help of the #28 Robert Yates-prepped T-Bird. Both cars now belong to North Carolina's Kim Haynes.

1965 Galaxie chassis, Moody first installed screw-jack-adjustable spring mounts at all four corners. A four-link trailing-arm, live-axle rear suspension based on the Ford 9-inch differential came next, along with a special handmade rear cross-member. A cross-chassis sway bar and a Watts link were then mounted fore and aft respectively, along with enough shock mounts to accommodate a pair of shocks at each wheel. Brakes consisted of massive finned 11x3 drums that were acted on by reinforced, fully-metallic shoes. When

fitted with a six-point roll cage, Moody's 1965 Galaxie chassis wasn't all that removed from Cup cars of the modern era. In fact, the rear-steer cars that continue to compete on the circuit still carry what is essentially a 1965 Galaxie chassis (albeit a fully fabricated one) beneath their slippery flanks.

Ford Boycotts: 1966

NASCAR's late season concessions to the Mopar hordes in 1965 had allowed them once again to run the 426 Hemi engine in lightweight

Fast Freddie Lorenzen carried on as a Holman & Moody team driver in 1965. His #28 Galaxie signaled Ford's dominance that season with a win in the Daytona 500. Kim Haynes has recently returned one of Lorenzen's cars to pristine condition.

Dodge and Plymouth unit-body cars. Those same rules were slated to govern in 1966, too, and Chryco was planning to eliminate all doubt about the Hemi's production status by finally offering it for sale as an RPO option. Ford's response was to again seek approval of the 427 SOHC engine. Much to the corporation's disappointment, Big Bill and the sanctioning body rebuffed all of Ford's efforts to that end, even after Ford announced that it, too, was building regular production versions of the 427 Cammer (which turned out to be not true).

When France hung tough, it was Ford's turn to boycott the Grand National series—a step taken after Ford Galaxie teams were trounced by Hemi cars at the Daytona 500. (Richard Petty finished

Hutcherson took in the rapidly passing scenery from this perch in 1965. Note the add-on bolster that more (or less) transformed a regular production bucket into a racing seat.

Hutcherson swept out of the midwestern corn fields in a cloud of dirt-track dust to become a Holman & Moody team driver in the mid-1960s. In 1965, he campaigned this block-long Galaxie on both dirt and asphalt.

All of Fred Lorenzen's H&M cars carried the words "Think! W.H.M." on the passenger side of the dash panel. That script was put there originally by Ralph Moody to keep Fast Freddie focused on "What the Hell Matters." Other "details" of note in a 1967 Fairlane control cabin such as this include the stock dash pad, production-based seat, and RPO steering wheel. Also, if you look closely, you can see the roll cage-mounted strobe light that driver Lorenzen used (in concert with a floor-mounted trap door) to check on right front tire wear during a race. When in use, the strobe "froze" a section of tread for visual inspection.

one lap ahead of Cale Yarborough's Banjo Matthews-prepped Galaxie.) Beginning with the short track race at Hickory in April, Ford teams, for the most part, elected to stay home on Sunday afternoons and watch football. A few independent

When Ford decided to boycott the 1966 season, not every Fomoco team elected to follow suit. Bud Moore, for example, opted to continue to enter selected events. By the middle of the season, he'd begun to field lithe little Comet race cars that had been built out of a combination of 1965 Galaxie (front) and reinforced unit body (rear) suspension components. The end result was the first Fomoco "half chassis" car. Moore's win with driver Darel Dieringer at the Southern 500 helped convince other Ford racers to start racing intermediates upon their return from the boycott late in the season. *JDC Collection*

thinkers like Tiger Tom Pistone, Junior Johnson, and Bud Moore did make appearances at a handful of events—with NASCAR's decided encouragement. It is perhaps those appearances that ultimately had more significance for Ford racers than the losses conceded by the factory-backed boycott.

Junior Johnson, for example, showed up at the Dixie 400 in Atlanta with a radically modified 1966 Galaxie that had been so twisted and distorted away from stock in the pursuit of improved aerodynamics that wags in the garage area took to calling the yellow car the "Banana." NASCAR let the car run (along with an equally novel-bodied Chevelle built by Smokey Yunick), and the car's creative sheet metal led directly to the first use of the now-common body templates. Bud Moore's diminutive little Mercury Comet also made a handful of very

Ford teams elected to run destroked 427 Tunnel Port engines at some tracks during the 1967 and 1968 seasons. Horsepower figures were still high enough to produce 27 Torino and Cyclone wins that year. Cale Yarborough (#21) and David Pearson (#17) were both regular fixtures in victory lane in 1968. *JDC Collection*

significant appearances on the tour during the boycott. Built not from a full-sized, full-frame Mercury but instead from a much smaller, unit-bodied Comet, Moore's #16 car was more than a little innovative. It was, in fact, the wave of Ford's future and the beginning of the end for the Galaxie line in NASCAR circles. Like its Hemi rivals, the red, white, and black car that Moore built for Darel Dieringer featured a unit-body chassis that had been beefed up for use with a 427 Medium Riser engine. When fitted with Galaxie suspension components and the front half of a Galaxie frame, the little Comet became a formidable race car—so much, in fact, that Dieringer bested all comers at the grueling 1966 Southern 500, even without the assistance of a Hemi engine under the hood.

When Fomoco drivers trickled back to the tour late in the season (just as their Chryco rivals had done the year before), they too rode into battle in intermediates that had been outfitted with "half chassis" Galaxie underpinnings and firebreathing Medium Riser big blocks. Fred Lorenzen used just such a car to win the Old Dominion 500 at Martinsville in September upon the Holman & Moody team's return to the circuit. Dick Hutcherson also found his way to victory lane late in the season in a scaled-down Fairlane race car. Even so, those late season triumphs (Ford and Mercury drivers notched a total of 12 Grand National wins in 1966) could not come close to matching the 24 triumphs turned in by Hemi drivers during the boycott.

A Sign of Good Things to Come: 1967

The Cammer was still unwelcome on the NASCAR circuit for 1967, but NASCAR tried to level the playing field by permitting Fomoco racers to install a pair of deep-breathing Tunnel Port head castings atop their 427 short blocks. Tunnel Port heads picked up that moniker due to the fact that their intake passages were so large that the engine's pushrods had to run right through the middle of them (in specially sealed tubes). Horsepower figures climbed significantly with their use, but as the NASCAR record book reflects, it wasn't enough to slow the Hemi-car stronghold on victory lane.

Parnelli Jones got the year off to a good start with a Ford win at Riverside in January, and Indy ace Mario Andretti made a "guest" appearance at the Daytona 500 in February that resulted in a trip to the winner's circle for his #11 Holman & Moody-built TP Fairlane. Fred Lorenzen's win in one of the pre-race "Twin" qualifiers, coupled with his second-place finish in the 500, seemed to portend a successful year for Fomoco teams on the tour. Unfortunately for Blue Oval lovers, 1967 was the season that Richard Petty was crowned the King of Stock Car Racing by winning a phenomenal 27 Grand National races. All told, Petty and his Plymouth and Dodge stablemates won a dominating 36 of 49 events they contested.

The new Mercury intermediates that debuted in 1968 were the last word in aerodynamics. Blessed with a swoopy fastback roofline and a sleek-angled hood line, the cars were fast right off of the trailer. And that's just what similarly named (but unrelated) drivers LeeRoy Yarbrough and Cale Yarborough proved at superspeedways all season. *JDC Collection*

145

The big news for Ford racers in 1968 was what was behind them—specifically, the swoopy, fastback roof panels. The all-new aerodynamic silhouette on cars like this A. J. Foyt/Jack Bowsher Torino made them nearly impossible to beat that season.

But as bleak as 1967 was overall for Ford and Mercury drivers, there were a few bright spots that foreshadowed the successes of the upcoming season. Darel Dieringer led from the pole at the Gwyn Staley 400 at North Wilkesboro to record Junior Johnson's first Grand National win as a car owner. Interestingly, Johnson attributed the win to his decision to outfit his #26 Fairlane with a destroked, 374-cubic-inch version of the 427 Tunnel Port that provided greater reliability than the full-sized version of the engine. Dick Hutcherson, in his last full season as a driver, also scored wins for Ford (and car owner Bondy Long) in the Smokey Mountain 200 and the Dixie 500. Bobby Allison accounted for a couple of

Fomoco victories, himself, when he used his Holman & Moody #11 car to win the last two races of the year at Rockingham and North Wilkesboro.

Cale Yarborough scored two other Ford wins that year—at the Atlanta 500 and the Firecracker 400—that in many ways served as a preview of the success that he and the Wood Brothers team would enjoy just one season into the future. And that phenomenal year got underway at Daytona in February of 1968.

Aero Wars: 1968–1970

As was the custom in the 1960s, the official beginning of the 1968 Grand National season was in

November of 1967. Bobby Allison won race number one for Holman & Moody in a 1967 Fairlane at Macon, and Dan Gurney continued his dominance of the Riverside Road course in a Wood Brothers-prepped 1968 Ford. But for all practical purposes, the "real" 1968 season began when the Wood Brothers parked their all-new fastback Mercury Cyclone in the garage area at Daytona just prior to the 500.

Nineteen sixty-eight was a model-change year for Ford and Mercury car lines, and the new year brought with it an all-new intermediate body style that looked fast even while standing still. Principally responsible for that illusion of speed was an exaggerated fastback roofline that began at the "A" pillars and swept in an unbroken arc to the cars' rear deck lids.

Mercury referred to its new intermediate variously as the Montego and the Cyclone. Ford intermediates soldiered on behind the Fairlane moniker, and high-line iterations came to be called Torinos. Whatever they were called, the two new intermediates were fast. Significantly faster, in fact, than the stubby little 1967s they had replaced—even when powered by the same twin-four-barrel inducted Tunnel Port engines.

Bud Moore returned to stock car racing in 1968 after a one-year stint in Trans-Am. His driver that season was the popular Tiny Lund. Moore's race car of choice for 1968 continued to be a Mercury. Check out the stock door handles that were still required by the rules book that season. *JDC Collection*

Behind the wheel of a 1968 Mercury Cyclone, Cale Yarborough rocketed around Daytona at 189.222 miles per hour during qualifying for the 500 and won the coveted pole starting position. Cale's velocity was nearly 9 miles per hour faster than Curtis Turner's pole-winning speed of just one year before. The secret of Cale's new-found speed was, of course, aerodynamics. And that did not bode well for Mopar drivers in general, and Plymouth drivers in particular, for the coming season. Though totally dominant during the 1967 season, Plymouth drivers were consigned to redesigned Satellite bodies that were every bit as boxy as their 1967 mounts. Benighted with barn-door-like vertical grille panels and formal sedan-style roofs, the new-for-1968 Satellite body styles were just about as aerodynamic as a brick. Dodge drivers had higher hopes for their new "fuselage" bodied Chargers, but those cars turned out to have hidden aerodynamic peccadillos of their own.

And so it was that 1968 turned out to be a "Total Performance" year for Ford and Mercury drivers on the tour. Yarborough translated his first-place starting berth at Daytona into a dominating performance during the 500. All told, his red and white Wood Brothers Cyclone led 86 of the event's 200 laps, including the all-important final one. Yarborough's closest competition that day was similarly named (but no relation) driver LeeRoy Yarbrough, who'd recently signed on to drive Junior

Floridian LeeRoy Yarbrough signed on to drive for Junior Johnson in 1968. He drove slippery Cyclones like this replica of his #26 team car. Though Mercurys that season featured vertical grille panels like their Torino siblings, a Cyclone still was better at air management due to its more angled hood line.

Nineteen sixty-eight became the Cale and LeeRoy show as both Mercury drivers were almost always running at the front of the pack. The secret of their success was the superior aerodynamics of their fastbacked Cyclone stock cars. By season's end, they scored 8 wins (including Cale's Daytona 500 triumph) and 27 top-five finishes between them. *Courtesy Ford Motor Company*

Johnson's #26 Mercury Cyclone. Cale and LeeRoy's one-two finish signaled the beginning of the Cale and LeeRoy show that dominated just about every superspeedway race during the 1968 season.

The Mercury duo reprised their Daytona finish at Atlanta in March with another one-two sprint across the line in the Atlanta 500. And that's just how Cale and LeeRoy finished in the Firecracker 400 at Daytona in July. LeeRoy finished out in front in the Dixie 500 at Atlanta when Cale crashed early in the event, and Cale's flashy #21 car crossed the stripe first at Darlington in the Southern 500 after LeeRoy's engine expired in that fabled event.

While Cale and LeeRoy were stealing the headlines in 1968, David Pearson was methodically racking up the points for the Holman & Moody team with a string of short-track wins and top-10 finishes. Pearson's #17 car finished first at Weaverville, Darlington (in the Rebel 400), Beltsville, Hampton, Macon, Bristol, Nashville, Columbia, Winston-Salem, Augusta, and Hickory. By season's end, his steady, methodical performance produced 16 wins, 36 top-5 finishes, and his second Grand National driving title (and the first won by the Holman & Moody team). All told, Ford and Mercury drivers scored wins at 27 of the 49 events on the 1968 schedule.

149

Mopar teams were none too happy with that result and resolved to trump Ford and Mercury's aero-advantage in the coming season.

The weapon that Chryco engineers devised to slay the Fomoco dragon was a slightly revised version of the Charger body style referred to as the Charger 500. In an attempt to cure the car's aerodynamic shortcomings, modifications had been made to the Charger's beak and roofline areas. More than a little overconfident that they'd solved their aero problems, Dodge execs took the unusual step of unveiling the new officially-approved variant at the fall 1968 race in Charlotte.

Unbeknownst to the Dodge boys, Ralph Moody was cooking up his very own aero-warrior in the super-secret back room of Holman & Moody's Charlotte Airport racing complex. Like his pentastar rivals, Moody spent time cleaning up the front end of the Ford Fairlane mule he was working on. To that end, he grafted on a new nose that extended the car's silhouette a full 6 inches and then finished it off with a flush-fitting grille and a labor-intensive front bumper rewelded to serve as an airfoil. Finishing touches were worked out by Ford stylists and wind tunnel engineers in time for Speedweeks 1969 at Daytona. And while they

Nineteen sixty-nine was David Pearson's second full season with Holman & Moody, and he spent that year behind the wheel of a blue and gold Talladega. As in 1968, Pearson proved to be the man to beat, and by season's end few had. As a result, he scored the second straight Holman & Moody national championship. *Courtesy Ford Motor Company*

were at it, the Fomoco aero-team cooked up a similarly configured aero-beak for the Mercury Cyclone line as well.

Fomoco execs called the new long-nosed Fords Talladegas after Bill France's still-under-construction palace of speed in Alabama. The Mercury version was dubbed the Cyclone Spoiler II. Ford plans called for the simultaneous introduction of its long-lusted-after corporate Hemi racing engine at Daytona. After having been denied track access for the Cammer 427 engine, Ford engineers had set to work on a cam-in-block version of the new (for 1968) "385" big-block engine that featured hemispherical combustion chambers cast in aluminum. When Dodge drivers showed up at Daytona with their sleek new Charger 500s, Ford teams were already in residence with a fleet of even slipperier Boss 429-powered Torino Talladegas.

With certain doom looming on the horizon, NASCAR stepped in at the last minute in an attempt to save the Mopar teams from total defeat. It seems that Big Bill France wasn't satisfied that Ford had actually built the requisite number of Boss 429 Mustangs in order to gain approval of the engine for use on the Grand National tour. As a result, France ordered that all the Boss engines be yanked out and replaced with last year's Tunnel Port 427s.

It was an interesting edict to be sure—and one that was more than a little suspect since, as history records, Dodge never came close to building the supposedly required 500 street-going versions of the new Charger 500 body style. But when the bombast and political maneuvering settled, Ford drivers were little hindered by France's last minute decision to "86" the Boss 429. David Pearson convincingly won one of the twin qualifying heats in his H&M-prepped (and Robert Yates-engined) Talladega. And in the race itself, LeeRoy Yarbrough translated a 19th-place starting position into his first Daytona 500 win.

Adding to the trounced Dodge drivers' depression as they filed out of the infield, tail

Fomoco's "A" team in 1969 consisted of (clockwise from right) LeeRoy Yarbrough, Donnie Allison, David Pearson, Cale Yarborough, and Richard Petty. They are all smiling here because they know they get to race Boss 429 hemi engines. *Courtesy Ford Motor Company*

between legs, was the fact that some of the slings and arrows of the unkind aerodynamic fate that had befallen them at Daytona had been hurled by former Plymouth partisan Richard Petty. Just before the season had begun, Petty had stunned the Mopar faithful by announcing his switch to cars of the Blue Oval persuasion. The reason for that unprecedented move was the exact same thing that had been the undoing of his former Dodge and Plymouth partners: aerodynamics. Simply put, when Petty got wind of Ralph Moody's swoopy new Talladega, he knew his chances of winning with a Plymouth in 1969 were just about nil. And so the King jumped ship to Ford's "Going Thing" for the 1969 season. It turned out to be a wise choice since, as he'd predicted, Plymouth drivers had more than a little trouble finding the way to the 1969 winner's circle (making it there just two times that season).

Though Ford teams were deprived of their "Blue Crescent" Hemis at Daytona, Big Bill relented in time for the Atlanta 500 in March and gave the all-new engine his official stamp of approval. Ford upped the aerodynamic stakes at that race even further with the simultaneous unveiling of the all-new Cyclone Spoiler II. Making matters even worse for Charger 500 drivers was the fact that the new long-nosed Mercs proved to be even faster than their Talladega siblings. That was due to the steeper angle that had been designed into the II's front sheet metal. Though only a matter of a few degrees, the extra angle added up to a 1- to 2-mile-per-hour advantage on the superspeedways.

Cale Yarborough put that asset to good use at Atlanta, where he led a dominating 308 of 334

Richard Petty broke Mopar lovers' hearts everywhere when he jumped ship to Ford in 1969. The reason for his change of heart is pictured here: a Ford Torino Talladega. King Richard knew his factory Plymouth ride was no match for the new Ford Aero-variant and decided, if you can't beat 'em, join 'em. He won 10 races in his long-nosed Ford that season.

total laps on his way to the winner's circle. It was a humbling defeat for the Dodge and Plymouth drivers, and one that, no doubt, sent them into an even deeper funk. For Fomoco drivers, it was the beginning of an incredibly successful season. LeeRoy Yarbrough scored a second Spoiler II win in May in the Rebel 400 and yet another two weeks later in the World 600. Cale upped the Mercury total to 4 with a win in the Motor State 500 at Michigan in June. Talladega drivers like David Pearson, Donnie Allison, and Richard Petty (and later in the season, LeeRoy Yarbrough) did their part in securing Blue Oval glory by winning big-track events at Rockingham, Dover, and Charlotte while also scoring 16 short-track triumphs. Petty's first road-course win (scored at Riverside) brought the Ford and Mercury win total to 30 for the season (26 Ford and 4 Mercury). David Pearson's Dick Hutcherson-led H&M team came out on top in the points chase, handing Holman & Moody their second straight Grand National title.

Fomoco's domination was so complete in 1969 that not even Dodge's desperate mid-season introduction of the radically winged Daytona (of which fewer than 500 were ever built—go figure) was not enough to derail the Blue Oval's winning ways. As things turned out, Dodge's gaudy new winged thing won but two superspeedway events. And one of those came at the inaugural Talladega event where most major teams (and every single Ford Talladega team) boycotted the event as the result of a safety dispute with Bill France.

Unfortunately, changing events behind the scenes in Dearborn would prove to be the undoing of Fomoco's aero-warriors during the 1970 season. Nineteen seventy was slated to be a model change year for Fomoco's intermediate lines. Longer, larger, and wider were the themes that held sway in styling studios circa 1970, and things were no different in Dearborn. Recognizing early that the new Fairlane and Montego body styles would not compare with their Talladega and Spoiler II predecessors

Talladegas and Spoiler IIs started out the 1969 season under 427 Tunnel Port power. When Bill France was satisfied that a sufficient number of Boss 429 Mustangs had been built to homologate that engine, Petty and other Fomoco teams shifted over to Boss '9 motorvation.

without help, Ford stylists like Larry Shinoda (who'd also designed the split window Corvette coupe, the Z-28, and the Boss 302) penned a radical new nose for both car lines that was designed to keep their aerodynamics apace with both their in-house and Brand X competition. In final form, Shinoda's design produced a front clip that rose in a smooth arc from pavement level to windshield base. Ford versions were called Torino King Cobras, while their Mercury siblings picked up the name Super Spoiler II.

Preliminary work on the two new aero-variants had progressed to the prototype stage by late 1969 when the rug was suddenly pulled from beneath the entire Ford racing program. The catalyst that brought that change was Lee Iacocca. It was Iacocca who got the nod from Henry Ford II when inveterate racer Bunkie Knudsen was booted from the Fomoco presidency. Unfortunately for Fomoco fans everywhere, as president, Iacocca

Ralph Moody and Larry Shinoda conspired to smooth out the aerodynamic flaws of the Cyclone and Torino car lines during the waning months of the 1968 season. Their solution was to graft on an all-new nose panel that both narrowed and lowered both cars' front body line. Fomoco execs called the new Mercury design the Cyclone Spoiler II. Cale Yarborough won the new line's first outing at the 1969 running of the Atlanta 500.

was diametrically opposed to continued corporate sponsorship of motorsports activities. One of his very first moves as Ford chief was to cut the corporate racing budget by a withering 75 percent across the board. As a result, the King Cobra project died before coming to fruition, and none of those sleek aero-warriors ever took a competitive lap on the Grand National tour. Worse yet, Talladega and Spoiler II teams that had been gearing up to campaign the new cars were forced at the last minute to abandon all of the R&D work done and hastily prepare their 1969 teams' cars.

The secret behind the Talladega's aerodynamic success was the special nose panel cooked up by Ralph Moody (with input from Larry Shinoda). It consisted of fenders that were extended 6 inches forward, a special header panel that tied the fenders together, a labor-intensive front bumper (cut and welded from a rear bumper), and a flush-fitting grille section. Donnie Allison drove the #27 car for legendary mechanic Banjo Matthews in 1969 and 1970.

LeeRoy Yarbrough had a phenomenal year for both Ford and Mercury in 1969. He kicked the season off by winning the Daytona 500 in a Talladega and then went on to score 6 more wins and 16 top-five finishes in both Talladegas and Spoiler IIs. He is shown here at speed in a long-nosed Mercury. *JDC Collection*

And, of course, Iacocca's budget axe also cut the flow of support dollars that flowed to factory teams to nearly a trickle. As a result, Fomoco's racing fortunes were mortally wounded before the first Boss 429 barked to life at Daytona, and the 1970 season was lost before it began.

A further impediment to Fomoco success in 1970 was the off-season introduction of yet another Chryco winged car. Stung by King Richard's 1969 departure for Ford, Plymouth engineers set out to seduce him back with an all-new winged Plymouth called the Superbird. That new aero-variant (coupled with several truck loads of money) was all it took to induce Petty to change his brand allegiance back to the Mayflower division.

And yet, with seemingly the whole world conspiring against them, Ford and Mercury drivers still managed to turn in a number of superspeedway wins during the 1970 season—with inadequate funding and absent radically pointed snouts or soaring rear deck wings.

The first of those wins almost came at the 1970 Daytona 500 where Cale Yarborough overcame a flock of winged cars in qualifying to turn in the pole-winning lap with his #21 Wood Brothers Spoiler II. Cale led the preliminary laps but was sidelined with engine failure early in the event. Holman & Moody driver David Pearson next picked up the Ford standard and late in the race appeared poised to win. Unfortunately, worn tires allowed Superbird driver Pete Hamilton to slip past just before the flag to take the win. Pearson did win at the spring Darlington race, and Donnie

Allison won both the World 600 and the Firecracker 400 in a Banjo Matthews-prepped Talladega. Cale Yarborough and LeeRoy Yarbrough scored superspeedway wins for Mercury at Michigan and Charlotte, and Cale's #21 car visited victory lane one more time on a big track (at Rockingham) before the year was over.

Though not a winning season overall for Ford and Mercury, the underfunded superspeedway wins scored with last year's race cars in 1970 helped secure final aero-war victory for Fomoco teams. When Bill France brought the aero-wars to an end in 1971 by restricting special aero-bodied cars to a maximum engine size of just 305 cubic

Nineteen seventy saw the introduction of an all-new Torino body line. Larry Shinoda penned an aeroversion of the new body style that featured a swoopy, Datsun Z-like front end that came to be called the King Cobra. Though the car showed promise, it died before it saw any racing time when Bunkie Knudsen was fired from Ford.

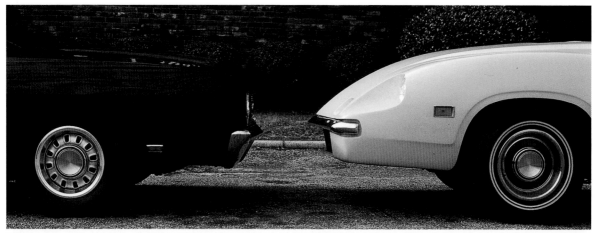

Here's a nose-to-nose comparison of the Talladega and the King Cobra. Early tests of the KC conducted by Holman & Moody showed that the new nose stuck to the ground like glue. Unfortunately, the car never got a chance to prove itself on the track.

Bud Moore bought two King Cobra prototypes from Ford and thus saved them from the crusher. Today, one of the two is in private hands and has been restored to Boss 429 trim. The other still belongs to Moore. Just imagine if Ford had gone forward with the KC race program.

Talladegas made appearances in a variety of racing venues. Benny Parsons, for example, raced in a Big T in both NASCAR and ARCA. His #98 Talladega finished up the 1969 season as the ARCA champ. *JDC Collection*

inches, Ford teams had won a grand total of 14 superspeedway races, with Mercury teams accounting for 8 additional mile or more wins. Winged Daytonas won just 6 superspeedway events during the same period and Superbirds just 7. Dodge Charger 500s accounted for but 1 big track win over the two-season affray. With a final tally of 22 superspeedway triumphs to Chryco's 14, it's clear that, pointy noses and soaring wings notwithstanding, Ford Talladegas and Mercury Spoiler IIs were the true champions of the factory-backed aero wars waged 1968 through 1970.

Ford went to war with the NASCAR sanctioning body over the legality of the SOHC Hemi engine. Ford lost that battle but ultimately won the war (the aero war that is) with the Boss 429 Hemi engine in 1969 and 1970.

The lights went out on Holman & Moody's fabled racing operation in 1972. Abandoned by Ford for a second time at the close of the 1971 season, the team built its last race car (pictured here) in 1972. The Boss 429-powered Torino was driven by Indy ace Bobby Unser at Riverside in 1973. Note the right-side fuel fill that was used on Riverside cars (where cars circled the track in a clockwise rather than counterclockwise fashion).

3

Ford's Lean Years for Racing

Though few appreciated the fact at the time, 1971 was destined to be Ford's last season of factory-backed racing on the Grand National (soon to be called Winston Cup) circuit for the next 12 years. With funding cut to the bone by Iacocca's gutting of the racing budget, most teams that decided to continue campaigning cars of the Fomoco persuasion opted to cut back and only field cars at the most lucrative stops on the circuit.

And with Talladegas and Spoiler IIs relegated to the scrap heap by the vagaries of the official rules book, just about every Blue Oval operation switched over to 1969 Cyclone sheet metal, since it was felt those cars were more aerodynamic than any Fomoco intermediates that had been built since. Holman & Moody fielded blue and gold Mercurys first for David Pearson that year, for example, and then (when Pearson left the team) red and gold Coca-Cola Cyclones for Bobby Allison. The Wood Brothers also switched to 1969 Cyclones for A. J. Foyt after Cale Yarborough's departure. That same move to Mercury was made by Banjo Matthews for his driver Donnie Allison. Long-time Ford partisan Junior Johnson jumped ship entirely for 1971 and elected to campaign Chevrolets for the first time since 1963.

In another interesting twist, most Ford teams ultimately abandoned their Boss engines in favor of tried and true 427 Tunnel Port engines when the restrictor plate regulation NASCAR had first introduced in 1970 began to choke the competitive life out of the "Blue Crescent" 429 engines

1971–1980

(because NASCAR's always-arbitrary rules book more severely restricted Hemi motors than conventional wedge engines).

As things turned out, 1971 was actually a pretty successful season for Holman & Moody. With Pearson still at the helm, the team won one of the twin 125s run every year before the Daytona 500 and finished fourth in the race. Pearson also turned in a win at Bristol before resigning from the team. Bobby Allison's first 1971 H&M effort produced a second (behind brother Donnie's Cyclone) at Talladega. The team then went on a superspeedway tear and won the World 600, the Mason Dixon 500, the Motor State 500, the Yankee 400, the Talladega 500, the Southern 500, and the National

500. Ralph Moody today recalls Allison's #12 Cyclone as his all-time favorite competition car (quite a statement when all of the cars that Moody drove or worked on are considered!). And on reflection, the stellar success enjoyed by the Holman & Moody effort that year was a fitting swan song for the team. For that's just what the season turned out to be as, when Ford removed all factory backing at the close of the year, the fabled Holman & Moody operation essentially ceased to exist.

The Wood Brothers' Stuart, Virginia, operation was also undergoing a transition away from factory sponsorship in 1971. Cale Yarborough had decided to leave the team at the close of the 1970 season to pursue his Indy car options, and A. J. Foyt had

When the sanctioning body effectively outlawed all special aerobody cars with a 5-liter limit in 1971, most Fomoco teams switched over to 1968/1969 Cyclone body styles. That proved to be a good move for the Holman & Moody team. When Bobby Allison stepped in for the departing David Pearson, he drove the #12 team car to wins in the World 600, the Motor State 400, the Yankee 400, the Talladega 500, the Southern 500, and the National 500. *JDC Collection*

Though not apparent at first, the 1970/1971 Cyclone body style turned out to be one of the most successful superspeedway body styles of all time. David Pearson and the Wood Brothers proved as much by winning just about every superspeedway race on the tour during the early 1970s. Pearson is shown here out in front at Daytona. *Daytona Racing Archives*

been signed to replace him. Foyt got off to a good start by finishing third in the Daytona 500 and then quickly found the way to victory lane at Ontario (an exact duplicate of the Indy circuit Foyt was master of) in the Miller High Life 500 in late February. Win number two for the team came in the Atlanta 500 in March. Donnie Allison hopped in Foyt's #21 "W" nose Mercury at Talladega and led older

brother Bobby across the stripe in the Winston 500 in what turned out to be the last win of the season for the Woods. All told, Mercury drivers scored 11 wins in 1971, while Ford drivers accounted for 4.

With Ford fully out of racing at the close of the 1971 season, it became increasingly challenging for the few remaining Fomoco teams to achieve victory. By the end of the decade, only a handful of diehard Ford partisans were still on a tour that by 1975 was almost exclusively a GM show.

Yet even during the darkest moments of that decade of despair, there were a few bright moments for Ford fans in the stands at Winston Cup stock car races. And more than a few of those moments were provided by the driver of a Wood Brothers Mercury.

A. J. Foyt, for example, gave a hint of the superspeedway domination the Woods' team would display in the mid-1970s when he convincingly won the 1972 Daytona 500 in a team Cyclone. One of the secrets behind Foyt's dominating success that day (he started second and lead the last 300 miles of the event) was the overlooked

aerodynamic prowess of the 1970 Mercury Cyclone body. Foyt used that advantage to win at Ontario just three weeks after Daytona. Though only allowed a vestigial 1 1/2-inch rear deck spoiler by the official rules book, the 1970/1971 Cyclone body was actually one of the best superspeedway chassis to ever wear a coat of racing livery.

Proof of that fact is the incredible string of superspeedway wins scored by David Pearson after he signed on to drive the car in April of 1972. Pearson, who was soon to earn his now famous "Silver Fox" nickname, won the first time out in a #21 Mercury at Darlington in the Rebel 400. A win in the Talladega 500 came next and was quickly followed by victory lane visits at Michigan (twice), Daytona, and Dover.

Independent drivers like Cecil Gordon also selected the slippery 1971 Cyclone body style as the basis for their racing efforts. This particular example has been restored by Davidson, North Carolina's Alex Beam.

Nineteen seventy-three found the Silver Fox once again behind the wheel of a 1970/1971 Cyclone, and once again that combination proved to be a winner. The team (and Pearson) had cut back its schedule to just 18 events that year, and all of those were super-speedway contests. Nonetheless, Pearson and the Woods won 11 of the events they entered. In that number were triumphs at Rockingham, Atlanta, Darlington, Martinsville, Talladega, Dover, and Daytona.

Though long associated with General Motors cars, Darrell Waltrip actually cut his NASCAR teeth on Mercury race cars. Ol' DW's first Grand National outings came in this #95 1971 Mercury which he's recently restored to race-ready condition. *Craft Collection*

While Pearson was wowing the crowds (and the competition) with high-speed Mercury victories, cars carrying Ford's Blue Oval badge never got closer to victory lane than pit road the whole season. Even so, canny mechanic Bud Moore was laying the ground work for future Ford greatness that very season. You see, though Pearson was still mopping up on the high banks with the help of big block (Boss 429) power, the sanctioning body was taking an increasingly jaundiced view of 7-liter powerplants. As a result, the ever-changing rules book was making life increasingly difficult for big-block-based teams. Innovative types like Moore (just back from the Trans-Am wars where small blocks reigned) quickly discovered that smaller displacement engines were far less regulated by the infernal rules book than mountain motors were.

As a result, Moore set out to build a competitive Winston Cup car that was motorvated by a racing version of the 351 Cleveland small block first introduced in 1970. Beginning in 1973, Moore built cars for Bobby Isaac, Darrell Waltrip, Donnie

Allison, George Follmer, Buddy Baker, and Bobby Allison, and every one of those #15 Fords was pulled around the race track by a small-block Ford engine. It was one of Moore's Cleveland-powered cars, in fact, that ended Ford's three-year drought with a win in the 1975 Winston 500 at Talladega. Proving that win was no fluke, Baker flat-footed his way to a second 1975 Talladega win in the Talladega 500. Baker also scored firsts at Atlanta and Ontario that season, and by year's end, more than a few teams were reevaluating their reliance on big-block engines.

The Wood Brothers continued their super-speedway mastery throughout the mid-1970s, winning 7 events in 1974, 3 in 1975, and 10 in 1976. The most famous of those wins is, without doubt, the dramatic Daytona 500 triumph Pearson scored in 1976. When the 1970/1971 Cyclone body style that had served the team so well was rendered obsolete by the rules book in 1974, the Wood Brothers team switched to the newer (and not nearly as aerodynamic) Mercury Montego body style. The team had also elected to follow Bud Moore's (and the rule book's) lead at about the same time and rely on small block motorvation.

Pearson had used the 600 or so ponies cranked out by his Merc's Cleveland to qualify seventh for the race. Nonetheless, he had the boxy Montego out in front of the pack by lap 5 of the event. By lap 155, the race had become a two-car affair to be decided between Pearson and his arch-rival at the time, Richard Petty. They traded the lead back and forth for the next 50 circuits. Petty had claimed the lead with 13 laps to go, and Pearson stayed glued to his bumper. As the speeding duo approached Turn 3 on the last lap of the event, Pearson made his move. He'd completed his pass but then drifted up

This is the view that most of the NASCAR field had of David Pearson's 1971 Cyclone during the early 1970s. The car's native speed coupled with Pearson's crafty driving won more than a few superspeedway events.

Bud Moore returned to the NASCAR fold (from the Trans-Am ranks) in 1972. The first cars he built that season were for team driver Bobby Isaac. One of those gape-nosed Torinos has recently been restored by North Carolina's Kim Haynes.

the banking in a fight for traction. Petty took the opportunity and attempted to slip back by on the low side of the track. Petty too lost his purchase on the asphalt, and there was contact between the two cars that sent both spinning wildly into the tri-oval at nearly 180 miles per hour. Pearson's car hit the outside wall hard in the front, crazily distorting the sheet metal back over the engine and chassis. Petty's STP Dodge was similarly wounded, and when both cars came to rest, for a moment it appeared that neither would win the race. Fortunately, Pearson had the presence of mind to keep the clutch down and the revs up while spinning out of control (they didn't call him the Silver Fox for nothing), and so he was able to coax his heavily damaged Mercury across the line ahead of both Petty and the onrushing field. It was a spectacular win, and one that was broadcast live to a country full of television viewers who were perched on the edge of their seats.

The car that Pearson limped into victory lane with was a reflection of the technology that dominated the Winston Cup scene from the mid-1970s until nearly the present. Unlike the unit-body-based "half-chassis" cars that had been introduced by Bud Moore during the boycott 1966 season, by 1974 Fomoco teams had shifted to full-perimeter chassis that featured fully fabricated front and rear snouts. For a time in the middle of the decade the rules book still required the use of stock chassis side rails, but even that wink at stock appearance had gone by the wayside by the end of the decade. Suspension components under Pearson's Merc were a mix and match of Ford and GM components. A familiar Ford 9-inch live axle was mounted aft, but it was reined in by a pair of Chevy-truck-derived trailing arms and a set of screw-jack-adjusted coils. Four shocks were employed to keep jounce in check. Fabricated "A" arms were used at the bow, and they captured another set of screw-jack-adjusted springs. A 1965 Galaxie steering setup was used to dial in directional changes. Two more pairs of shocks and a wrist-thick, through-the-chassis sway bar rounded out the front suspension.

Disc brakes had become increasingly popular in the garage area ever since Mark Donohue had scored the first NASCAR disc brake win in 1972 (in a Rambler of all things!), so Pearson's Mercury that day was stopped by a stout set of aftermarket rotors and calipers.

The rest of his Mercury's chassis consisted of the jungle gym's worth of tubing that the NASCAR rules book had mandated by the late 1960s. Four bars were mounted per side, and the basic cage had expanded to eight major mounting points. A Petty Bar and a handful of diagonal braces had also

become part of the safety recipe by the time of Pearson's last lap shunt, and they no doubt helped to keep him safe and sound and able to drive across the stripe first.

The whole package rolled on 15x9.5 aftermarket rims and treadless Goodyear bias-ply tires—treaded racing rubber having gone to its eternal reward in 1971. Other significant bits and pieces of the package included a safety fuel cell (first required by the rules in 1967), a foam-based fire system (first required in 1971), and, of course, a full-race Cleveland small block cooked up by Leonard Wood.

Ford performance, on the other hand, was not exactly noteworthy during the mid-1970s. Buddy Baker won yet another Talladega race in a Bud Moore Ford in 1976, but that would be the only entry in the Ford win column until 1978.

When NASCAR determined that speeds were too fast for safety (sound familiar?) in the early 1970s, the sanctioning body set out to eliminate the use of 7-liter engines. Bud Moore countered that assault with a series of small-block (Cleveland) based race cars. Buddy Baker (pictured here during a pit stop) and others drove for Moore during the 1970s and scored a handful of superspeedway wins despite their pioneering use of 5.8-liter powerplants. *Daytona Racing Archives*

Exiting the NASCAR scene in 1972 was the famed Holman & Moody race car-building team. It is perhaps fitting that their last car built (pictured at beginning of chapter) rolled out of the Charlotte shop under the power of a full-boogie Boss 429 engine. Note the late-style ram air system the car came equipped with.

Bobby Allison was an on again/off again Fomoco driver throughout his career. The late 1970s were an "on again" period for Allison, when he drove for Bud Moore's Spartanburg, South Carolina-based team. Though bulky, the T-Birds he drove did enjoy superspeedway success. *Daytona Racing Archives*

Pearson continued to turn in Mercury wins for the Woods, but at a much reduced pace compared to the early 1970s. He scored two wins in 1977, (including the Southern 500), and four in 1978 (including the Firecracker 400) before ending his association with the Wood Brothers on an unhappy note at Darlington (after he left the pits with no lug nuts in place). Neil Bonnett took Pearson's place during the next two seasons and scored five more Mercury wins (including superspeedway wins at Dover, Daytona, Atlanta, Pocono, and Talladega). The last of those wins came at the 1979 Talladega 500 where Bonnett started second on the field and then went on to lead Cale Yarborough's Junior Johnson Chevrolet across the stripe. It is more than a little ironic that Bonnett's win that day, just ahead of former Mercury star Yarborough, should have been the very last to be recorded by a Mercury driver in current NASCAR history. Though some teams have built and tested Lincoln Mercury-based race cars in the nearly two decades since that day in 1979 (Cale Yarborough's team experimented with a Cougar in

the 1980s, and Michael Kranefuss' team tested a Lincoln Mark VIII in the 1990s), no other Mercury drivers have visited victory lane. Indeed, there are no Mercury-based teams in competition on the circuit today and likely will not be in the near future.

As Mercury's star was in decline in the late 1970s, Ford drivers (at least one Ford team, that is) were experiencing some measure of success. When Buddy Baker and Bud Moore parted ways in 1978, Bobby Allison signed on to campaign the team's block-long #15 Thunderbirds. Allison had driven Cam 2 Mercurys for Roger Penske the season before, but that operation had folded its tent at the end of the year (which resulted in the sale of several team Mercurys to a young Georgia fellow named Bill Elliott who then used them in some of his earliest NASCAR appearances). So the senior member of the Alabama gang was amenable to Moore's offer when it came during the off season. It proved to be a very successful pairing.

Evidence of that fact is provided by the 1979 win that Allison turned in for the team at the all

Fomoco racers in the 1970s relied on the junkyard (rather than Dearborn) for racing parts. This Wood Brothers 351 C engine, for example, was built around a scavenged Australian block and regular production heads. Fortunately, Ford's interest in factory-backed racing would awaken from its dormancy in the early 1980s.

important Daytona 500. Though Bobby had only qualified his boxy T-Bird 33rd that day, by the end of the event he placed the car's block-long hood out in front of the Chevrolet hordes. It was the first win in the "Super Bowl of Stock Car Racing" for both Moore and Allison. Also of note that day was the 8th-place finish turned in by that young red-headed fellow named Elliott in one of Allison's old Cam 2 Mercurys. It was Elliott's first top-10 finish on the Winston Cup tour, but it was to be far from his last. Allison finished 2nd at Rockingham in the #15 car before snagging his second win of the year at Atlanta. Win number three came at Dover in

Red Farmer was a charter member of the Alabama gang. As a result, the superspeedway at Talladega, Alabama, was one of his favorite tracks. The 1973 Torino he raced there is fairly typical of Ford stockers of the 1970s: aerodynamically impaired and down on power. Better days were ahead for Ford racers in the 1980s. *Mike Slade*

Here in a picture is Fomoco's problem during the late 1970s: aerodynamics or, specifically, the lack thereof. Where once slippery aero-warriors like the Torino Talladegas had knifed through the air, by the late seventies, the Ford styling studio had regressed to parasitic-drag producing grilles like the one on this Wood Brothers Mercury. Lack of factory support, of course, didn't help put Fomoco cars in the winner's circle either. *JDC Collection*

September, and Allison went on to win at Charlotte and in the season finale at Ontario. Allison stayed with Moore's Spartanburg-based operation through the 1980 season, and during that time he scored nine more wins for the team.

Things were looking bleak for Ford teams and fans as the 1980s dawned. Save for the efforts of the Wood Brothers and Bud Moore teams, the 1970s would have been a winless decade for Blue Oval partisans. Chevrolet and its GM clone divisions mopped up in the Winston Cup division during Fomoco's absence. Though not openly funding Bow Tie-based racing programs, as in the early 1960s during the AMA ban, Chevrolet engineers had left the back door of the high-performance division open throughout the 1970s. Ford, with Iacocca at the helm, instead had focused its attention on such stunning concepts as the Maverick

Grabber, the Mustang II, and the Pinto wagon. The end result was a lost decade for Ford racers—except of course—for those like Junior Johnson who had jumped ship to Chevrolet.

Though it's hard to imagine now, by 1979 it was becoming nearly impossible for even diehard Fomoco teams like Moore's, the Woods', and Junie Donlavey's to press on, due to the increasing rarity of usable Cleveland engine components. With that engine out of production and junkyard parts dwindling, Ford teams were forced to prowl Australian junkyards in search of race-worthy blocks and heads. Fortunately, Iacocca was soon to depart Ford for Chrysler (where he fathered the boring "K" car line), and with his departure, racier lights in the Ford executive class (in whose number was no lesser personage than Edsel Ford II) began to move the corporate tiller back towards motorsports competition.

172

Left
Though the late 1970s were the doldrums for Ford fans on the NASCAR tour, they did produce future reasons for enthusiasm—like Bill Elliott. The yet-to-be-Awesome Bill got his NASCAR start at the wheel of dirigible-class Mercurys like this one during the latter part of the leisure-suit decade. *JDC Collection*

Below
Ford and Mercury race cars had become all angular and bulky by the late 1970s, as can be seen in this trio of Mercurys and Fords. Bill Elliott is piloting the #9 Mercury, Bobby Allison the #15 Thunderbird, and David Pearson the #21 Merc. Rounded edges and regular returns to the winner's circle were still several years in the future. *JDC Collection*

Davey Allison, pictured here at speed, had his racing career tragically cut short by a freak helicopter accident in 1993. He was a bright, personable young man whose future was unlimited. In that regard he had more than a little in common with Fireball Roberts, Joe Weatherly, and Alan Kulwicki—all Ford racers who came to an untimely end.

4

Ford Racing
Roars Back to Life

Nineteen eighty-one was the year that NASCAR downsized its chassis from 116-inch wheelbases to the 110-inch standard that is currently in effect. The new smaller Thunderbirds produced by this rules change were both nimbler and more competitive than the Frank Cannon-mobile full-sized cars they replaced. And that fact is borne out by the nine wins that teams fielding those cars scored in 1981 and 1982.

Bill Elliott scored his very first Winston Cup win in the Winston Western 500 at Riverside (November 1983) at the helm of a downsized 1982 Thunderbird. Bud Moore fielded winning Fords for Benny Parsons and Dale Earnhardt (that's right, Ford fans, "Ironhead" once drove Fords!), and Neil Bonnett also added to the Wood Brothers Fomoco win total.

Though Ford teams once again began to taste stock car victory in the early 1980s, it wasn't until 1983 that the changes necessary to return Ford to a position of dominance began to occur. The most important event in that number was the decision taken in the Ford styling studio to move away from sharp edges and towards rounded, flowing surfaces. That change of focus led directly to the totally restyled Thunderbird line that took a bow in 1983. As in 1968, the power of superior Ford aerodynamics began to be felt at tracks all across the circuit.

At the same time those curvy new creations began to roll off of the assembly line, "Glass House" execs gave the green light for the production of a new run of 351 Cleveland-based engines and high-performance parts.

1981-Present

NASCAR rules dictated downsizing in 1981 from the traditional 116-inch wheelbase of years gone by to a new shorter 110-inch wheelbase. That change brought about the introduction of Fox chassis-based Thunderbird race cars. The Wood Brothers carried their familiar red-and-white #21 livery into the 1980s with Neil Bonnett as their driver (seen here during a pit stop at the North Carolina Motor Speedway). *Mike Slade*

More encouraging yet was the fact that, for the first time in nearly two decades, the corporation began to offer a catalog full of over-the-counter high-performance aftermarket parts. While Ford's revived interest in factory high performance wasn't exactly a rebirth of the halcyon Total Performance days of yore, it was a dramatic change in focus compared to Iacocca's days of thrifty fuel sippers.

Ford drivers Dale Earnhardt, Buddy Baker, Bill Elliott, and Ricky Rudd scored eight wins in 1983 and 1984. Their on-track success did not go unnoticed. Soon (and for the first time since the late

1960s) new Ford teams began to form. One of the first GM-based teams to switch back to Ford was Cale Yarborough's Ranier Lundy-backed operation. Yarborough's name already appeared many times in both the Ford and Mercury win columns, so his return to the Blue Oval was something of a homecoming. So, too, was the reunion of Ranier Lundy chief mechanic Robert Yates with the new and improved Cleveland-based engines that were slated to power Cale's #28 Hardee's car. As history records, a much younger Yates was once a Holman & Moody line mechanic and had, in fact, built the Tunnel Port engine that had powered LeeRoy Yarbrough to victory lane in the 1969 Daytona 500. Yates-built Ford engines were soon making themselves right at home in victory lane again.

Nineteen eighty-five was the year that Ford teams signaled that they intended to dominate the Winston Cup series in the same way their spiritual predecessors had in the 1960s. Bill Elliott fired the first volley of that assault in the Daytona 500 where, with the help of a high-revving small block built by brother Ernie, Awesome Bill swept qualifying with a record shatter-ing 205.265-mile-per-hour qualifying lap. Elliott used his car's speed advantage during the race itself to wear down the competition with a frantic 192-mile-per-hour average pace. He went on to lead 136 of the 200 laps that made up the event, including the all important final circuit. Elliott also turned in wins in Atlanta, Darlington, Talladega, Dover, Michigan, and Pocono. Along the way he captured the Winston Million and became the media's darling. His total tally of wins came in at 11, and his earnings topped two million simoleons. Interestingly, though Chevy

Dale Earnhardt's Fox-based Thunderbird wasn't any more aerodynamic than the rest of the breed, but that didn't stop him from winning the 1982 Rebel 500 in one such car.

Bill Elliott took his first checkered flag from a cockpit just like this one in 1983. The Melling team was less than generously funded in those days. Evidence of that fact was found in this particular car during its restoration by Alex Beam: the driver's seat was found to be made up from a "liberated" Georgia State road sign.

Previous pages
Fomoco racing fortunes took a dramatic turn for the better in 1983. The reason for that change was that old reliable physical force—aerodynamics. After years of building sharply-creased, vertically-paneled cars, Ford stylists went ovoid in 1983. The end result was super-slippery race cars like this Cale Yarborough Hardee's T-Bird. *Mike Slade*

rival Darrell Waltrip won but 3 Winston Cup events that year, the always-confusing NASCAR points system made him the Winston Cup champ. Superspeedway wins by Cale Yarborough and Ricky Rudd brought Ford's win total to 15 for the season.

As fast as Ford's first generation of rounded-off Thunderbirds had proven to be, even faster velocities were in the offing for 1987. That heightened performance came as a result of yet another styling change that refined the Thunderbird silhouette to what many still consider to be its most

aerodynamic form. Of greatest significance were the changes made to the car's bustle that both raised and widened the body line. The nose received refinement, too, and in race trim the body line rose from the racing tarmac to the "A" pillars in a smooth arc. When coupled with the ever-increasing levels of horsepower that were being found by Ernie Elliott and Robert Yates, speeds well in excess of the double ton were just a tickle of the throttle away.

Bill Elliott literally drove that point home during qualifying at Daytona in February when he scorched the track with a 210.364-mile-per-hour lap. Starting from the pole, he went on to humble the rest of the field by leading over half of the event and taking the checkered flag. Even the new add-on noses and bubble-back rear windows that the GM intermediates had sprouted to break the Thunderbird's stride proved unable to slow Awesome Bill's pace. Ford wins came quickly at other superspeedways on the tour. Ricky Rudd won at Atlanta and later at Dover. Rookie Davey Allison scored his first NASCAR win at Talladega behind the wheel of a Robert Yates missile (after Elliott eclipsed the field by qualifying with a record-setting 212.809-mile-per-hour pace lap). Allison won again at Dover. Elliott claimed the Talladega 500 (where the summer heat slowed his qualifying speeds to a tepid 203.827 miles per hour). He won at Michigan, then again at Charlotte, once more at Rockingham, and for the final time at Atlanta.

All told, Ford drivers won 11 times in 1987. And that was enough to persuade the sanctioning body that something would have to be done about, ahem, safety (yeah, that's it; it's just plain unsafe for Ford teams to win so many races). Reaching into the tech inspector's golden oldie bag of tricks, NASCAR announced that the 1988 season would see the reintroduction of the dreaded restrictor plate. Even so, Bill Elliott still visited victory lane a total of 6 times and scored 9 other top-10 finishes on his way to the 1988 Winston Cup driving title. It was the first such win for a Fomoco driver since David Pearson's 1969 triumph for Holman & Moody and had certainly been a long time in coming.

With those horsepower-robbing plates in place, the 650-plus horsepower that folks like Yates could coax from just 5.7 liters of Ford small block were trimmed a substantial 200-odd ponies. And that was enough to keep Ford teams out of victory lane at more than a few events. And, oh yes, the resulting bunch-up of cars that often led to huge chain reaction wrecks was much safer indeed than when Ford drivers were lapping the field twice at Talladega under green flag conditions. Unfortunately, the dreaded restrictor plates first rolled out in 1988 are still with us today.

Early 1980s' T-Birds sported formal, chopped-off rooflines that were great at creating drag. No restrictor plates were needed in those days to keep speeds in check.

Davey Allison was a rookie driver during the 1987 season. But his lack of experience did not keep his Robert Yates-prepped Ford out of victory lane. Young Davey became the first rookie to win more than one race in his freshman season since Dick Hutcherson earned that same honor as a Holman & Moody driver in 1965.

When Ford decided to get reinvolved in racing, the corporation began to crank out sorely needed high performance engine parts. By 1983, it was again possible to build a full race 351 C-evolved engine from all new components. No more junkyard shopping was required.

Even in the face of NASCAR's best efforts to slow the Ford contingent down, more and more teams began to make the switch to Thunderbird-based teams. Whereas in the 1970s, there might have been just one or two Fomoco-based teams on any given starting grid, as the 1990s dawned, oftentimes more than half of the field was comprised of cars bearing the Blue Oval. The Thunderbird's slippery shape, coupled with an increasingly robust behind-the-scenes support from Ford, made it a no-brainer for many teams to switch to Ford.

The 1990s have been marked by continued Ford success. Nineteen ninety-two saw Ford drivers visit victory lane no fewer than 16 times. In that number was a memorable (and sentimental)

When Ford stylists revised the Thunderbird body style in 1987, part of the program was to raise the car's rear deck lid several inches. The line's front silhouette was also freshened up that year and made more aerodynamic. The end result was the fastest NASCAR stock car of all time. Bill Elliott's 212.809-mile-per-hour qualifying lap at Talladega in 1987 will likely never be topped.

win scored by Davey Allison in the Daytona 500. Young Davey, whose life would be taken in a tragic flying accident less than a year later, started the race sixth that day (behind fellow Ford driver Sterling Marlin who had a 192.213 qualifying lap in the Junior Johnson Ford). Though he didn't make it to the front of the pack until lap 56 of the event, Davey led the last 29 circuits convincingly to take the win. Bill Elliott (running for Junior Johnson) and Davey Allison both wound up with 5 wins each that season, but it was the doggedly independent Alan Kulwicki who came up with the points to secure the Winston Cup driving title. Kulwicki's formula for success included a handful of Thunderbirds (sometimes called "Underbirds" due to his

Bill Elliott took in the very rapidly passing scenery from this perch in 1987 and 1988. Interestingly, just beneath the floorboards lurked most of the same suspension components that cars like Fred Lorenzen's 1965 Galaxie had rolled on.

Into the 1990s, the Wood Brothers are still fielding competitive cars of the Ford persuasion. Though no longer painted in the Wood's traditional red-and-white livery, the race cars that they build in Stuart, Virginia, still carry the familiar #21 racing number. Michael Waltrip is the most recent of the team drivers.

The Wood Brothers continued their winning ways in the 1980s with drivers like Neil Bonnett and Kyle Petty. Here the team services young Kyle's T-Bird on the way to a win in the 1987 World 600.

Ricky Rudd proved to be one of the most consistent Ford drivers in the 1990s, winning at least one Winston Cup race every season for nearly a decade. His Tide-backed T-Birds were both flashy and fast.

independent status), 2 wins (at Pocono and Bristol), 17 top-10 finishes, and lots of hard work. The end result was $2,332,561 in winnings and the second Winston Cup driving title secured by a Fomoco driver in the modern era.

Ford drivers scored a modern-era high of 20 season victories in 1994, and Jack Roush driver Mark Martin came within a hair's breadth of winning the third Winston Cup title of the modern era. The 1990's iterations of the Thunderbird chassis are much the same as the early 1980's Fords they succeeded. All are built around a purpose-built tubular-steel chassis that has never been closer to a UAW assembly line than a North Carolina fabricator's shop. A 9-inch solid-axle differential forms the focus of the car's rear suspension, and its movements are checked by a pair of Chevy-derived trailing arms, a cross-chassis panhard rod, and a pair of screw-jack-adjusted coil springs. One gas-charged shock per wheel keeps

Bud Moore's #15 Fords continue to make regular appearances well into the 1990s. Recent drivers of Moore-prepped T-Birds include Ricky Rudd, Geoff Bodine, and Dick Trickle. In 1998, the Spartanburg native celebrated his 50th year in stock car racing.

oscillations in check. At the box, most teams have now switched to Chevrolet Camaro-derived front-steer (steering box ahead of center line) suspension components that allow greater flexibility in header and oil pan configuration. Another pair of gas shocks and a cross-chassis spline-ended sway bar complete the front suspension. Special manhole-cover-sized discs and six-piston caliper brakes are mounted at all four corners, and they act on 15x9.5 rims that roll on special Goodyear Eagle radial tires.

Power for a modern Winston Cup T-Bird is churned out by an alloy-headed evolution of the 351 Cleveland engine. A single 850-cubic-feet-per-minute-based Holley carb sends combustibles to the engine's poly-valved combustion chambers

Alan Kulwicki was the epitome of the rugged individualist. Though offered several "big time" rides with long-established teams, he chose to go his own independent way. That course led him to the 1992 Winston Cup championship.

through a highly massaged single-plane aluminum intake. A cobby roller cam incapable of idling below 2,000-odd rpm governs timing events, and a high-energy ignition (HEI) system fires the engine to life. A low-parasitic-drag dry-sump system carrying 20-plus quarts of synthetic provide the engine's life blood, and handmade large-diameter stainless headers send hydrocarbons out towards the ozone layer. In peak Robert Yates tune, a modern high-compression Ford engine can be relied on for in excess of 725 ponies. Absent the restrictor plates that NASCAR still mandates at Daytona and Talladega (among other superspeedways), it's likely that a Winston Cup "Bird" would be circling the track in excess of 220 miles per hour.

Not happy with that fact, the sanctioning body has low compression ratio 9:1 engines waiting in the wings and is moving in the direction of cutting speed on the track by reducing the allowable squeeze in each engine's combustion chambers.

In addition to these changes, Ford itself has discontinued the Thunderbird line for 1998. It appears that 1997 will be the last year for a Thunderbird on the circuit (at least until the new Thunderbird line makes a bow in 1999 or the year 2000). However, for the 1998 season Ford introduced a Winston Cup version of the four-door Taurus economy car that is showing promise.

Evidence of its potential was provided by Rusty Wallace's Taurus triumph in the 1998 running of the Bud shootout—the new body style's first competitive outing. More Taurus victories

Ned Jarrett won the 1965 Grand National driving championship in a Holman & Moody-built Ford Galaxie. In the 1990s, his son Dale has shown the same flair for piloting a race car that his dad had in the 1960s. The younger Jarrett will without doubt duplicate his dad's NASCAR driving title in the very near future.

Mark Martin's #6 Taurus quickly established itself as a championship contender during its first season of Winston Cup Competition.

were quick to follow. As this is being written, the 1998 season is winding down to a head-to-head battle between Mark Martin's #7 Taurus and Jeff Gordon's Monte Carlo. Though few predicted that Ford's new body style would show championship potential right out of the blocks, that's how things have turned out. But then again, Ford does, after all, stand for First On Race Day, doesn't it?!

Since the very first strictly stock race in Charlotte in 1949, Ford drivers have visited Grand National and Winston Cup victory lanes more times than any other manufacturer (as of press time that figure is 479). And that's a winning tradition that's likely to continue well into the next century.

Ricky Rudd's Taurus was one of the most colorful cars on the tour in 1998 regardless of brand affiliation.

Appendix

First Model Wins

First	Laps/ Track Length	Place	Date	Driver/ Team/Car
Lincoln Win	150 laps 3/4-mile dirt	Charlotte, North Carolina	6/19/49	Jim Roper Mecklenburg Mtrs 1949 Lincoln
Mercury Win	200 laps 1/2-mile dirt	Vernon, New York	6/18/50	Bill Blair 1950 Mercury
Ford Win	200 laps 1/2-mile dirt	Dayton, Ohio	6/25/50	Jimmy Florian Euclid Motors 1950 Ford
Thunderbird Win	110 laps .9-mile dirt	Hillsborough, North Carolina	3/1/59	Curtis Turner Holman & Moody 1959 T-Bird

First Championship

First	Year	Driver	Team/Car	Wins	Top 5 Finishes	Purse
Ford Grand National Championship	1965	Ned Jarrett	Bondy Long Galaxie	13	42	$93,624.40

First Race Wins

First	Year	Driver	Team/Car	Avg. Speed (mph)	Purse
Ford Daytona 500 win	1963	Tiny Lund	Wood Brothers Galaxie	151.566	$24,550
Mercury Daytona 500 win	1968	Cale Yarborough	Wood Brothers Cyclone	143.251	$47,250
Ford Southern 500 win	1956	Curtis Turner	Schwam Motors Fairlane	95.067	$11,750
Mercury Southern 500 win	1966	Darel Dieringer	Bud Moore Engineering Comet	114.830	$20,900
Ford World 600 win	1962	Nelson Stacy	Holman & Moody Galaxie	125.552	$25,505
Mercury World 600 win	1969	LeeRoy Yarbrough	Junior Johnson Cyclone Spoiler II	134.361	$29,325
Ford Talladega 500 win	1975	Buddy Baker	Bud Moore Engineering Torino	144.948	$28,725
Mercury Talladega 500 win	1971	Donnie Allison	Wood Brothers Cyclone Spoiler	147.419	$31,140

First Pole Positions

First	Year	Driver	Team/Car	Speed (mph)
Ford Daytona 500 Pole	1985	Bill Elliott	Melling Racing Thunderbird	205.114
Mercury Daytona 500 Pole	1965	Darel Dieringer	Bud Moore Engineering Marauder	171.151
Ford Talladega 500 Pole	1985	Bill Elliott	Melling Racing Thunderbird	209.398
Mercury Talladega 500 Pole	1971	Donnie Allison	Wood Brothers Cyclone Spoiler	185.869

Fomoco Driver Records

Most Ford Grand National/Winston Cup Championships: David Pearson—2 (1968 and 1969)

Most Ford Grand National/Winston Cup wins: Ned Jarrett—43

Most Mercury Grand National/Winston Cup wins: David Pearson—44

Fomoco Team Records

Most Ford Grand National/Winston Cup Championships: Holman & Moody—2 (1968 and 1969)

Most Ford Grand National/Winston Cup wins: Holman & Moody—84

Most Mercury Grand National/Winston Cup wins: Wood Brothers—63

Other Fomoco Records*

*Ford Manufacturer's Points Championships:
11—1956, 1957, 1963, 1964, 1965, 1967, 1968, 1969, 1992, 1994, and 1997

*Most Grand National/Winston Cup wins of any manufacturer: Ford—479

*Most Grand National/Winston Cup wins scored in a single season: Ford—48 (1965)

*Winningest Ford car line: Thunderbird—173 (1959–1997)

*Winningest Mercury car line: Montego—77 wins (1968–1980)

*Winningest Ford body style: 1989–1997 Thunderbird—115 wins

*Winningest Mercury body style: 1968–1969 Cyclone Spoiler—24 wins (1968–1971)

*Greatest number of top-five finishes in a single season:
Ned Jarrett (1965 Bondy Long Galaxie) and David Pearson (1969
Holman & Moody Torino Talladega) are tied with 42

*Largest margin of victory: Ned Jarrett (1965 Southern 500 in Bondy Long Galaxie)—14 laps

*NASCAR's first Most Popular Driver: Ford driver Curtis Turner (1956)

Chrysler, Plymouth & Dodge
Stock Cars

1971

196

FOREWORD

Though Ford Motor Company and General Motors cars have come to dominate the NASCAR ranks of late, there once was a time of greater automotive variety along pit row. From 1949 until the mid-eighties, cars of the Chrysler Motor Company (Chryco) played a major role on the NASCAR tour.

From the earliest races in the Grand National series, Chryco race cars took an important rank on the tour. Early NASCAR star Lee Petty scored the first win for Plymouth in only the seventh race of the fledgling NASCAR series, for example. Many more visits to victory lane were in the offing for Plymouth, Dodge and Chrysler drivers.

During the fifties, Chrysler 300 drivers so dominated the competition that for a time the financial health of the series was placed in peril. When "Letter Series" drivers like Tim Flock and Buck Baker won dozens of races, non-Chryco fans began to stay away in droves. It would not be the last time that Chryco drivers would go on a winning tear through the starting field.

In the sixties, Dodge and Plymouth upped the performance ante by rolling out an all-new Hemi-headed 426ci big block engine that churned out enough torque to tow Amarillo to Anchorage. The engine helped crown Richard Petty the "King of Stock Car Racing," while humbling the Ford and Mercury hoards. By the end of the sixties, Chryco race cars had sported pointy beaks and soaring wings that helped keep Dodge and Plymouth race cars a regular fixture in victory lane.

So fast were Hemi-powered comp cars that the NASCAR dons felt compelled to introduce the first iteration of the now-dreaded restrictor plate. When increasingly restrictive induction rules choked the life out of the fearsome Hemi, Mopar teams switched to wedge-headed big blocks and later to high revving corporate small blocks—even so, Dodge and Plymouth drivers continued to enjoy superspeedway success.

Unfortunately, changing corporate interests ultimately left the Dodge and Plymouth fans and drivers without support in the late seventies and by the middle of the next decade, Chryco stock cars had become but a memory in the garage area. It is in the hopes that those golden memories of Dodge, Plymouth and Chrysler glory will never be forgotten that this book was written.

197

CHAPTER ONE

PLYMOUTH TAKES THE LEAD
Lee Petty Sets the Stage

The date was October 2, 1949, and the place was Heidelburg Speedway in Pittsburgh, Pennsylvania. The event in question was a 100-mile (200 lap) race around the half-mile dirt track there. It proved to be a memorable affair. The fledgling National Association for Stock Car Automobile Racing (NASCAR) sanctioned the race held that day, and it was only the seventh such stock car event to take place in the new for 1949 series.

A driver named Al Bonnell was the fastest qualifier during preparations for the race and his "Strictly Stock" (the original name for the NASCAR series) Olds claimed the pole starting position with a hot lap of 61.475 miles per hour. Though Bonnell and his Olds were not destined for greatness that October day (he ultimately finished dead last) the race's ultimate winner was. And so, too, was the car line that driver had elected to campaign. The driver was a fellow named Lee Petty and his competitive mount was a 1949 Plymouth that carried the number 42. It

There once was a time when Chryslers were the hottest thing on the track. That was during the mid-fifties, when Karl Kiekhaefer's big white fleet of Chrysler 300s won just about every race on the NASCAR tour. Mike Slade

199

Lee Petty switched to a lightweight Plymouth midway into the inaugural 1949 NASCAR season. A short time later, he scored the first Chryco win in Grand National (then "Strictly Stock") history. Though far from fast, the little flathead six-powered car was able to out handle its rivals on the rutted dirt tracks of the day.

was the first stock car win scored by the North Carolina driver and the first NASCAR triumph for a Chrysler competition car in the series. It wouldn't be the last—for either Petty or Chrysler. Petty went on to visit victory lane a total of 54 times before hanging up his helmet and gloves. He and other Chrysler, Plymouth and Dodge drivers collaborated to win a grand total of 365 Grand National stock car events between 1949 and 1973. As you can see, Petty's winning performance was truly the start of something big.

Like all of the other cars on the starting grid at Heidelburg, Petty's Plymouth was absolutely stock. And that's just the way that Bill France, NASCAR's founding father, wanted things to be. The official racing book of the day was a brief one, page affair that in sum dictated the use of totally unmodified cars in the series. In point of fact, many of the cars that showed up for the eight races that made up the inaugural 1949 NASCAR season were so stock that they were driven both to and from the track on race days.

Petty's lightweight little Plymouth was no different in that regard. Based on the nimble little business coupe chassis, Petty's race car rolled on a 217.8-inch wheelbase and was powered by a stone stock 97 horsepower flathead six-cylinder engine. While not exactly a powerhouse, what the little two-door coupe lacked in ultimate velocity, it made up for in low weight and nimble handling. As history records, that is exactly why Petty had selected the car in the first place. Petty's first NASCAR outing had taken place at the very first NASCAR-sanctioned strictly stock car race in June of 1949. Race prep for that 150-mile dirt track event consisted mostly of persuading one of Petty's (perhaps gullible) North Carolina neighbors to let the Randleman native drive his 1946 Buick Roadmaster in the event.

Though Petty's Roadmaster was fast on the straights, it lumbered through the turns like a

A replica of the little Plymouth that Indy driver Johnny Mantz piloted to victory in the very first Southern 500 is today enshrined in the National Motorsports Press Association Hall of Fame in Darlington.

wounded rhino. That trait ultimately led to a spectacular series of flips on lap 105 of the 197 that made up the race. It was THE first recorded racing accident in NASCAR history. The shunt put Petty out of the race and off of racing big heavy cars like the Buick. Shortly after the race (and the return of his neighbor's crumpled car) Petty vowed never to field a heavy vehicle in competition again. Three races later he showed up with a lithe, little Petty Brothers sponsored Plymouth and promptly finished seventh at the fourth ever NASCAR stock car race, held at the famed oval in Langhorne, Pennsylvania. Petty scored his second top ten finish at NASCAR event six in Martinsville (a second) before notching his already reported first "Strictly Stock" win in Pittsburgh.

Petty finished up his first season of stock car racing with a second at North Wilkesboro and wound up second only to Red Byron in the first ever seasonal points competition. It was a

As incredible as it sounds, the Plymouth that won the very first Southern 500 in 1950 had served as Bill France's "go-fer" car during the week before the race. A set of truck tires helped the street legal race car tame the Lady in Black. Mike Slade

promising start to a long racing career and one that caused other drivers to sit up and pay attention to the performance of Petty's diminutive Plymouth. It wasn't long before more cars from the Mayflower division began to show up on stock car starting grids all across the country.

Plymouth win number two came in September of 1950 at a soon-to-be-famous paved oval in a South Carolina town called Darlington. Opened just in time for the 1950 racing season, the new 1.25-mile banked superspeedway in Darlington was one of the first paved race tracks in the country. The inaugural race for the new track was

scheduled for the Labor Day weekend and organizers referred to the event as the Southern 500. A $25,000 purse was posted for that very first Southern 500 and, coupled with the high speeds made possible by the track's banked surface, it attracted scores of drivers. When the green flag fell, fully 75 stock cars roared off into the first turn. In that number was a West Coast driver named Johnny Mantz who had been saddled with the sobriquet "Madman Mantz" during his Indy car days. Mantz's competition car for the event was a rather unimposing-looking Plymouth coupe that had served as an errand runner during the days just prior to the race. NASCAR president "Big" Bill France, chief starter and flagman Alvin Hawkins and mechanic Hubert Westmoreland were listed as co-owners of Mantz's Plymouth. Even so, the car was anything but a pre-race favorite and, in fact, qualified dead last for the race with a hot lap of just 73.460 miles per hour. Though down on speed to the rest of the field, Mantz had a plan for victory that was based on his open wheel paved track experience. Mantz knew that 500 miles of competition would take the measure of most of the stock passenger car tires of the day, so he opted to mount harder compound truck tires under his light little #98 Plymouth. It proved to be a savvy move. Once the green flag fell, Mantz maintained a steady if somewhat sedate pace. Soon other drivers began to experience repeated tire failures (Red Byron experienced no fewer than 24 flats, for example) while Mantz continued to motor around the track without interruption. By lap 50, Madman Mantz had put his little Plymouth out in front of the rest of the field and that's just where the car stayed for the rest of the 400-lap event. Mantz's post-race trip to victory lane at Darlington would not be the last one made by a Chrysler driver after a Southern 500.

Plymouth drivers continued to visit victory lanes on the circuit through the 1952 season. Lee Petty was the most successful of the lot and he racked up wins at Hillsboro, North Carolina; Rochester, New York; Morristown, New Jersey; Macon, Georgia; and Langhorne, Pennsylvania. Herb Thomas took time out from his Hudson Hornet driving duties to score a Plymouth win at Martinsville, Virginia, in 1950 and at Macon in 1951 to round out Plymouth's stock car wins at ten for the 1949 through 1952 seasons. As things turned out, it would be seven more NASCAR seasons before a Plymouth would spend time in a Grand National victory lane. But that didn't mean that Mopar fans were left with little to cheer about during the interim. Not by a long shot.

Dodge Out in Front

The dawning of the 1953 Grand National season brought with it a wholesale defection of drivers from the Plymouth ranks. Fortunately for Mopar fans, that shift in driving allegiance was an "all in the family affair" for the most part that saw drivers like Lee Petty switch to cars of the Dodge persuasion for 1953. The reason for that shift was the all-new "Red Ram" Hemi engine that became a regular production option in the Dodge line that same year. And what an engine it was.

Though Chrysler Corporation had first unveiled a hemispherically combustion-chambered OHV V-8 engine in 1951, it was not until 1953 that the new and promising high-performance engine was assigned to duty in anything other than a "luxo-land yacht" Chrysler. In Dodge trim, the new engine was referred to as the "Red Ram." The new Dodge engine displaced 241.3 cubic inches and featured an over square 3.44-inch bore and 3.25-inch stroke. The cast iron cylinder heads that reciprocating assembly was nestled under were cast with true hemispherical combustion chambers and fitted with generously proportioned (for their day) valves. Street Red Ram V-8s were factory rated at a modest 140 horsepower. But it's certain that racers like Lee Petty were able to coax significantly more ponies out of a race-ready Hemi since the engine was fairly dripping with potential. But that potential was only available for Dodge (and Chrysler drivers) in 1953 since the Plymouth line was denied access to Hemi power that year. Hence, the wholesale shift to Dodge by Plymouth drivers.

The Dodge chassis of choice for drivers on the tour was the two-door Coronet hard top. Stretched over a 114-inch wheelbase, the redesigned for 1953 Coronet line weighed in at just short of 3,500 pounds and featured rounded, if unremarkable, bodywork. Like the lithe little Plymouths that Lee Petty and Johnny Mantz campaigned in previous seasons, the Hemi-powered

Dodges that showed up for the 1953 NASCAR season were smaller and more nimble than the lumbering behemoths that GM and Ford (Fomoco) drivers were forced to field. That fact, coupled with the power potential of the new Hemi engine, made a Dodge stock car circa 1953 a formidable package, indeed. And that's just what Lee Petty proved in spades at the very first race of the new Grand National season.

Palm Beach Speedway in sunny Palm Beach, Florida, was the site of the 1953 season opener. The race held there in February of that year was a 20-lap affair around a half-mile dirt track. Lee

Petty was on hand for the event and he qualified his Red Ram motorvated Dodge seventh on the field. When the flag fell the early laps were dominated by Hudson Hornet drivers. But by lap 49 of the 200 that made up the total, Lee Petty had muscled his Dodge into the lead. That's just where it remained for the balance of the race. When the dust (literally) had settled, Petty had turned a 60.220 miles per hour average speed into Dodge's first ever Grand National stock car victory. And so it was that the driver who'd claimed first blood for the Plymouth division in the NASCAR ranks also notched that same honor

This is the view that most competitors had of a Mercury Outboards sponsored Chrysler 300 in 1956. Team drivers like Buck Baker and Tim Flock won an incredible 30 races that season. Sixteen of those triumphs came in a row! Mike Slade

A Petty Plymouth was pulled around the track by a 97 horsepower flat head six-cylinder engine. Though that sleepy little six was far from a record breaker in the power production department, its lineal ancestors were soon striking fear in the hearts of Brand X drivers on the Grand National tour.

for Dodge. Making Petty's win even sweeter was the fact that Jimmie Lewallen claimed second place in the Petty Engineering 1952 Plymouth that was also fielded by the team that day. Petty's triumph was but a harbinger of the racing glory that would ultimately be won by Hemi-powered Grand National stock cars in the years to come.

Petty went on to score wins at Richmond, Martinsville, Shreveport and Spartanburg in 1953. Jim Paschal claimed a second Martinsville win for Dodge and along with Dick Meyer added top ten finishes in the Southern 500 to the Dodge tally of top performances that year. Petty and

Paschal's win came on dirt at short track events that made up the bulk of the 1953 NASCAR schedule. When the season was over, Petty's five wins and 25 top five finishes had earned him $18,446.50 and second place in the seasonal points chase (to Herb Thomas' Hudson effort). He was destined to improve on that performance the following season.

Chrysler Dominates

Chrysler race cars had been a presence on the NASCAR trail since the very first Strictly Stock race in 1949. Chrysler win number one came in

A stock bench seat, dash and controls confronted Plymouth drivers like Lee Petty in 1949 and 1950 on the NASCAR tour.

1951 at one of the most anticipated races staged that season. The event in question was dubbed the Motor City 250 and was held at Michigan Fairgrounds in August. Just staging the race was a major coup for Big Bill France and the NASCAR series, and it coincided with the 250th anniversary of the city of Detroit. When France got wind of the gala that city fathers had planned for the occasion, he quickly suggested a motorsports event featuring the same makes and models that rolled off of the nearby UAW assembly lines.

When race day arrived, just about all of Motown's movers and shakers had turned out for the dirt track affair that featured one circuit of the one-mile fairground course for every year of Detroit's existence. Fifty-nine cars qualified for the field and there were no fewer than 15 different makes of cars on the starting grid. In that number was a 1951 Chrysler driven by Tommy Thompson that had qualified fifth just a tick or so off of Marshall Teague's pole winning 69.131 miles per hour Hudson hot lap.

Though Teague's Hudson had dominated qualifying, by lap 25, Thompson had nosed his Chrysler into the lead. Curtis Turner hotly contested the point with Thompson for the bulk of the remaining laps (in his unfriendly, fender rubbing way) and on several occasions both he and Thompson slewed off the track in a shower of dirt and dust. But Thompson was not to be deterred and when the flag fell he roared across the line first. Chrysler executives at trackside that day no doubt left the fairgrounds with a bit more swagger than when they'd arrived. Lee Petty gave those same executives even greater bragging rights three seasons later when he won the first Grand National manufacturer's title for the Chrysler Corporation (as well as his own first driving championship).

Petty's championship season began with a third place finish at the season opener in West Palm Beach, Florida, where he campaigned a new Dodge. By the time the tour rolled into Daytona two weeks later for the famed beach race, Petty had swapped mechanical allegiances to the Chrysler line. The car he towed to Daytona from North Carolina was a San Juan Motors sponsored #42 New Yorker Deluxe that was powered by a 235 horse Chrysler Firepower Hemi. In 1954 trim the hottest corporate Hemi displaced 331ci and mounted an all-new four-barrel carburetor. Though compression ratios were kept low (7.5:1) by the factory, the engine was rated an industry high 235 horsepower. When installed in a 125.5-inch wheelbase, 4,000-pound New Yorker chassis, impressive performance was just a stab of the throttle away. And that's just what Petty provided at Daytona.

In the days before Bill France opened his banked superspeedway, stock car racers duked it out at Daytona on a 4.1-mile long oval that consisted of a sandy beach straight and paved surface street back stretch tied together by two sweeping sand-packed corners. Then, as now, the race at Daytona was the most prestigious on the tour. Petty signaled his arrival on the beach with a pole winning qualifying speed of 123.4 miles per hour. When the green flag fell, Petty quickly translated his horsepower advantage into the lead. Petty's primary competition during the race was Tim Flock's 1954 Oldsmobile, and in fact, it was Flock's #88 car that crossed the finish line first. That victory was a short-lived one, however, as NASCAR tech officials disqualified Flock when a post-race tear down turned up illegally polished carburetor passages. As a result, Lee Petty was awarded the win.

Petty followed up on that first place finish with a string of top five finishes after Daytona. Petty alternated between his Dodge and Chrysler race cars at those subsequent races and it was in a #42 Chrysler that he notched his second win of the year in a 100-mile event at Sharon, Pennsylvania. Chrysler wins at Rochester, New York;

Grand Rapids, Michigan; Charlotte, North Carolina; Corbin, Kentucky; and Martinsville, Virginia, brought Petty's win total to seven. Coupled with the 24 total top five wins Petty turned in 1954, those first place finishes made him the Grand National champion that season. As things turned out, that championship season was not to be the last for either Petty or cars of the Chrysler persuasion.

During the off-season, Chrysler executives decided to up the performance ante by unveiling an all-new luxury high-horsepower car called the Chrysler 300. So named because of the 300 horse Hemi engine that came factory stock in every iteration of the marque, the Chrysler 300 quickly became a legend on NASCAR tracks all across the country. In fact, Chrysler 300 drivers were so successful the next two Grand National

Street clothes and "washable" racing livery were fixtures on the 1949 NASCAR tour. And so was a young fellow from Randleman, North Carolina, named Lee Petty. Though Petty had begun the season at the helm of a GM car, he soon switched mechanical allegiances to cars of the Plymouth persuasion. That move turned out to be the start of a very long and rewarding association. Daytona Speedway Archives

seasons, they caused many a sleepless night for Big Bill France.

You see, NASCAR's sanctioning officials have never been fond of race cars that steal the show. And that's because it's been the show that's packed the grandstands since the inception of the series. The possibility of one car or make of car winning the majority of races on the circuit is not an inviting one for race promoters and sanctioning officials alike. Though the fans of one particular driver or marque may wish for an all-conquering season and wins at every stop on the tour, there's little doubt that the equally fervent fans of the also-ran teams would quickly lose interest in the series and spend their discretionary income elsewhere.

Close competition and "pro-wrestling like" driver rivalries keep ticket sales high and local track owners happy. Consequently, the sanctioning body has felt little compunction in modern times about "tweaking" the official rules book in the name of parity on the track. Restrictor plates, spoiler rules and body template requirements have all been used in the modern era to keep things nearly equal once the green flag falls. But it wasn't always that easy for folks like competition director Gary Nelson to bunch up the racing pack. That was especially true in the mid-fifties, when the stock cars that duked it out every weekend were just that—stock. During those days, when any given manufacturer produced a stock car that possessed superior performance to that of the rest of the field, there really wasn't much that NASCAR could do to keep that car from winning and winning and winning. And that's just what happened during the 1955 and 1956 Grand National seasons.

As mentioned, the cars in question were Chrysler 300s and the reason behind their dominance during the 1955 and 1956 seasons was a fellow named Carl Kiekhaefer. Kiekhaefer was the owner of the Mercury Marine outboard engine company and a hard-nosed businessman who knew how to make a buck. Far from being a racer or even a fan, Kiekhaefer was rather just a businessman looking for a way to advertise his wares in 1955 when he decided to jump into Grand National stock car racing in a big way. When market research identified the typical NASCAR race as a gathering place for potential Mercury Marine customers, Kiekhaefer was literally off to the races.

The first step he took upon setting up his 1955 team was to select cars from the 1,725 examples of Chrysler's new "Letter" series built that year as the basis for the effort. That choice was a natural one since the all-new 300s were literally the fastest street-legal American made cars of the day. Designed from the start with racing in mind, the new 300s were two-door versions of the normally sedate New Yorker line that had been treated to a mechanical dose of steroids. Rolling on revised underpinnings, designed to produce greater cornering resolve, and powered by Hemi-headed 331ci versions of the Chrysler Firepower V-8, the new cars were formidable machines.

Kiekhaefer's next task was signing a team of drivers. Reaching deep in his pocket, the Mercury executive decided that only the best would do, and soon he'd hired a number of the top drivers on the tour. In that number was 1952 series champ, Tim Flock.

Though Kiekhaefer didn't sign Flock to drive for the team until just days before the Daytona Beach race in February of 1955, Tim outpaced the rest of the field during qualifying to secure the pole position of that race with a speed of 130.293 miles per hour. During the race proper it was pretty much all Flock and his #300 Chrysler as that duo lead the race from start to finish. Fellow 300 driver Lee Petty finished in second with his Petty Engineering car to make it a one-two sweep for the Letter series' competition debut.

Flock went on to win no fewer than 18 poles and a matching 18 Grand National races during the 1955 season. Top five finishes in 14 other events earned Flock both $37,779 in winnings and his second Grand National championship. It was an incredible season for Kiekhaefer, to be sure. The grand total of 27 Chrysler wins notched by Flock, his fellow Mercury Marine drivers Speedy Thompson, Norm Nelson and Lee Petty had to be encouraging to both Kiekhaefer and Chryco executives. But Kiekhaefer wasn't satisfied with the results, and he redoubled his efforts during the off-season by signing Buck Baker and Frank "Rebel" Mundy to drive for the burgeoning team in 1956. Later that year, he also added Herb Thomas to his list of drivers, making the Mercury Marine operation truly a dream team.

Kiekhaefer's racing preparations left little to chance. In addition to fielding both the best drivers and fastest cars, Kiekhaefer also employed a team weatherman to predict track conditions on race day and he even hired scientists to take dirt track soil samples to help in selecting just the right tire and chassis combination.

In a first for the series, in a day when many competitors simply flat towed their race cars to and from the track, Kiekhaefer equipped each of his teams with a "box-type" truck and a wealth of spare chassis and engine parts. Kiekhaefer's teams also spent more than a little time testing their team cars in advance of a race, and drivers were required to keep track of engine and chassis performance during those sessions for analysis in post-test debriefing sessions.

Kiekhaefer's thoroughness in the preparation department extended to renting an entire hotel for the team to stay in during the days leading up to a big race. Bed checks were made to make sure that his strict curfew was enforced, and he sometimes required that drivers and their spouses stay in different rooms to keep pre-race "distractions" to an absolute minimum.

Kiekhaefer's military-like discipline and advance planning paid off, as mentioned, in 1955 with a total of 22 NASCAR wins and the series championship. With Baker adding to the talent pool in 1956 the team won just about every race they entered. The first race of the season actually took place in November of 1955 at Hickory, North Carolina. Tim Flock won that event convincingly in his #301 Chrysler leading all but 16 laps of the race. Buck Baker notched his first 300 win at the fifth race of the season in Phoenix, in a similarly dominating fashion. When the series rolled into Daytona, Flock made it two in a row on the beach course when he won from the pole and led all but two laps of the event. All told, Kiekhaefer's team Chryslers won an incredible 30 of the 50 features they entered. At one point during that historic season, team drivers won an unbelievable 16 straight events. By year's end, Baker had secured Kiekhaefer's second straight NASCAR crown and the team had won more than $70,000 in prize money.

Unfortunately for Kiekhaefer, his teams' on-track success did not translate into the fan goodwill he'd hoped for. In fact, NASCAR spectators took to throwing bottles at team cars by the middle of the season and some stayed away from the track altogether. Big Bill France was equally displeased with Kiekhaefer's success. With gate receipts in jeopardy, France had his tech inspectors tear down Kiekhaefer team cars and inspect them for any rules violations. When none were found, all France could do was hope the cars would break. And that didn't happen with any great regularity.

The 300Bs that Buck Baker and his co-drivers used to romp through the 1956 competition were all second generation members of the vaunted "Letter" series that had debuted in 1955.

For 1956, Chrysler engineers turned up the underhood heat a notch further by offering a 354ci, high-compression version of the hemi-

Lee Petty won the 1954 running of the fabled Daytona Beach race in this Hemi-powered Chrysler New Yorker. As you can see, stock cars were pretty darned stock in the days when Ike was still in the White House. Note the factory bright work that is still in place and the huge chrome bumpers that most cars of the day carried. Daytona Speedway Archives

spherically headed Chrysler Firepower engine that was rated at 355 horsepower. Built on Chrysler's marine assembly line, these engines featured forged internals, solid lifter, long duration camshafts and twin Holley carburetors. When installed ahead of a heavy-duty three-speed manual transmission and working with the upgraded suspension componentry common to the letter series line, these engines afforded spectacular performance, as Kiekhaefer's NASCAR opponents found out to their dismay.

Beyond the obvious steps taken to remove street-legal dead weight such as running lights

and sound deadener, the 300Bs that Buck Baker and others drove in 1956 were disconcertingly stock. Kiekhaefer's race cars all carried the same side trim, fender badges and roll-up windows that they and the other 1,102 1956 300Bs had originally received on the Chrysler assembly line.

Things were much the same in the control cabin, too. Seating consisted of a stock bench that had lost its passenger's side seat back. The factory dash panel was augmented with a brace of analog gauges. The stock truck-sized steering wheel was retained unchanged as was the spindly looking column shifter. The most rudimentary of roll cages

Karl Kiekhaefer was serious about winning races on the NASCAR tour and he spared no expense in that pursuit. The Chrysler 300 teams he fielded were the class of any starting grid they graced. In a day when most drivers flat towed their race cars to and from the track, Kiekhaefer outfitted his teams with transporters and a staff meteorologist. And yes, the Grand National tour did make a road race stop at Road America in 1956! Daytona Speedway Archives

was relied upon for safety, and a single, quick release lap belt was all that kept Baker and the other team drivers from sliding wildly about the car's interior. The most notable racing changes made to a 300B's ergonomics were the deletion of carpeting and the removal of the rear seat. Another more subtle modification was a hole cut in the passenger side floorboard just behind the right front wheel. When a strobe light mounted nearby was turned on, it allowed the driver to see how much tread was left on the critical right front tire—an important bit of information in days when treaded street tires served double-duty on the race track.

The factory stock theme was followed fairly closely both under hood and under car in keeping with the NASCAR rules book. Suspension components were beefed up and extra shock absorbers were used, but overall, Kiekhaefer's cars had a lot more in common with regular production Chryslers of the day than do the current crop of silhouette stock cars running on the Winston Cup circuit.

It's been said that Kiekhaefer was more than a little surprised at the way the fans received his team's racing success. The respect and goodwill he had hoped to generate for his outboard motor company by competing in NASCAR was most definitely not forthcoming. And so, he folded his racing operation and left the stock car circuit as abruptly as he had entered it in 1957.

Lee Petty campaigned Hemi-powered Dodge Coronets in 1956, and the two wins he scored when added to the nine other Dodge victories recorded that season helped bring the total number of Grand National wins notched by Mopar drivers to 33. An impressive number indeed when one considers that figure represented fully 60 percent of the 56 NASCAR events contested in 1956.

Unfortunately, 1956 turned out to be the high-water mark of the decade for Dodge, Chrysler and Plymouth drivers in the fifties. By the time the next season rolled around, Fomoco and General Motors had elected to get involved with factory-backed NASCAR competition in a big way.

The high dollar contracts their arrival on the scene ushered in, were accompanied by a number of high horsepower mechanical packages, such as Ford's supercharged 312 engines, Chevrolet's fuel injected small block and Oldsmobile's J2 Rocket motor. The combined effect was more than even the most avid Mopar supporters could resist. Even Lee Petty swapped mechanical allegiances to General Motors for 1957. As a result, it was to be two long years before a Plymouth driver would visit a NASCAR winner's circle again and yet still another season before a Dodge driver would make that same trek. Chrysler's next (and final) NASCAR win took even longer to come about and didn't make it into the record book until 1961. Though Mopar fans found little to cheer about during 1957 and 1958, better days were just around the corner.

1959 "Fin" Cars Take Flight

NASCAR's first decade ended on a positive note for Chryco fans. That's because 1959 was the year that Lee Petty returned to the Plymouth fold after his dalliance with General Motors. The car that lured him back to the Mayflower division was a finned Sport Fury that was powered by Plymouth's new for 1959 361ci, 305 horsepower wedge motor. Interestingly, Petty didn't make that switch until the twentieth race of the 1959 season and only after winning the inaugural Daytona 500 in a 1959 Oldsmobile. The race that put Petty back in a Plymouth took place in June at Atlanta. Pre-race qualification for that 150-mile dirt track affair placed Petty far towards the back of the pack in thirty-seventh. Yet when the race was over Petty had bested the rest of the 40-car field to finish first. At least that was the way

things finally turned out, since at first it appeared that Petty's then unknown son, Richard, had crossed the line first in one of his dad's hand-me-down Oldsmobiles. When the elder Petty protested the result, a post-race reexamination of the scoring chart reversed the order of finish, handing Petty and Plymouth the win. Petty backed up that performance with a second Plymouth victory just four days later (again on dirt) at a hundred miler in Columbia, South Carolina.

Petty added five more notches to Plymouth's win belt for 1959 on his way to a second Grand National driving title. In addition to the $49,219 in winnings Petty pocketed that season, another high point had to be the emergence of his son, Richard, as one of NASCAR's rising stars. The younger Petty's performance in the Southern 500 brought particular distinction when he led the event early (in a Plymouth identical to his dad's) and then went on to finish fourth—outpacing his dad and many established stars in the process.

Papa Petty went on to score four more "Fin car" wins in his 1959 Fury and three more top five finishes. When coupled with his first of the season Oldsmobile finishes, Petty's Plymouth work earned him a then unprecedented third Grand National driving championship.

The first full decade of NASCAR, sanctioned stock car racing produced a total of 58 Chrysler wins, 20 Dodge triumphs and 17 Plymouth visits to victory lane. In addition, Chryco drivers had claimed the NASCAR championship four times. Though Chrysler drivers had but one more GN win waiting for them in the following seasons, for Dodge and Plymouth drivers, the best was yet to come.

CHAPTER TWO

THE SIZZLING SIXTIES
Birth of the Hemi

When the 1960 season dawned, the NASCAR series was on the cusp of dramatic changes. Though rough-and-tumble dirt track events had been standard fare for stock racers in the fifties, by 1960 Bill France and Curtis Turner had opened banked (and paved) superspeedways in Daytona and Charlotte, and yet another was slated to open in Atlanta. Those paved palaces of speed, coupled with the well-established superspeedway in Darlington, signaled an unmistakable trend towards asphalt racing and much higher speeds.

Lee Petty and son, Richard, continued to campaign big finned Plymouths for 1960, and that was the season that the yet to be crowned "King" of stock car racing would make his first trip to the winner's circle. Young Richard signaled that he was going to be a season contender at the Daytona 500 where he translated a nineteenth place starting position into a third place overall finish—one position ahead of his dad.

Richard Petty's "finned" Plymouths had picked up their soon-to-be-famous electric blue paint schemes by the 1960 NASCAR season. Petty started that season by finishing third in the Daytona 500. By the sixth race of the season, young Richard had scored the first of what would be 200 career Grand National/Winston Cup victories.

215

The control cabin in Petty's 1960 Fury was still mostly stock. A production-based bucket seat kept the future King in close proximity to the stock dash and three on the tree shifter. An oscillating-style house fan provided a bit of air conditioning during muggy summer events in the Deep South.

Fins were all the rage in 1960 among most American auto makers. There's even the chance that their soaring fins helped a bit in the handling department. Plymouth Furys came out-fitted with a particularly fetching pair. Richard Petty made them take flight at tracks like Daytona and Darlington.

As in 1959, the cars that Petty Engineering fielded had started out on a regular production assembly line as Golden Commando powered Sport Furys. In stock trim those cars stretched out over a 118-inch wheelbase chassis that rolled on torsion bar/"A" frame and leaf spring/live axle underpinnings. When stripped for oval track duty, the cars weighed in at just under 3,400 pounds. The raised block, 361ci wedge motors that powered Petty Engineering Plymouths for 1960 came factory rated at 305 horsepower and race-ready produced 325. That package was capable of speeds in excess of 145 miles per hour at Daytona

in 1960, and by season's end had generated eight wins and 37 top five finishes for the two-car team.

Win number one for both Richard Petty and the 1960 Petty Enterprises effort came at the sixth race of the season. The site of that event was the Charlotte fairgrounds and the race there consisted of 100 miles around a half-mile dirt track. Young Richard qualified his Fury seventh for the race and kept race leaders in his sights until the closing stages of the event. He passed race leader Rex White for the top spot on lap 183 and kept his Blue and White #43 car out in front until the checkered flag fell 17 circuits later. Petty's purse

Dodge drivers in the early sixties campaigned Polaras. Though afflicted with novel styling, full-sized 1962 Dodges were plenty fast. Unfortunately, their Plymouth and GM rivals were a tad faster. Though the 413ci Max Wedge engines they carried into battle churned out an advertised 380 ponies, the Pontiac's SD 421 was good for even more.

was a meager $800, but even more rewarding days at the track were, of course, just around the corner.

Lee Petty notched his first 1960 season win at the next stop on the tour in North Wilkesboro, and Richard got one win closer to his ultimate total of 200 less than a month later with an asphalt triumph at Martinsville in the Virginia 500. Though Petty's first Darlington win was still in the future, he did turn in a second place finish (to Joe Weatherly) in the Rebel 300 and a sixth in the Southern 500. Richard scored his third and final win of the 1960 season in a 99-mile dirt track event at Hillsboro, North Carolina. When the dust and asphalt had settled at season's end, Richard Petty had finished the season second (behind Rex White's Chevrolet) in the points chase with dad Lee four places further back in sixth. Dodge drivers were not as fortunate and managed just one GN win for 1960 while Chrysler fans had nothing to cheer at all that same year.

1961 saw Chryco wedge engines increase in size to 383 cubic inches. The extra displacement resulted in increased under-hood heat, and for 1961, the hottest wedge motors were factory rated at 330 horsepower. Unfortunately, that increase was not enough to hold off the

Top of the line power for 1962 was the 413 Max Wedge motor. In street trim, that engine carried twin four-barrel carburetors and cranked out 380 horsepower. More cubic inches and an all-new set of Hemi heads were just around the corner for "RB" Mopar big blocks in 1962.

Though the race cars that Plymouth drivers campaigned in 1962 were as challenged in the styling department as their Dodge stablemates, they were able to out score them 11 to zero (in terms of Grand National wins).

ever-increasing number of factory backed Ford and General Motors drivers. Though both of those car manufacturers were supposed to be honoring an Automobile Manufacturers of America ban on factory-backed motorsports competition, the back door at both factories was wide open, and the special high performance parts that flowed through those portals went straight to the track—the NASCAR track, that is.

Unfortunately for Chryco fans, the most spectacular event of the season for Plymouth drivers was a career-ending, two-car shunt in the Daytona 500 that catapulted Lee Petty and a Chevrolet driver outside of the track in turn four. Though

Petty returned to the series after a long period of recuperation, for all practical purposes, the three-time champion's racing career as a driver came to an end in a smoking heap that day at Daytona. Son Richard's 1961 tour at Daytona didn't go much better, as his own Plymouth took an off-track and over-the-wall excursion during a qualifying race that knocked him out of the 500 itself. Richard did bounce back to score two short track wins for Plymouth later in the season, but on the whole, 1961 was an off year for Mopar fans on the circuit.

Things didn't get much better the following two seasons. Pontiac drivers had the hot ticket in 1962 with their Super Duty 421 wedge-powered

Catalinas. Pontiac executives had decided to go racing in earnest in 1961, and opted to make a special big block 421ci engine an "over the counter" option in order to legalize the package for stock car competition. That engine became a regular production option in 1962. Chryco engineers tried to counter with a hogged-out version of the 383 that displaced 413ci inches. Based on the Raised Block (RB) engine family, the new Max Wedge 413 was rated at 410 horsepower and no doubt cranked out a few more ponies in full race tune. Though the new big block was quite successful in NHRA drag race competition, it proved to be less than a match for either the 421 Poncho motor or Chevrolet's really fine 409 big block in NASCAR circles.

The 1962 season opened with a big win for Pontiac at the Daytona 500, where the legendary Fireball Roberts bested all comers in a Super Duty powered Catalina that had been prepared by Smokey Yunick. In a display of mechanical domination that none had seen before, Fireball claimed the top starting spot during qualifying with a hot lap of 156.999 miles per hour, and then went on to win both his pre-race qualifying race and the 500 itself. One bright spot for Chryco fans was Richard Petty's second place finish just 27 seconds behind Roberts' black and gold Pontiac. And that's just the way Petty's 1962 season wound up—in second place to a Pontiac driver. Though the soon to be "King" had turned in eight short track wins with his 413 powered Belvedere, it was Poncho driver, Joe Weatherly, who sat atop the points standings for the Grand National title. Three other wins scored by Mayflower division driver Jim Paschal in the second Petty Engineering Plymouth brought team wins to 11 on the season. Dodge drivers had another dismal season and failed to win a single event.

In an effort to answer the Pontiac and Chevrolet power advantage, Chryco engineers broke out the boring bar during the off-season and widened the corporate big block engine to a full 426 cubic inches. Horsepower increased to an advertised 425 ponies. It was hoped by all in the Mopar fold that the extra grunt afforded by the new engine would be the ticket to victory lane and the Grand National championship in 1963. And it might have been were it not for a couple of new 427ci racing engines unleashed by the competition that same season.

The all-new big block engine unveiled by Chevrolet for 1963 was shrouded by so much mystery that in time, teams on the circuit took to calling it the Mystery Motor. After tiring of being "whupped" by their Pontiac corporate cousins, Chevy engineers set out to devise an all-new, race-only engine for the 1963 NASCAR season. Topped with polyangle valved, free flowing head castings and featuring a beefy, four bolt main journaled block, the new engine churned out well in excess

Dodge drivers got back in the habit of winning Grand National races in 1964. The all-new 426 Hemi engine turned out to be the key that unlocked the door to victory lane for Dodge drivers like Anthony Joseph Foyt that season. A.J. drove a Ray Nichels prepped Polara to victory in the 1964 Firecracker 400 at Daytona, for example, with the help of Hemi power. Author Collection

221

of the 427 horsepower that Chevrolet modestly claimed for it. So promising was the new power plant that a number of former Pontiac drivers like Junior Johnson jumped ship and built Impalas. And though the new Bow Tie mill was far from being a regular production option (only 48 total Mystery Motors were ever built according to Smokey Yunick), NASCAR officials deemed it legal for competition.

Ford rolled out a new 427 of its own in 1963, too—and a new, more aerodynamic Galaxie body to race it in. Unlike the Mystery Motor, though, Ford's 427 was an actual production power plant that was based on the 406 FE big block engines that had been raced the year before. That having been said, the big incher Fomoco engine was far from being a sedate station wagon puller and in race trim was capable of cranking out in excess of 425 ponies for 500 miles at a time. Which is what Tiny Lund proved at the 1963 Daytona 500, where he drove a Wood brothers prepped #21 Galaxie to victory in the event. Junior Johnson set a new qualifying record to capture the pole of the 500 (with a hot lap of 165.183 miles per hour) and he and fellow Mystery Motor driver Johnny Rutherford captured both of the pre-race qualifiers to make speedweek's headlines a Chevrolet or Ford affair in 1963.

Chryco introduced the awesome Hemi, in part, as a response to Fomoco's high revving 427 wedge motor. The 1964 season's results left little doubt that the Ford motor was no match for the all-new hemispherically combustion-chambered motor.

Richard Petty finished sixth in the 500, making him the highest placing Chryco driver, but he was never a factor in the event's outcome. Petty took steps to right that wrong by winning the next two events on the schedule at Spartanburg and Weaverville, but Chevy and Ford drivers continued to be the "big dogs" on the 1963 superspeedways. At year's end, Petty had recorded 14 short track wins and 16 other top five finishes. An impressive performance to be sure, but not enough for a national title, which for the second year in a row was snagged by Little Joe Weatherly (who drove Pontiacs and Mercurys in 1963). Petty's stats did earn him a second consecutive second place

points total, and coupled with teammate Jim Paschal's Plymouth wins, brought Mayflower division triumphs to 19 for 1963. Dodge drivers were locked out of victory lane again on the NASCAR tour. That fact and many others would be radically changed in just one more season.

Birth of the Hemi

The 1962 and 1963 NASCAR Grand National seasons taught Chrysler engineers that more would be needed to win stock car championships in the sixties than a Max Wedge motor was capable of providing. And so it was that a team of engineers including Willem Weertman,

In street trim, Chryco's 426 Hemi often came dressed in dual four-barrels. It was a large and attractive power plant with valve covers suitable for basting a turkey in.

Race Hemis were limited to just one four-barrel fuel mixer. For 1964, that induction system made possible an "advertised" 405 horsepower: more than enough to win the Daytona 500 and just about everything else worth winning that season!

The combustion chamber configuration of choice was a familiar one for the old-timers on the new engine team. Tom Hoover and Bob Rarey are given credit for the ultimate choice made, but in truth, the decision to build a Hemi-headed version of the 426 RB engine can actually be attributed to the engineers who perfected that design in the early fifties. With combustion chamber configuration and valve layout established, the other bits and pieces of the new engine package quickly fell into place. By early 1963, the foundry process needed to produce the engine was under way.

The first 426 race Hemi assembly took place the last week of November 1963—just two short months before speedweek 1964 in Daytona kicked into gear. Dyno testing of the new engine took place in December with more than promising results. When horsepower figures exceeded the 400 maximum that were registerable on the in-house dynamometer, a bit of slide rule work by engineers yielded a gross horsepower figure in the 425 range. Keeping in mind that that figure represented only the starting point of a race Hemi's ultimate horsepower potential, you'll easily understand the great deal of optimism that Hemi team engineers had about the coming Grand National season.

But all was not perfection with the new engine. In fact, as late as January 28, 1964, the Hemi engineering team was struggling with a cylinder cracking gremlin that suggested serious durability problems for the engine under racing conditions. The team literally worked around the clock to solve the engine's teething problems. Incredibly, the factory-backed teams who were slated to campaign the Hemi at Daytona didn't ultimately receive their engines until just days before the race. But when those engines arrived, they were ready to race—and win!

Qualifying for the 1964 500 got under way on February 7, 1964, and all eyes were on the Dodge and Plymouth teams as they queued up for their turn at two hot laps around the 2.5-mile banked

Tom Hoover, Bob Roger and Don Moore set out to build a world beating big block engine during the winter of 1962 and 1963. Their goal was to have the new engine up and running in time for the 1964 Daytona 500. That goal above all others dictated making use of as many pre-existing engine castings as possible. The decision to retain the already race proven block casting developed for the Max Wedge 426 was, therefore, a natural. Keeping the planned engines the same basic dimensions as the pre-existing 426 wedge motor was also a choice that was dictated by the project's incredibly tight time budget. Cylinder bore centers were accordingly kept at 4.80 inches and the engine was designed to maintain a 4.25-inch stroke and 3.75-inch bore yielding 426 cubic inches of displacement. Those decisions having been made, Weertman's team set out to design an all-new induction system that was capable of taking on all comers on the NASCAR tour.

track. Paul Goldsmith was one of the first Hemi drivers to pull out onto the track, and two laps later his Ray Nichels prepped Plymouth Belvedere had shattered the old track record of 160.943 by nearly 14 miles per hour! Richard Petty proved that incredible velocity was no fluke just a few moments later when he rocketed around the track at 174.418 miles per hour, just five-tenths of a mile per hour slower than Goldsmith's record shattering speed. The Ford and GM teams who watched

qualifying trackside must have felt like condemned prisoners just strapped down in the electric chair. Truth be told, they truly were doomed.

When the green flag fell at 12:30 p.m. on February 23, 1964, fans in the stands knew they were about to see something special take place out on the track. Goldsmith led lap one of the event before handing off to Petty. Bobby Isaac in a second Ray Nichels prepped Hemi car (a Dodge) mixed it up with Petty and Goldsmith for

To call the 1966-1967 Belvedere line boxy is an exercise in understatement. Characterized by sharp edges and 90 degree angles, the car was less than optimally aerodynamic. But who cares about air flow when you have a full race Hemi to punch holes in the air with? Mike Slade

Next
Richard Petty earned the title "King of Stock Car Racing" in this 1967 Plymouth Belvedere. Though it was essentially the same car he'd campaigned the year before, for 1967, the car was just about unbeatable. At one point during the season, for example, Petty visited victory lane at ten straight events. Mike Slade

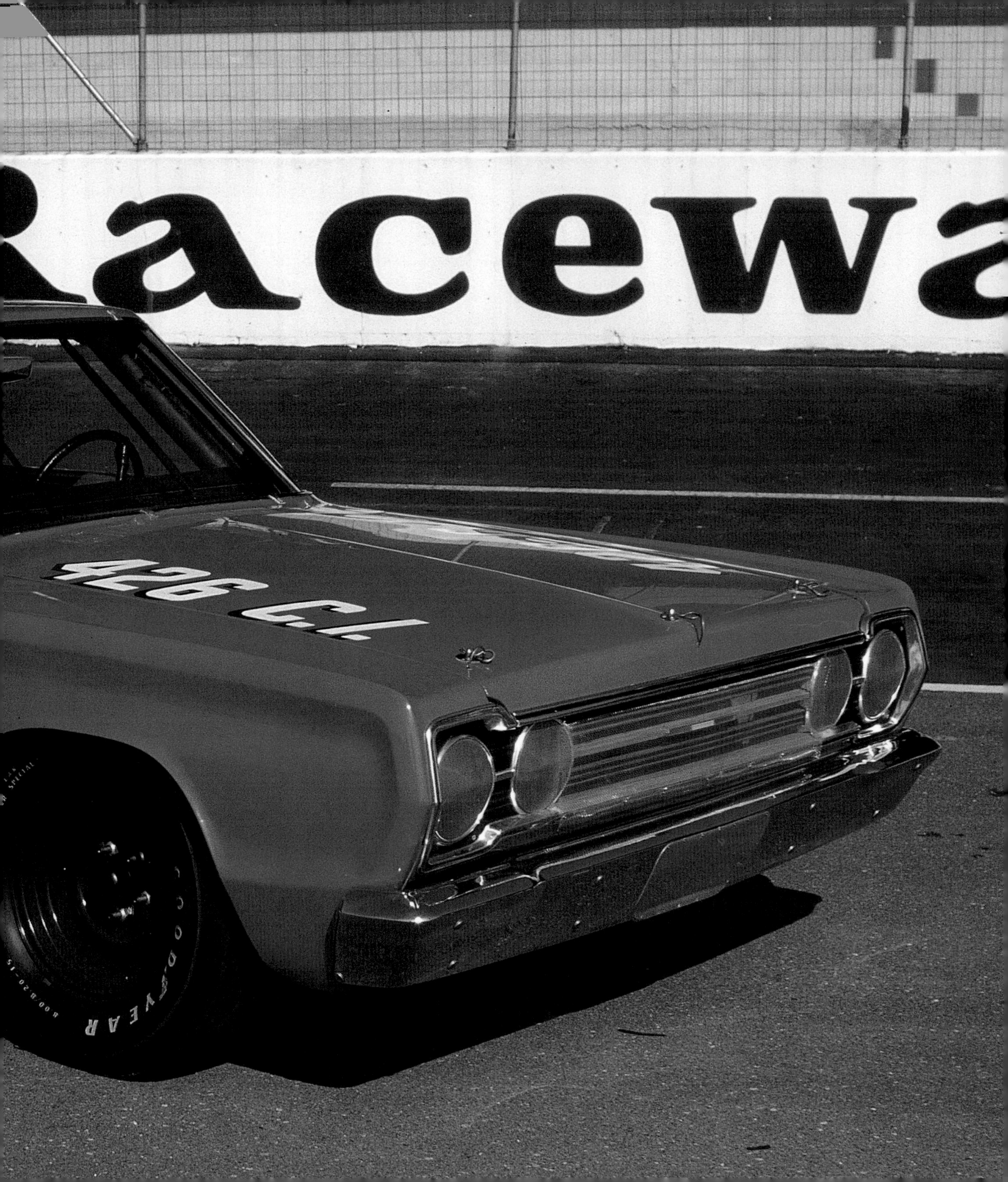
Racewa
426 C.I.
GOODYEAR

Dodge Polaras didn't get much slicker in the years that followed, but they did get a whole lot faster. That was especially true in 1964 when, along with their Plymouth counterparts, Dodge drivers picked up 426 Hemi engines. Pictured here is David Pearson's 1964 Cotton Owens' prepped Polara. Daytona Speedway Archives

a few laps and A.J. Foyt, driving a Banjo Matthews Ford, clawed his way to the front for two laps. Save for those two interruptions, the race was all Goldsmith, Petty and Hemi. In the end, Petty's #43 Belvedere crossed the stripe one full lap ahead of his closest rival, fellow Plymouth driver Jimmy Pardue. All told, Hemi Plymouth and Dodge drivers claimed four of the top five finishing positions. It was an impressive first outing for the new engine. And one that promised great success in the coming season.

The Hemi's all-conquering debut at Daytona also caused more than a little grumbling about it's non-regular production status—mostly from the Fomoco teams it had well and truly trounced. In time those complaints would grow in quantity and volume until the point that NASCAR officials were forced to take action. But not before Petty and his Hemi compatriots ran away with the 1964 Grand National season.

David Pearson scored the first Grand National win recorded by a Dodge driver in three seasons when he piloted his Cotton Owens prepped Coronet to victory in the Richmond 250, one race after

Daytona. He backed that up with a second Dodge Hemi win two weeks later in Greenville, South Carolina. Pearson won again at Hillsboro in April at yet another short track and Plymouth partisan Petty raced to a win at a hundred miler in South Boston, Virginia, one month later.

Jim Paschal came out on top in the grueling World 600 at Charlotte in May in his #41 Petty Engineering Plymouth. It was the second superspeedway win for a Hemi car in 1964 and Paschal's four lap margin of victory was a sign of just how bulletproof and dominating Chryco's new engine really was.

LeeRoy Yarbrough added his name to the Mopar winner's list with a victory at Greenville, and Buck Baker notched another win for Dodge at Valdosta in June. A.J. Foyt earned some bragging rights for USAC drivers at Daytona in July when he piloted a Ray Nichels prepped Hemi Coronet to victory in the Firecracker 400—a race that saw Hemi-powered cars sweep the top six finishing positions. Buck Baker won his third Southern 500 in August at Darlington in a Ray Fox Dodge and, as in the Firecracker, his Hemi car's only competition that day was the four other Hemi Plymouths and Dodges that crossed the stripe just behind him. Even long "retired" team owner Cotton Owens got on the Hemi bandwagon with a Dodge win at Richmond in the Capitol City 300 in September.

By the end of the incredible 1964 season, Dodge and Plymouth drivers had won 26 of the 62 races contested that year. The cars that made all that success possible were lightweight unit body repetitions of the Plymouth Belvedere and Dodge Polara car lines. The trim little Plymouths were the lightest and smallest of the pair and rolled on a 3,225-pound (street weight), 116-inch wheelbase. Torsion bars, reinforced "A" frames and a quartet of shocks were used to provide suspension movement at the bow, while a corporate live axle, parallel leaf springs and another double duo of shock absorbers were used to bring up the

Lee Petty's driving career was cut short by a wreck he had in the 1961 Daytona 500. It started in turn four when Petty's #42 Plymouth became entangled with Johnny Beauchamp's Chevrolet. Both cars ultimately catapulted over the top rail of the track and plunged into the parking lot outside. Petty's car was demolished and he was in the hospital for a number of months afterwards.
Author collection

Richard Petty's 1963 Belvedere was fast—but not fast enough to beat the special motored Pontiacs he had to run against that season. Relief was just one season away. In 1964 Petty's Plymouth was to be powered by a full race 426 Hemi engine. Daytona Speedway Archives

rear. Special heavy-duty hubs (full floaters at the rear) were used all around, and they carried heavy-duty, fully metallic shoes and drums to help scrub off speeds.

A Dodge Polara carried a bit more weight and stretched out over a 119-inch wheelbase. Even so, a race-ready 1964 Dodge still tipped the scales hundreds of pounds lighter than a Holman & Moody Galaxie. Light weight, coupled with superior horsepower, has always spelled racing success. So the dominance displayed by Plymouth and Dodge drivers in 1964 shouldn't come as a big surprise.

Plymouth and Dodge drivers that year took in the rapidly passing trackside scenery from within a disconcertingly stock control cabin. A single factory-based bucket seat served as the central focus in both cockpits and that perch was encapsulated in a fairly rudimentary (by modern standards) roll cage. A stock but gutted dash panel carried a brace of aftermarket gauges just ahead of the stock steering wheel and four speed floor shifter.

Most regular production Plymouth and Dodge race cars circa 1964 were the class of every

starting grid they blessed, and they won just about everything in sight.

All told, Richard Petty made eight trips to victory lane and turned in a total of 37 top five finishes that earned him his first Grand National driving championship and $114,771.45 in winnings. David Pearson's eight wins and 29 top five finishes in his Cotton Owens Dodge gave him a third overall berth in the seasonal points race. Both Petty and Pearson would go on to win other Grand National driving championships and more than a few races for Plymouth and Dodge teams in the future. And most all of those wins would be earned with the help of the incredible 426 Hemi racing engine that first roared to life in 1964.

1965 The Hemi's Bellow Is Silenced

But none of that future greatness was destined to take place in 1965. And that too was a result of the 426 Hemi engine. As mentioned, Fomoco teams were none too happy with the sudden and immediate success enjoyed by Dodge and Plymouth Hemi teams in 1964. Their displeasure was based on the portion of the official NASCAR rules book that required a certain number of "units or models" to be produced in order to be legalized for Grand National competition. Fact of the matter was, a Hemi fan in the stands at a typical NASCAR race would have been hard pressed to find a regular production Hemi car on sale down at his local dealership. There just weren't any made (and wouldn't be until 1966). Access to "over the counter" Hemi engines was also pretty doggone limited too, unless you happened to be named Petty or Owens or Nichels.

Folks at Ford began to make noises about building a decidedly non-regular production Hemi-headed single overhead cam version of their 427 engine for use in 1965 at about the same time that some drivers took to complaining about the significantly faster speeds, characteristic of races in 1964.

Early word on the new Fomoco Cammer engine was that power production topped 600 ponies. That calculated amount of power promised to push superspeedway speeds well into the 180s, even when saddled with the bulk of a Galaxie chassis. Chrysler executives, jealous of the competitive advantage their new Hemi had earned in 1964, wasted little time in rising to meet the new Ford menace. Their theory was that if one overhead cam was good (as in the SOHC 427 Ford motor), then two just had to be better. Bill Weertman, Tom Hoover and many of the engineers who'd contributed to the original race Hemi project went back to the drawing board and penned an all-new set of dual overhead cam equipped, hemispherically chambered cylinder head castings that flowed better. Four valves per cylinder were part of the new head program as was an eight runner intake manifold. With Gilmer belt-driven cams acting directly on valves (in modern motorcycle engine fashion), the new engine was capable of more than 10,000 reliable rpm. Awesome horsepower figures were projected for the Chryco cammer, with some estimates exceeding 900 ponies in race trim! Best of all, like the original 426 Hemi, the new hemi heads were designed to simply bolt onto the existing 426 RB long block assembly.

NASCAR executives were well aware of the two new overhead cam engines that were coming down the pike. And they were equally aware of the complaints that many drivers were beginning to make about the much faster racing speeds on the 1964 circuit. When notorious leadfoots like Junior Johnson and Fred Lorenzen began to voice their concerns, Bill France just had to sit up and listen.

Big Bill's response to driver complaints and the escalating Fomoco/Mopar horsepower war was announced on October 19, 1994. It came in the form of four new rules that would govern competition for the 1965 season: 1) Engine size was limited to 428ci and the engine was required to be of a production design. 2) Hemi-headed engines and Ford high riser head castings (a set of non-production wedge castings that Ford teams had been allowed to use in 1964) were outlawed. 3) Cars legal for superspeedway competition had to carry a 119-inch wheelbase. A 116-inch wheelbase was permitted for short track competition. 4) Carburetion was limited to a single four-barrel that carried 1 11/16-inch throttle bores.

The news about the new rules hit Plymouth and Dodge teams like a thunder clap. In one fell swoop, both the race-proven 426 and the proposed dual overhead cam hemi were sidelined. Worse yet for Plymouth drivers, their lithe little Belvederes had been banned from the high banks for 1965 no matter what engine they elected to run.

The rules were slated to go into effect on January 1, 1965, just in time for the Daytona speedweeks that season. Chrysler executives were dismayed. Chrysler's Bob Anderson lamented, "Racing has always prided itself on being progressive. Here we are backing up." Racing Chief Ronnie Householder went further and said bluntly, "The new rules NASCAR announced have put us out of business down South." Ten days after France announced the new 1965 rules, Householder made an announcement of his own on behalf of Plymouth and Dodge factory-backed NASCAR teams. It read in significant part: ". . .[U]nless NASCAR rules for 1965 are modified or suspended for a minimum of twelve months to permit an orderly transition to new equipment, we have no alternative but to withdraw from NASCAR sanctioned events and concentrate our efforts in USAC, NHRA and SCCA. . ." And so it was that 1965 was the Grand National season that never was for Chryco teams on the tour. Richard Petty built a Hemi-powered Barracuda drag car called the 43 Jr. and David Pearson went quarter miling in Cotton Owens' drag race Dart dubbed the "Cotton Picker."

When Ford teams swept the first 13 places in the 1965 Daytona 500, France eased up a bit on the across-the-board Hemi ban and said that he'd let them run "If Chrysler makes a production line Hemi that is optional equipment for Plymouth Furys and Dodge Polaras." But Householder would not back down. The Moparless season progressed and with each passing race, track attendance decreased. Soon race promoters were raising a hue and cry and more than a few heated phone calls were made to NASCAR headquarters in Daytona Beach, Florida.

France's response to the pressure was to meet with USAC president, Henry Banks, to hash out a uniform set of rules for stock car competition in both racing organizations. It was a face-saving way for France to back off of his Hemi ban without having to publicly cave in to Householder's intransigence. The resulting NASCAR/USAC rules changes were announced in June of 1965. They established a minimum weight formula of 9.36 pounds per cubic inch of displacement; they permitted the still non-production Hemi engine to be raced in Polaras and Furys on tracks longer than a mile; and they permitted Hemi engines to be run in Belvedere and Coronet bodies on tracks that were shorter than a mile in length.

When the NASCAR tour showed up for the 1965 Firecracker 400, though factory-backed teams were still on the sidelines, Buck and Buddy Baker showed up with Hemi-powered Dodge Polaras (an engine and chassis combination that Householder had said just wouldn't work) and turned in credible performances. As a matter of fact, young Buddy finished the race second to only A.J. Foyt's Banjo Matthews prepped Ford.

It wasn't until July 25 that Chryco and Householder relented and returned to the NASCAR fold under the new rules. Though Richard Petty went on to win four races for Plymouth, and David Pearson three for Dodge, their late season success could not undo the months of inactivity that passed during the boycott. Ford drivers won an incredible 32 consecutive Grand National events in 1965 and all told, fully 48 of the 55 races contested that season. Ned Jarrett was the Grand National champion that year. But, as things turned out, it would be a good long time before a Ford driver visited a NASCAR victory lane again—or won the Grand National championship for that matter!

Return of the Hemi

1966 was the year that Dodge and Plymouth decided to unleash the 426 Hemi on an unsuspecting America. Responding (in part) to Bill France's challenge of 1965 to make the once pure race engine available to the general public, both Dodge and Plymouth car lines offered slightly detuned Hemi engines as regular production options. And both manufacturers wasted little time in letting Bill France know it. On December 13, 1965, France was given a tour of a Hemi engine assembly line. He was favorably impressed and remarked at the time, "I saw more Hemi engines today than Ferrari makes cars in a year." With that stamp of approval, the Hemi engine was made welcome at NASCAR tracks all across the country. As in the last part of the 1965 season, the 426 Hemi was allowed to compete in intermediate (Belvedere and Coronet) chassis on short and intermediate tracks at 426ci. New for 1966 was the option to run those same body styles with destroked, 405ci Hemi on superspeedways, too. As in 1965, full-sized Polaras and Furys could mount a full-sized 426 Hemi for superspeedway work without the need for destroking.

France was no doubt hoping that the new regular production status of the 426 Hemi engine would lead to a peaceful (read: profitable) season on the Grand National tour. But those hopes turned out to be very short lived. In fact, the very same day that France strode down the Hemi assembly line, Ford announced that it intended to campaign its 427ci overhead camshaft Hemi engine during the 1966 NASCAR season. The fact that Ford officials had chosen to make that declaration without notice to the sanctioning body no doubt made France more than a little agitated. His response was brief and to the point and delivered just four days after Ford's precipitous press release: The SOHC 427 engine would not be permitted to race.

Relations between France and Ford quickly became contentious. The first outburst of the coming battle of wills came just before the Christmas holidays when Ford executive, Leo Beebe, announced that Ford would not be able to field cars at either Riverside or Daytona since corporate competition plans for 1966 all revolved around use of the Cammer 427. High level negotiations between France and Ford produced some

concessions, and on Christmas Day, Big Bill announced that the Cammer would be viewed as an experimental engine (due to its non-regular production status) for 1966 and reviewed for competition in 1967. Ford, for its part, announced that it would continue to support stock car racing without interruption. Unfortunately for France, that seeming accord was undone by the superior performance turned in by Hemi teams at the 1966 Daytona 500.

Richard Petty shouted the Hemi's legal arrival at Daytona in 1966 with a hot lap around the 2.5-mile circuit of 175.163 miles per hour in a 405ci powered Belvedere. The twin qualifiers that preceded the 500 were an all-Hemi affair too, with Paul Goldsmith's Plymouth taking one race and Earl Baumer's sleek new "flatback" Charger the other. When the green flag fell on race day, Petty and Goldsmith traded the lead among

Richard Petty used a 426 Hemi engine to bludgeon the competition in 1964 at Daytona where he won just about everything in sight, including the 500 itself. Here the as-yet uncrowned "King" leads Paul Goldsmith, Marvin Panch, Dan Gurney, Darel Dieringer and Sal Toyella through turn four at the Big D. Author collection

Things were quite different for Pearson and his Cotton Owens Dodge in 1966. NASCAR legalized the Hemi again and Ford drivers conducted their own boycott of the series. As a result, Pearson's new flat back Charger was the car to beat for 1966. Not many drivers did, as things turned out. Daytona Speedway Archives

themselves for the first 30 odd laps, and by the end of the event, Hemi-powered cars had led all but 40 laps of the race. It was a humiliating defeat for Ford and one that folks in Dearborn decided to not take sitting down.

Five days after the Daytona 500, Ford announced that the 427 SOHC motor was now a regular production option. Confronted with that assertion from Ford's highest executives, France looked to the Automobile Competition Committee of the United States (ACCUS) (a body that France, incidentally, had no small amount of sway with) for an out. On April 6th ACCUS announced its approval of the 427 SOHC for stock car competition with one significant caveat: Cammer equipped race cars would have to compete with a handicap of nearly 500 pounds.

France and NASCAR adopted that ruling and announced that Cammer 427 would be eligible to compete in 119-inch wheelbase cars (read: the Galaxie line with the specified handicap). As a sop to Ford's tender sensibilities, the sanctioning body also simultaneously

announced that two four-barrels would be legal for use on all wedge-headed Ford racing engines. The Chrysler Hemi was limited to one four-barrel carb, but was legalized for use in 116-inch and 119-inch wheelbase cars on all tracks without the need for downsizing.

Unfortunately for France, Ford executives didn't find the new rules provisions to their liking. Ford immediately announced that it was pulling its teams out of three short track races that were next on the schedule. A few days later on Friday, April 15, Ford chief Henry Ford II announced that it was the beginning of a boycott of all NASCAR races. "We can't be competitive under these new rules," Ford said. "We are giving away too much to the Chryslers. And besides that, the safety factor in this is quite important. We couldn't keep wheels on the car at this weight." For the second season in a row, the Grand National stock car series became essentially a one manufacturer show—only this time it was Mopar drivers' turn to have things their own way on the high banks.

Jim Hurtubise (in a Norm Nelson Dodge) and David Pearson had already won an event at Atlanta and Hickory before the Fomoco walkout. Once Ford drivers were safely on the sidelines, Hemi car drivers won the next eight races in a row. In that number were high profile superspeedway triumphs at Darlington in the Rebel 400 (Richard Petty), and at Charlotte in the World 600 (scored by former Ford driver Marvin Panch in a Petty Plymouth).

As in 1965, track owners were more than a little unhappy with the string of single marque wins, and soon Bill France was receiving pressure to modify his stance. France was so desperate to have Ford and Chevrolet drivers in the starting line-up that he had his tech inspectors look the other way when car owners like Smokey Yunick and Junior Johnson took more than a few liberties with the rules book. That willful blindness eventually led to Smokey's allegedly 15/16 scale Chevelle and Johnson's Yellow Banana Galaxie. Though both of those radically rebodied race cars have become legends, their NASCAR permitted deviations away from "stock" still weren't enough to slow the Hemi movement of stock car wins.

Ultimately, Ford drivers returned to the series late in the 1966 season after NASCAR officials modified the rules book to permit Fomoco teams to run intermediate Fairlane and Comet cars that had been fitted with front chassis members borrowed from the 1965/1966 Galaxie line. Interestingly, that rules change was probably the first step towards the totally fabricated chassis that compete on the NASCAR tour today. Though Ford drivers still weren't allowed to run the SOHC 427 engine (which never ran a competitive lap in the NASCAR ranks as things turned out), their downsized intermediate race cars were more of a match for the Hemi-powered Plymouths and Dodges than the block Galaxies they had fielded at the beginning of the season. Darel Dieringer proved that point in spades when he drove a 427-wedge powered Comet to victory in the 1966 Southern 500.

While Fomoco drivers were able to score a few late season wins once they returned to the fray, by the time the rubber dust had settled after the last race of the year, Plymouth and Dodge drivers had won fully 34 of the 49 events contested in 1966. Dodge driver David Pearson came out on top in the seasonal points chase to win his first Grand National driving championship. The 15 wins and 26 top five finishes he turned in that year with his #6 Cotton Owens Dodge earned him $78,193.60 in purse money.

A King Is Crowned; The 1967 Season

When the year 1967 rolled around, it is fair to say that all in the Grand National garage area were hoping for a controversy-free season of NASCAR races. The two boycott years that led up to the 1967 season had been damaging for both the sport and the teams involved in it. All of the top teams and drivers were on hand for Daytona speedweeks 1967 and, at first, harmony prevailed. Mopar drivers were back in force with 426 Hemi-powered Plymouth Belvederes and Dodge Chargers. The cars were just as fast as before. Truth be known, the flat back Chargers were probably even better than before, since NASCAR had allowed Dodge teams to add a rear deck spoiler to aid aerodynamics (a first in the NASCAR ranks). Ford drivers were fast too, especially since the 1967 NASCAR rules book allowed them the use of two four-barrel carburetors and a set of decidedly non-production "Tunnel Port" cylinder heads. Though those castings carried a conventional wedge-shaped combustion chamber, they had been cast up with relocated intake ports so huge that special sealed tubes were needed to run push rods right through the middle of each intake runner (hence the name "Tunnel Port").

Curtis Turner was fastest during qualifying in his more or less "legal" Smokey Yunick prepped Chevelle. The race itself was primarily a battle between Tunnel Port- and Hemi-powered drivers, though, and both LeeRoy Yarbrough's Charger and Fred Lorenzen's Fairlane were fast. USAC star Mario Andretti turned out to be the fastest of all, however. At race's end it was his Tunnel Port-powered Holman & Moody prepped Fairlane that was parked in victory lane. And that fact made Mopar executives more than a little unhappy. Bob Roger was a particularly vocal critic of the non-production heads that had helped power Andretti's Ford to victory. Soon Chrysler executives were making noises about staging another boycott unless the new Ford heads were ruled illegal by the sanctioning body. When NASCAR stood fast behind its ruling that the heads were legal, Chrysler executives sent out the word to their team that they'd appreciate it if those teams would not run the March race in Atlanta as a protest. Unfortunately, there was much less unity among Plymouth and

Dodge drivers in 1967. Richard Petty said publicly that "We (Petty Engineering) race for a living. If they are having a race at Atlanta, we'll be there. In fact, we'll take two cars. If we get a notion, we'll take three cars." That statement pretty much spoke for the rest of the Hemi teams on the tour, too. And so, the threatened Chryco boycott of

Cotton Owens is one of the Grand National (now Winston Cup) series' legendary mechanics. He had a special touch with the 426 Hemi engine and the drivers who campaigned his #6 Dodges won many races as a direct result. Daytona Speedway Archives

1967 died aborning. As things turned out, Ford's new Tunnel Port heads proved to be no match for Chrysler's Hemi engine anyway.

Though Andretti had snared the Daytona 500 win for Ford, the next handful of races fell to Plymouth and Dodge drivers without much effort being expended. Cale Yarborough interrupted that string with a Tunnel Port Fairlane win at Atlanta, but Hemi drivers returned to dominance after the Atlanta 500 and won 20 of the next 25 events contested. Petty Engineering was the big winner in that string as both Richard Petty and team driver Jim Paschal turned in multiple wins. New factory driver Bobby Allison also added to that string of Hemi wins in a Cotton Owens prepped Charger.

In August, Richard Petty went on a tear that's likely to never be duplicated again. Starting with the Meyer Brothers Memorial on the 12th, Petty won the next ten consecutive races. In that number was the 1967 Southern 500 that he won handily, more than five laps ahead of new Holman & Moody driver David Pearson.

Petty's string of wins was broken by Buddy Baker in the National 500 at Charlotte, where Baker whipped the field in a Ray Fox built Hemi Charger. At season's end, Petty had won an incredible 27 events (of 48 starts) and scored 11 other top five finishes. Factoring in Jim Paschal's four wins for Petty Engineering brought that team's total to a stunning 31 for 48 total. Petty's performance won him both a second Grand National driving crown and the now familiar title as the "King of Stock Car Racing." Interestingly, when recently asked the secret of his phenomenal 1967 success, Petty was unable to put his finger on a reason besides lots of luck. Petty went on to say "We were running the same car we had in 1966. Had the same people working on it, same motors. Everything was just naturally a little better. We had another year of experience and we just had phenomenal luck. You run ten races in a row—and finish every lap for ten races in a row—it was quite a season, let alone win the cotton pickin' things. We weren't doing anything different. It was just one of those things." One of those things indeed.

As in 1966, the Hemi Plymouths that Petty drove to glory had all started out as regular production "Bodies in White" Belvederes that had been "bucked" on a UAW assembly line. After arrival in Randleman, North Carolina, the Petty Enterprises crew reinforced the chassis and added a four sidebar roll cage. Race strength torsion bars and "A" frames were added at the bow. A kidney pummeling set of parallel leaf springs and a corporate live axle fitted with floating hubs were mounted aft. Dual shocks were employed to govern each wheel's movement and 3x11-inch fully metallic drum brakes were mounted to scrub off speed. A single four-barrel Hemi was nestled under the Belvedere's stock front sheetmetal and it transferred power to the pavement through a corporate four-speed and a set of track specific gears. Petty kept rein over that 600+ horsepower drivetrain from a production bucket seat perch and with the help of the stock steering wheel and a Hurst Shifter. The car's final cosmetic silhouette was little changed from its assembly line configuration. In fact, save for the slightly flared wheelwells and the 1 1/2-inch rear deck spoiler that the rules book had started allowing in 1967, the car's sheetmetal was pretty much stock. Boxy stock, in fact. And the same was true for the Dodge Chargers that campaigned alongside Petty's #43 Plymouth during the 1967 season. It was just that boxiness that proved to be the two Chryco intermediates' undoing during the 1968 Grand National season.

1968 First Shots of the Aerowars Fired . . . Pictures at Eleven

If Dodge and Plymouth drivers had planned on reprising their "win everything in sight" roles for the 1968 season, they were quickly disabused of that notion during speedweeks at Daytona that year. Though nothing had happened during the off-season to stifle the high horsepower bellow of their 426 Hemi racing engines, there had been a significant change that would greatly affect the on-track fortunes of Plymouth and Dodge drivers during the 49 race 1968 series. That change was improved aerodynamics. Specifically, the greatly improved aerodynamics of the new for 1968 Ford Fairlane and Mercury Montego car lines. Whereas the 1967 iterations of both those intermediate body styles had been squat, sawed off and boxy in configuration, the new model year produced stretched out sleek bodies that featured an exaggerated fastback roofline which flowed unbroken from "A" pillars to the tip of the rear deck lid. Though the 1968 rules book still limited those cars to the same 427 Tunnel Port motors that had been used the season before, their greatly improved aerodynamics promised improved performance without the necessity of improved power production.

Dodge and Plymouth stylists had also been hard at work during the off-season and both the Satellite and Charger lines featured rounded and smoothed body panels that were easier on both the eye and the air than their 1967 counterparts had been. The new for 1968 Dodge Charger line was the most radically changed and seemed to be a sure bet for superspeedway wins. The car's new nose swept from the windshield forward to a slit-like grille that was surrounded by gently curving sheetmetal. The roofline at first glance was swoopy too and seemed to flow smoothly into the deck lid. Unfortunately, the car was not a true fastback as the "flying buttress" "C" pillars that were part of the design actually surrounded a fairly vertical back light. The sleek new nose also had some problems, since it featured a recessed grille sure to catch the superspeedway air just like an open parachute would.

Richard Petty earned the title "King of Stock Car Racing" in 1967 with the help of this Hemi-powered GTX. Petty dominated the series that season winning a grand total of 27 events along with the Grand National championship. Daytona Speedway Archives

Things were even bleaker aerodynamically for Plymouth drivers in 1968. Though their new Road Runners were rounded all over, they carried billboard upright grilles and a sedan style roofline that did not promise to be very efficient at air management.

Still and all, both Mopar chassis carried the potent and by now race-proven 426 Hemi engine. And that was certainly a force that Fomoco drivers had to reckon with. Or, at least, that's what Mopar drivers hoped.

South Carolina driver Cale Yarborough began giving Dodge and Plymouth drivers fits during qualifying for the Daytona 500 when he piloted his Wood brothers Mercury around the track at an average speed of 189.222 miles per hour. Though still relying on one of "last year's" 427 Tunnel Port engines for power, the sleek new sheetmetal that surrounded that #21 car had allowed Yarborough to up the qualifying ante at Daytona by nearly nine miles per hour.

Richard Petty clawed his way to the second

starting spot with a curiously vinyl top equipped Road Runner, but the rest of the top ten qualifiers were pretty much all of the Fomoco persuasion.

That's about how things stayed when the race got under way beneath overcast skies. It wasn't until lap 35 that Buddy Baker's Ray Fox Dodge made it to the front of the pack to lead a lap for Mopar, and that visit was only for one more circuit. Baker ultimately led but one more lap, and his three lap stint out in front, coupled with the one lap lead that Al Unser had posted in Cotton Owens Dodge, represented the only trips around the track led by anything other than a Ford or Mercury. Cale Yarborough's #21 Mercury and LeeRoy Yarbrough's #26 Cyclone spent the most time up front. Cale ultimately led his similarly named but unrelated Mercury rival across the stripe by a bare 1-second margin at the end of the 200 laps that made up the event. It was a humbling defeat for Dodge and Plymouth drivers.

Unfortunately, Mopar drivers didn't fare much better for the balance of the season. Ford and Mercury teams took the next three races after Daytona, and it wasn't until Richard Petty won a 100 miler at Hickory on April 7 that a Mopar car got to visit victory lane. Though NASCAR officials tried to even things out by permitting Mopar teams to run two four-barrel carbs at and after the Rebel 400, Ford and Mercury drivers went on to win 27 of the 49 races run in 1968 including the Rebel 400, the Atlanta 500, Carolina 500, Firecracker 400, Dixie 500 and Southern 500 events.

Buddy Baker did break the Fomoco flow with a big win in the World 600 (in a Ray Fox Charger). Chargin' Charlie Glotzbach made it a Dodge sweep of Charlotte Motor Speedway when he won the National 500 in a Cotton Owens Charger later in the year. And King Richard turned in one superspeedway win at Rockingham in the American 500 in October. But save for those three mile-or-more wins, 1968 was pretty much a blow-out for Fomoco's "Going Thing" and that was all due to aerodynamics.

CHAPTER THREE

1968: THE AEROWARS BEGIN IN EARNEST

As you might have guessed, Chryco executives were none too happy with the result of the 1969 NASCAR season. In just one short season, Plymouth and Dodge drivers had gone from winning almost every race on the tour to being nearly shut out at every superspeedway (and the sports pages that reported race results on Monday morning). It was, to say the least, an intolerable situation. And one that would have to change immediately.

As mentioned, the problem with the Charger's aerodynamics was twofold. The recessed grille that street Chargers carried trapped so much air at racing speeds that it created hundreds of pounds worth of lift. Since lift at the bow of the race car translates into understeer, Dodge drivers had a very hard time getting their cars to turn without backing out of the throttle. Not a good situation when your Fomoco rivals are able to negotiate the same corners with their throttle pedals flat on the floor.

Imagine this in your rearview mirror and you'll understand how intimidating a Dodge Daytona was for Ford and Mercury drivers in 1969. Dodge Daytonas look fast even when they're standing still.

The new Charger's back light caused more than a little consternation, too. Though the car's roofline appeared to be of a fastback design, the "C" pillars were actually hollowed-out to accommodate a nearly vertical back light. Air flowing over the roof at speed tended to become roiled over the hollowed out window recess and that created lift. Not nearly as much of that destabilizing force as the grille did, but more than was optimal for racing purposes.

With the Charger's aerodynamic peccadillos identified, Chrysler engineers set out upon a crash course to correct them in time for the 1969 season. Work got under way with a sketch that had been drawn by engineer John Pointer. The new design featured a grille insert that had been moved forward to a position flush with the front body work and then sealed to it to prevent the admission of any unwanted air. The Charger's rear lift problem was solved by fitting a sheetmetal plug over the hollowed-out "C" pillar area of the roofline. The new plug carried a smaller and flush-fitted back light and created a true fastback roofline. Engineers in Chryco's Special Vehicle Group quickly reproduced Pointer's sketch in clay and soon were testing a 3/8th scale replica of the proposed design in the wind tunnel at Wichita

When the new for 1968 Charger line proved to be aerodynamically challenged, Chryco engineers went back to the drawing board. The end result was the Charger 500. It was the first special body car purpose-built for use on the NASCAR tour. All told, just 392 street-going homologation versions of the 500 were built. That low production number marks cars like the one pictured here (which belongs to Central Florida's Dan Andrews) as some of the rarest built during the musclecar era.

State University. When those wild tunnel tests produced positive results, Dodge executives gave the green light for the production of the 500 street-going "homologation" versions that the NASCAR rules required for any special body style intended for use on the tour. Dodge's answer to the sleek new Fairlanes and Montego line was dubbed the Charger 500. It represented the first time that an American auto manufacturer had created an entirely new car line solely to compete in a form of factory-backed motorsports.

Street-going versions of the new 500 rolled off of the assembly line powered by either 440 wedge-headed single four barrel engines or 426 Hemi big blocks. A number of exterior color combinations were available as were a variety of interior appointments. In every instance, homologation Charger 500s carried the special grille and backlight treatment that had first been suggested by John Pointer's inspired sketch.

Bob Roger's Special Vehicles engineers were convinced they'd created a winner in the new

While street Charger 500s came with both 440 wedge and 426 Hemi engines for power, their racing counterparts relied exclusively on Hemi engines for motorvation.

Charger 500 variant and wasted little time in telling the world so. A press car was made available to motoring scribes at the Chrysler proving grounds as early as June of 1968 and a PR Charger 500 was on hand at Charlotte Motor Speedway for the National 500 in October. In addition to the favorable coverage those early outings received, the new aero-variant's fortunes were also given a boost by the sanctioning body's less than rigorous adherence to its own 500 unit minimum production requirement. Though the Dodge brass had promised that at least 500 street 500s would be built, records available today suggest that no more than 392 of the new NASCAR specials ever rolled off of the assembly line. Then, as now, the NASCAR rules book could become only an "advisory" document when the "good of racing" was involved.

While Dodge drivers had every reason to expect great things from the 1969 Grand National season, their Plymouth stablemates took little cheer in the coming of the new season. That's because their lot that year was to race the same old boxy body styles they'd campaigned the year before. Richard Petty was particularly peeved about that fact and began politicking for a Petty

When the NASCAR circus rolled into Daytona for Speedweeks 1969, there was a flock of aerodynamic Charger 500s in the procession. Bobby Allison's #22 Mario Rossi prepped Charger was in that number. **Author collection**

Blue Charger 500 to campaign in 1969. Unfortunately for Petty (and ultimately for Plymouth fans everywhere), the Chryco executives he talked to were more than a little short-sighted—and perhaps just a wee bit too confident of both themselves and Petty's Chryco allegiance. As it happens, Ford's racing tsar, Jacque Passino, had been courting Petty for some time. His plan was to make Petty a card-carrying member of Ford's Going Thing. When Petty's request for a new Charger 500 was summarily denied, he picked up the phone and dialed Passino's Dearborn number. A short time later, he signed a one-year contract as a Ford driver.

But it wasn't just money that persuaded Petty to jump ship and throw in his lot with Ford. In point of fact, it was aerodynamics. What Dodge drivers didn't know as they looked eagerly towards the 1969 season is that they wouldn't be the only drivers campaigning an all-new aero-variant during the next year.

Unbeknownst to them and the rest of the racing world, Ralph Moody and Ford stylist Larry Shinoda had been hard at work on a slicked-up version of the Fairlane fastback body. Moody's task was made easier by the fact that the Fairlane (and Montego) car line did not suffer from the same unwanted lift problems over the rear window that the standard Charger body did. So Moody concentrated his efforts solely on cleaning up the Fairlane's front end. Part of the program cooked up by Moody in the super secret back room at Holman & Moody's Charlotte complex was moving the Fairlane's normally recessed grille approximately six inches ahead of stock. Next, Moody grafted on a set of sheetmetal stampings that both narrowed and tapered the car's profile on their way towards mating with the moved-up grille. A special header panel was used to connect Moody's newly extended fenders just ahead of the stock hood. A new front bumper cut and welded to form a rudimentary air foil rounded out the new variant's design. Ford executives called the new car the Torino Talladega, after Bill France's then under construction superspeedway in Alabama. When wind tunnel tests provided positive results, Ford boss Bunkie Knudsen gave the green light for Talladega homologation. All told, 754 street Talladegas were built in time to satisfy NASCAR's production requirements. When Ford teams began rolling into the garage area for Daytona speedweeks 1969 they came packing long-nosed Talladegas. In that number was one particular Petty blue car that carried familiar #43 markings.

Pre-race preparations for the 500 got under way on a high note for Dodge drivers. That's because superspeedway specialist Buddy Baker drew first aerodynamic blood for Charger 500 drivers by snatching up the pole with a 188.901 miles per hour hot lap. David Pearson took some of the edge off of that triumph, when he tripped the clocks at 190.029 just a few days later, to become the fastest qualifier for the race. Pearson

When Charger 500s fell short of the mark, Dodge engineers returned to the drawing board in search of aerosuperiority. Their answer was to graft on a radical new beak and soaring rear deck spoiler to the basic 500 package. The end result was the Charger Daytona. Chargin' Charlie Glotzbach drove winged Daytonas for Ray Nichels during the aerowars. Glotzbach was a notorious lead-foot and he wasted little time tapping into the new aerocar's potential. During testing at the Chrysler proving grounds, for example, Glotzbach quickly had his winged car running in the 240 mile per hour range. Author collection

backed up that performance with a solid win in the first of the two traditional pre-500 qualifiers. Bobby Isaac scored the first Charger 500 (and ultimately only) superspeedway win just a few hours later when his K&K Insurance Charger 500 crossed the stripe first in the second qualifier.

Buddy Baker translated his pole starting berth into the lead for the first three laps of the 500 itself. Cale Yarborough claimed the top spot for Ford on lap four and Talladega drivers went on to lead 118 of the race's 200 laps including

the all-important final one. LeeRoy Yarbrough's Big T was first across the line and finished one car length ahead of Charlie Glotzbach's day-glo #6 Charger 500.

To say that Dodge drivers were disappointed by the results of the much-anticipated Daytona 500 is an understatement. Special Vehicle's engineer, Larry Rathgeb, was forced to admit that the Talladega "was superior in aerodynamics and in performance to the Charger 500." His colleague George Wallace added that "Overall,

Bobby Allison ranks as one of the greatest drivers in NASCAR history. In 1969 and 1970, he campaigned a flashy Dodge Daytona for Mario Rossi. With Allison at the helm, that car was powered by a full race 426ci Hemi engine. In 1971, Dick Brooks drove the same car in the Daytona 500 under the power of a 305ci small block engine. That race turned out to be the last event on the Grand National tour for a Chrysler winged car. Author collection

Dodge teams weren't any better off than they had been the season before." Fortunately, though Chrysler engineers like Rathgeb and Wallace were dejected after Daytona, they were far from being defeated. And that was a good thing, since Mopar racing fortunes were destined to get a whole lot worse that year before they improved. David Pearson snapped up wins at the next two short track races on the 1969 tour before Bobby Allison was able to win a trophy for Dodge at Bristol in the Southwestern 500. Joy from that short track win was short-

lived for the "Dodge Boys" however, because Fomoco teams showed up one week later packing a new double whammy at Atlanta.

Ford's desire to field a Hemi-headed race engine of its own was well known. It was at Atlanta in 1969 that Fomoco realized that goal, when the sanctioning body finally allowed the all-new Boss 429 Hemi to compete. Ford teams had actually arrived at Daytona with Boss '9s parked under the hoods of their long-nosed Talladegas, but when Bill France balked at the engine's homologation status (France asserted that the necessary 500 street-going Boss 429 Mustangs hadn't been built), Ford teams were forced to yank the new motors and replace them with tried and true 427 Tunnel Port wedges. France lifted his Boss '9 ban just before the Atlanta race, the second super-speedway event of note on the 1969 schedule. As if things weren't bad enough for Dodge and Plymouth drivers at that race, the Atlanta 500 was also the race that Mercury drivers got an aero-variant of their own to campaign. The car was called the Cyclone Spoiler II, and like its Talladega counterparts, the new Merc sported a stretched and drooped nose. Worse yet for Mopar drivers, the new Spoiler II's body work was actually one to two miles per hour faster than the Talladega.

Cale Yarborough drove that point home (literally) by handily winning the Atlanta 500 in his first outing in a Boss '9 powered Spoiler II. The balance of the 1969 season was characterized by a string of Charger 500 victories on short tracks (where the 426 Hemi seemed to produce more low end grunt than the new Ford motor) bracketed by a string of mile-or-more superspeedway wins all captured by the aerodynamically superior Talladega Fords and Spoiler II Mercurys. Fomoco wins at high-profile headline-generating races like the Rebel 400, the World 600, the Motor State 500, the Firecracker 400, the Dixie 500, the Yankee 600 and the Southern 500 served to cause Special Vehicles engineers to redouble their efforts to overcome the Fomoco aero advantage. Their solution was both innovative and radical. The end result was a pair of purpose built stock car racing intermediates that set the racing world on its ear.

The Wing's the Thing

Shortly after the debacle in Daytona, Dodge engineers had returned to the drawing board in search of even better aerodynamic performance. As with the Charger 500 project, early work on Dodge's answer to the Torino Talladega came straight from the pen of John Pointer. Working

Racing exploits of Dodge Daytona drivers were made possible by a homologation run of street-going cars like this one. Like their racer counterparts, those street cars all carried pointy beaks and soaring rear wings. The rear spoiler on a Dodge Daytona consisted of three elements: a horizontal cross bar shaped like an inverted airplane wing and two tear drop-shaped upright struts. Working in concert those alloy components created both down force and stability.

closely with Bob Marcell, Pointer cooked up an all-new version of the Charger body which sported a pointy beak and radical rear wing that soared several feet above the rear deck lid. The essential purpose of those added appendages was, of course, to further smooth the flow of air at racing speeds.

Dodge product planner Dale Reeker and Special Vehicle engineer Larry Rathgeb were enthusiastic about the sketches and passed them on to higher-ups for production approval. That final okay came from Dodge Veep and GM Bob McCurry. After scanning the artwork that Rathgeb and Reeker had presented, McCurry simply asked

Next
The nose on a Charger Daytona was designed to slice through the air like a hot knife through butter. Formed out of sheet-metal, the radical new beak created nearly 200 pounds of positive down force over the front wheels of a race car at superspeedway velocities.

Dodge Daytonas and Plymouth Superbirds represented the last word in both aerodynamics and factory commitment to motorsports competition. It's unlikely that we'll ever see the likes of them again.

if the new car would win races. An answer in the affirmative was quickly forthcoming. So, too, was McCurry's corporate blessing. The only fly in the ointment for the new project was the necessity of having the new car in ready-to-race trim by September 1969—the scheduled date of the very first Grand National stock car race at Alabama International Speedway (aka Talladega). The new track's inaugural race was sure to capture a lot of media attention and Dodge executives wanted to capitalize on that gathering of scribes by debuting the new stock car at the same time. That deadline left an impossibly short seven months to turn Pointer and Marcell's sketches into functional sheetmetal let alone to build the 500 homologation cars needed to satisfy the sanctioning body. So the race was on for Special Vehicles engineers.

The starting point for the project was a 1968 Charger chassis that had been built for use by Charlie Glotzbach in the Firecracker 400. That particular chassis just happened to be on hand since it had originally been built to bend the rules book a

bit via non-stock lowering (two inches both front and rear). When NASCAR tech inspectors caught on to the car's "cheated up" configuration, its active racing days were over. First work on the as-yet-unnamed car's new beak began in late January. Two different versions of Pointer's original design were mocked up in 3/8ths scale first and then wind tunnel tested back at Wichita State. That test data was then translated into a full-sized clay nose that had been grafted onto the snout of Glotzbach's old Charger for further testing in the Lockheed aircraft wind tunnel in Georgia.

While one team of engineers was busy working on the aero-variant's beak, yet another group was endeavoring to recreate Pointer's soaring rear wing in sheetmetal. Differing wing heights and configurations were tested. With time and testing it was decided to make the wing's horizontal cross member an inverted airfoil that was designed to produce positive downforce. Dodge aerodynamicist Gary Romberg played a large role in final wing configuration and his work ultimately led to shaping of the wing's uprights as airfoils, too. The final decision was just how far to position the horizontal wing section above the car's rear deck. Test heights of 6, 12 and 15 inches were tried. Ultimately, an elevation of 23 inches was settled on for no other reason than that height allowed the abbreviated trunk lid to open fully—an important consideration when you factor in the rules mandated fleet of street-going cars that would have to be built.

As with the design changes charted up for the new design's nose, Romberg's rear wing prototypes were first tested in 3/8ths scale and then transferred to the Glotzbach car for full-size wind tunnel work. In addition to the new wing and nose work, the aero-variant was ultimately fitted with two rear-facing air scoops that mounted atop the front fenders directly over the tires. Though swoopy looking and seemingly aerodynamic in nature, in truth, the new scoops were last-minute add-ons designed to provide more tire clearance when the suspension was fully compressed at racing speeds.

And in a way, suspension compression was just what the new race car was all about. Wind tunnel testing of the new beak and bustle showed that when those components were bolted onto the basic Charger 500 unit body, 200 tire shredding pounds of positive downforce were produced over the front wheels and 600+ (depending on wing angle) at the rear. Actual track testing

with a race spec car left Dodge drivers like Buddy Baker and Glotzbach smiling from ear to ear and boasting that they could navigate Daytona with just one hand on the steering wheel.

Dodge executives opted to name the new car after that very track, Bill France's Daytona International Speedway. The wraps were pulled off of the new Daytona in April of 1969 when the motoring press was treated to a mockup that had been hastily cobbled from fiberglass components and a Charger 500 chassis. A photo op with a race car

Bobby Isaac drove winged Daytonas for Harry Hyde and the K&K insurance team in 1969 and 1970. Isaac was one of the only factory team drivers to stick around for the boycotted inaugural Talladega 500. One of Isaac's cars is currently on display at the International Motorsports Hall of Fame in Talladega today.

mockup sporting an early version of the rear wing was also arranged for the press at the Chrysler proving grounds in Chelsea, Michigan.

The Charger Daytona's debut left motoring scribes in a hyperbolic frenzy—just the result that Dodge PR types were hoping for. Yet while the new radically winged car looked fast during photo ops, the question as to its actual race track performance remained unanswered. Side-by-side top speed tests were conducted with a race spec Daytona and an equally racey Charger 500 at Chelsea in July of 1969. Those results were mixed. The performance goal set for the new Daytona during development was a five mile per hour increase in top speed without the introduction of additional horsepower (as a rule of thumb, it takes about 15 extra horsepower to generate each additional

Buddy Baker drove a Daytona for Cotton Owens during the aerowars. He won the Southern 500 in 1970 in a day-glo #6 car just like this one. This particular Daytona is on display at the Joe Weatherly Museum in Darlington. Mike Slade

Cotton Owens was a master at setting up a race Hemi engine. In peak tune, Owens was able to coax in excess of 650 ponies out of an engine like this one. When coupled with the Dodge Daytona's aero-package, that grunt translated into near double ton super-speedway velocities.

mile per hour of top speed at tracks like Daytona and Talladega). While the new Daytona proved to be faster than the old 500, it was only just. But within a week of taking it to the track, Dodge drivers and engineers had pumped up the top speed to an impressive 205 miles per hour average around the five-mile Chrysler banked track. By the time Chelsea testing was completed, Glotzbach had pushed the envelope out to an incredible 243 miles per hour. Soon all involved with the project were looking forward to September and Talladega with undisguised glee.

Charger Daytona teams began arriving in Talladega, Alabama, during the third week of August 1969. They had no idea what to expect of the new track because it had been built as the longest (2.66 mile) and steepest (banking at Talladega is 33 degrees) on the Grand National tour. But they were anxious to find out how their new winged car would perform on a real race track under drafting conditions.

Their first few laps around the track were an unsettling experience. As it turned out, the track surface was both green and very rough. Ripples in the corners caused drivers to bounce up and down about three inches in cycles of 40 seconds or so. That had to be an unnerving experience for a driver who was hurtling around the track at more than 190 miles per hour and under the influence of more than 2Gs (times the weight of normal gravity).

When Ford teams arrived, their drivers began to complain of the same high speed oscillations that the Daytonas had experienced. As Chryco and Fomoco testing continued, a new and even more ominous problem reared its ugly head: tire blistering. Though both Goodyear and Firestone had been hard at work on a tire that was up to the task of taming Talladega, their best efforts had fallen short of the mark. Sustained high speed running quickly caused blistering on the treaded tires of the day, which if left unchecked, resulted in potentially catastrophic

Like all race spec Daytonas, the control cabin in Baker's #6 car was purposefully spartan. A single production-based bucket seat kept Buddy behind the tape-wrapped wheel and within easy reach of the Hurst floor shifter. Note the engine electronics package that was mounted in the passenger's floor well.

high speed blow-outs. While testing continued, both tire companies burned the midnight oil in search of a compound and configuration that would take the gaff. Treadless stock car tires were even tried for the very first time on the NASCAR circuit. But nothing seemed to work.

Though drivers in both of the aero-warring camps were concerned about track conditions, testing and qualifying continued unabated and track speeds began to climb as teams came closer to sorting their cars out. Charlie Glotzbach was consistently fast in both his own #99 Nichels Engineering Daytona and during test sessions with the Chrysler engineering #88 Mule that was not slated to actually run in the event. Glotzbach's earliest laps topped the 185 mark with ease. On September 9, 1969, Glotzbach took the test mule out for a spin and topped 199 miles per hour (199.987 miles per hour to be

Buddy Baker became the first driver to officially break the 200 mile per hour mark in a stock car in March of 1970. He used this Chryco R&D Daytona to turn in a 200.096 mile per hour lap at Talladega to set that record. Baker's record setter is still at Talladega on display in the International Motorsports Hall of Fame that's located there.

exact). Glotzbach returned to a garage area characterized by equal parts jubilation and consternation. The new all-time record top speed was certainly something to crow about (if you happened to be a Dodge driver, that is) but Glotzbach was also in more than a little hot water since he'd been ordered not to exceed 185 miles per hour due to safety concerns.

When pole qualifying day rolled around, Bobby Isaac turned out to be the fastest driver on the track and his #71 K&K Dodge tripped the lights at an official new NASCAR record speed of 199.386 miles per hour. Though Glotzbach was

trumped on pole day, he still copped fastest qualifier laurels with a lap of 199.466 in his Dow Chemicals Daytona. The scene seemed to be set for a winged car blow-out on race day. But when race day dawned over Talladega, Glotzbach and most of the other top flight drivers were nowhere to be found.

A driver boycott of the event led by Richard Petty and the Professional Driver's Association (PDA) had pretty much emptied out the garage area. When Bill France had been unable to satisfy the drivers' concerns about track conditions (with no quick fixes available, France had been reduced to suggesting that drivers "race" more slowly!), drivers honoring the PDA boycott pulled their cars out of A.I.M.S. on Saturday evening before the scheduled Sunday race. France was forced to crazy quilt a starting field for the featured 500 out of the few remaining Grand National cars in the garage area and a score of the Grand American Mustangs, Camaros and Javelins that had run an "undercard" event and were still at the track. In that number was the #99 car that Glotzbach had used to set the fastest lap. But when the green flag fell it was journeyman driver Richard Brickhouse who flat pedaled the car across the stripe.

Bobby Isaac was one of the few name drivers who had not caravaned out of the track with the PDA, and his #71 Daytona led the field for its first trip around the track. None of the long-nosed Talladegas and Spoiler IIs that the winged Daytonas had been designed to humble were in the field. And even if they had been, any real test of aerodynamic supremacy between the two breeds of factory aero-warriors would have been undone by the great number of mandatory tire check pit stops that France had imposed on the event to prevent high speed shunts from occurring. Brickhouse got to kiss the pretty girl in

Baker's R&D Daytona was powered by a NASCAR spec 426 Hemi. Note the roll cage assembly that extended under the hood of the #88 car and tied into its reinforced, torsion bar chassis.

Chryco built three different aero-cars to do battle with Fomoco and the forces of evil during the 1969 and 1970 seasons—the Charger 500, the Charger Daytona and the Superbird. Whether wearing street plumage or race car war paint, a Chryco winged car is a radical looking beast. Tim Wellborn owns the two low mileage street wings pictured here, while the K&K car is on display at the International Motorsports Hall of Fame in Talladega.

Talladega's victory lane, but when all was said and done, the first Grand National victory scored by a Chrysler winged car was a hollow one indeed.

The first real test of superspeedway superiority came four races later at Charlotte in the National 500. With high speed oscillations and tire blistering problems behind them, Fomoco and Dodge drivers had no excuses for not turning in their best performances on the banked 1.5-mile Charlotte Motor Speedway. Though many in the C.M.S. garage area (including more than a few Fomoco drivers) predicted that the new winged Dodges would sweep all of the top starting positions during qualifying, things didn't turn out as planned. Cale Yarborough proved to be the fastest of all during qualifying and his long-nosed Cyclone Spoiler II set a record-setting speed of 162.162 miles per hour (a speed fully six miles per hour faster than Charlie Glotzbach's pole speed of one year before). Richard Petty's #43 Talladega was just a tick slower and claimed the outside pole. All told, Fomoco drivers claimed the first four starting positions and the closest a Daytona

driver come to the front of the pack was Buddy Baker's fifth place berth. Fastest qualifier Yarborough said of the new winged cars after qualifying, "We (Fomoco drivers) had looked at those cars and wondered quite a bit about how we would stack up. It's a great feeling to win the pole under these circumstances."

While Fomoco drivers were feeling great, Dodge drivers like Baker, Isaac and Glotzbach could only grumble. As things turned out, events during the race did little to improve their mood. When the field was given its head, Donnie Allison charged to the lead in his poppy red Banjo Matthews prepped Talladega and held onto the top slot for 25 laps. Dodge drivers Dave Marcis, Buddy Baker and Bobby Allison led the field in turn for the next 86 circuits before handing the baton back to Fomoco forces. When the white flag was shown to the field, it was Donnie Allison who was out in front again. He not only won the race that day, his #27 Talladega also led the most laps (154 of 334). After the event, Allison said, "Once I went to the front early, I knew I could handle just about anyone if nothing happened." Things had definitely not gone as planned for Dodge drivers in the first legitimate head-to-head test of aerodynamic superiority with Talladega and Spoiler II drivers. After the race, blame for that fact was placed on tire failure and Daytona drivers complained that their winged cars became undriveably loose after just 10 or 15 laps on fresh tires.

The next mile-or-more superspeedway race on the 1969 schedule came at Rockingham in the American 500. Daytona drivers, still licking their wounds from their defeat at Charlotte, hoped for better results at the Rock. Qualifying results provided reason for optimism as Charlie Glotzbach outpaced all comers with a 136.972 miles per

hour circuit of the 1.07-mile superspeedway. Bobby Allison was only a fraction of a second slower in his #22 Mario Rossi prepped Daytona and started the race on the outside pole. LeeRoy Yarbrough's Talladega was the fastest of all, however, and his Talladega turned in a top speed of 137.732 miles per hour during post pole day practice sessions. Though Daytona drivers had hoped to turn in their first superspeedway defeat of the long-nosed Fomoco hoards, it was not to be at Rockingham. At race's end, LeeRoy Yarbrough was awarded his seventh superspeedway trophy of the 1969 season. Talladega teammate David Pearson came home in second in his #17 Big T one lap behind Yarbrough. Buddy Baker's #6 Daytona finished six more laps

Dodge Daytonas were designed with high banked, superspeedway action in mind. Here's a gaggle of those cars in their element at Daytona in 1970. Author collection

Plymouth executives were distraught after Richard Petty jumped ship for Ford in 1969. They resolved to get him back no matter what the cost. The Plymouth Superbird was a direct result of that endeavor. Petty protege Pete Hamilton drove the #40 Superbird for Petty Enterprises in 1970. Author collection

down to the winner to claim third place. Though Baker and his Daytona teammates had spent their first two superspeedway outings getting a good look at the rear bumper of a long-nosed Fomoco product, big track victory was waiting for them just around the corner.

The last race of the season was a 500-mile affair contested on the two-mile superspeedway located just outside College Station, Texas. The Texas 500, though now but a memory from a

race no longer on the circuit, is still a race worthy of remembrance since it was the setting for the first wing car win over Fomoco's long-nosed aero-cars on a superspeedway.

Buddy Baker claimed the pole position for the event with a speed of 176.284 miles per hour. David Pearson's Talladega was only a few hundredths off of that frantic pace, though and started the race alongside Baker's Daytona in the second spot. Baker translated the top starting spot into the lead of the most laps during the race and all told, Baker's day-glo #6 Dodge was out in front dominating 150 of 250 laps contested. In fact, Baker's third Grand National win seemed all but in the bag, until on lap 228 he ran smack dab into the back of James Hylton's Daytona—while the field was running under caution! It seems that Baker had taken his eyes off of the track as he passed pit road in order to flash his crew the victory sign. That victory was lost in the resulting crash. Chryco officials along pit road were visibly upset about Baker's misstep as that shunt at first appeared to end their last chance for a big track winged car win in 1969. Fortunately, when Baker bowed out, Bobby Isaac stepped up to provide that hoped-for win. He wheeled his orange Daytona across the stripe two full laps ahead of second place finisher David Pearson's Talladega.

When the first full season of the factory-backed aerowars was in the books, David Pearson and Fomoco had come out on top. Pearson's 11 wins and 42 top five finishes had secured his second straight (and third total) Grand National championship. Richard Petty's first year in a Ford was also a successful one, and his ten wins placed him second in the points chase. Overall, Ford drivers scored 26 Grand National wins with their Mercury stablemates adding four more for a total of 30 wins. Dodge drivers turned in 22 mostly short track wins, and their Plymouth compatriots recorded two. Things would be very different indeed the following season.

Major changes were taking place behind the scenes at both Chryco and Fomoco well before the end of the 1969 season. The big news at Plymouth was the production of an all-new winged warrior that was based on the Satellite/Road Runner chassis. As already reported, folks in the Mayflower division were more than a little stung by long-time Plymouth partisan Richard Petty's departure for Ford and an aerodynamic Talladega. Shortly after his defection, Plymouth "powers

When Richard Petty lost an engine during the early laps of the 1970 Daytona 500, it seemed that the new Plymouth Superbird's competition debut would be spoiled. Pete Hamilton saved the day by slipping past David Pearson's Talladega during the waning laps of the race to cross the stripe first. Author collection

that be" came to their senses and resolved to move heaven and earth to get the King of stock car racing back behind the wheel of a Road Runner. Since the source of Petty's unhappiness was the lack of a slippery new aero-car built by Plymouth, it was an absolute no brainer for executives in that division to order up a winged car of their own. Covert overtures were made to Petty in June of 1969. When he indicted a willingness to return to the fold if a suitable winged Plymouth was built, the commitment was made to build just such a car that very same month. As with the Daytona project of one-half season before, George Wallace, Gary Romberg, Larry Rathgeb and the Special Vehicles team were given the task of cooking up a winged Road Runner.

Though one might have thought that creating a winged Plymouth would be easy for the

A soaring rear wing was a part of both the Dodge Daytona and the Plymouth Superbird packages. Though slightly different in configuration, a Superbird's wing was just as effective at creating a down force as a Daytona's tail feathers were.

team of engineers who had come up with similar aero-plumage for the Dodge Charger line, it was actually a tougher task than it appeared. First, RPO Satellite fenders were not easily adaptable to the fitting of a Daytona styled nose cone. Second, a Satellite's rear window could not be modified in exactly the same way that a Charger 500/Daytona's back light had been. Finally, whereas race engineers had been pretty much left alone while designing the Dodge Daytona, office politics and rivalry between Special Vehicles engineers and styling studio types was allowed to gum up the works during design work on the new

winged Plymouth. Adding to these difficulties was the new NASCAR rule that now required not just 500 homologation cars to be built, but 1,000—or one car for half of the total number of Plymouth dealerships, whichever was greater.

Those problems notwithstanding, work on the new winged car did get under way. One of the first steps in that process was the installation of Dodge Coronet fenders on the front of a Satellite unit body. As it turned out, Dodge fenders were much more suitable for the addition of a pointed Daytona style nose than standard Plymouth sheet metal was. With fenders in place, a new air

A Plymouth Superbird's beak came to a higher point than a Dodge Daytona's did. As a result, a larger front spoiler was needed to help manage the air that confronted the car at superspeedway velocities. Ramo Stott drove this Superbird in both NASCAR and ARCA events in 1970. Miraculously, it survived its racing career in remarkably good shape.

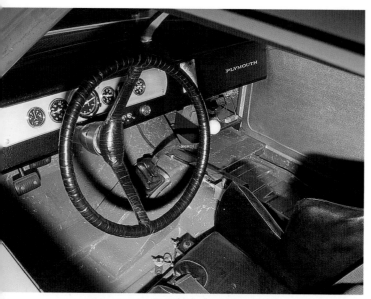

Race Hemis were part of the performance recipe for Plymouth drivers in 1970. This Petty Enterprises prepped mill sports a ram box single 4V intake and cowl induction fed induction system.

The cockpit of a race spec Superbird was an austere place. It contained little more than a production-based bucket seat and the basic (and non-power assisted) controls necessary to shepherd the car around a racing circuit with expedition. Note the essentially stock dash panel that was still part of the NASCAR program in 1970.

scything nose was formed from sheet steel and made to work in unison with the Dodge fender/Plymouth hood front clip.

Work at the rear of the car included the development of an air flow smoothing rear window plug that carried a smaller than stock backlight. A Daytona style three element wing was also part of the program. Interestingly, the wing devised for the new Plymouth was a bit different in size than the airfoil first developed for the Daytona.

As with Daytona R&D work, 3/8ths scale models of proposed designs were wind tunnel tested first, and then translated into full-sized components for further aerodynamic evaluation. By late summer 1969, Special Vehicles engineers were track testing a race car mockup of the new car and final negotiations were under way with Richard Petty regarding his return to Plymouth for 1970. Chryco executives called the new winged wonder the Plymouth Superbird, and scheduled its racing debut for the first race of the 1970 NASCAR season: the Motor Trend 500 at Riverside Raceway in California.

Over at Ford, work was also under way in preparation for the 1970 season during the early days of the 1969 series. Ford and Mercury car lines were scheduled to undergo a complete redesign for the upcoming model year and that necessitated the development of two all-new aero-variants of the Fairlane and Montego models. Famed stylist Larry Shinoda (designer of the split window Corvette, the Z-28 Camaro and the Boss 302 Mustang) was given the task of drawing up the aero-add-ons needed to make the new and larger 1970 Ford and Mercury intermediate bodies into superspeedway winners. The design Shinoda settled on featured a whole new front clip made up of a block-long hood and radically extended fenders that carried fared headlights. The overall look was quite similar to the nose on an early 240 Datsun Z car and the hoodline rose from just above pavement level in a smooth arc that terminated at the wind screen.

Research and development work on the new

aero-design had progressed to the point of naming the new Ford the Torino King Cobra (with the Mercury version referred to as the Super Spoiler II) by the middle of 1969. Fiberglass beaks were fitted to a number of street prototypes and at least one race chassis for evaluation. Early tests were conducted at Daytona with a Holman & Moody prepped car driven by Wood brothers Mercury driver Cale Yarborough. Preliminary results indicated that the new nose worked well. Too well, in fact. It struck the front tires to the tarmac so well that the rear tires lost traction. Ford engineers were hard at work on a new rear window, and

possibly even a Daytona style wing, when the bottom fell out of Ford motorsports funding.

The agent behind that change in Ford racing fortunes was Lee Iacocca. When Ford chief and inveterate racer Semon Bunkie Knudsen got the boot from Henry Ford II late in 1969, he was replaced by Lee Iacocca. Iacocca's vision of Ford's future focused on thrifty (read: boring) little commuter cars like the Pinto and Maverick and did not include factory-backed motorsports competition. One of his first acts as chief executive was to cut Fomoco racing budgets a withering 75 percent across the board. By the end of the 1971

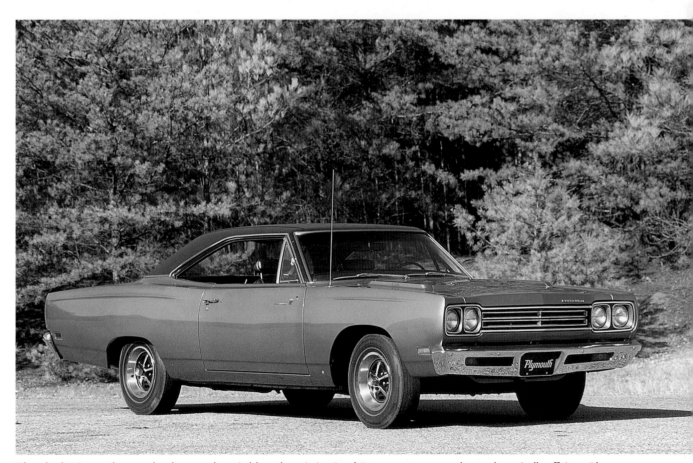

Though pleasing to the eye, the sheetmetal carried by a late sixties Road Runner was not exactly aerodynamically efficient. Plymouth engineers cured those deficiencies with an add-on beak and a radical rear deck wing.

Richard Petty was more than a little unhappy when he was told he'd have to campaign a boxy Plymouth Road Runner for the 1969 season. He was so unhappy, in fact, he jumped ship to run a Ford.

season, Ford was out of the racing business altogether. Iacocca's axe killed the Torino King Cobra project aborning and relegated Ford drivers to last year's Talladegas and Spoiler IIs for 1970. It also hamstrung the production of special racing high-performance parts and suspension components, and put corporate racing factory, Holman & Moody, on a bread-and-water diet. And so it was that Chrysler's record-shattering winged warriors won the second round of the factory-backed aerowars in 1970, well before the first race of that historic season was run.

1970 Winged Cars Take Flight

1970 was destined to be the high water mark of Chryco's factory-backed racing efforts, though few probably realized it at the time. The NASCAR season got under way with a road course race at Riverside that year and a whole new flock of winged Plymouths were on hand to show their tail feathers to the rest of the field. First and foremost in that number was King Richard Petty. Plymouth's all-new Superbird and the promise to make Petty Engineering the "Holman & Moody of the Mopar world" (read: Petty would pick up responsibility for the construction of all future Chryco stock car chassis) had brought the prodigal Plymouth son home. Not to be overlooked was the winged Plymouth fielded by former Ford partisan Dan Gurney's West Coast team. Signing Gurney for Trans-Am and NASCAR duty had been quite a coup for Plymouth executives and his Petty prepped 'Bird received more than a little ink. Gurney got the season off to a promising start with a pole winning lap around the challenging course at 112.060 miles per hour. Though A.J. Foyt went on to win the event in a Jack Bowsher Torino, great

things were waiting for Superbird drivers just down the NASCAR road.

When the NASCAR circus rolled into Daytona for speedweeks 1970 there were no fewer than 18 wing car teams in the van. Cale Yarborough proved that though poorly funded, Fomoco teams were far from defeated by cinching the pole position with a 194.015 qualifying lap. Yarborough turned that top speed potential into a win at the first of the twin qualifiers that precede the 500 each year. Charlie Glotzbach claimed top honors for Daytona drivers in the second Daytona "twin"

The car that persuaded King Richard to join Ford's Going Thing was a long-nosed Torino Talladega. Though Fomoco executives were happy he made the switch, Mopar fans were prostrate with grief. Author collection

While Dodge engineers were hard at work on the Charger 500 in late 1968, their Fomoco rivals were not resting on their laurels. Ralph Moody, Larry Shinoda and a team of Fomoco aerodynamicists pooled their talents to create the Torino Talladega. Though wingless, Talladegas (and their Mercury counterparts, the Cyclone Spoiler II) ultimately won the aerowars by scoring 23 super-speedway victories to Dodge and Plymouth's 13 during the 1969 and 1970 seasons.

to make it Fomoco 1, Mopar 1 heading into the 500 itself.

Yarborough outdistanced outside pole sitter Buddy Baker's Daytona as the pack headed into the first turn of lap one in the 500 and held that lead for the first few circuits. Glotzbach and a series of Daytona drivers took command next, and when King Richard blew an engine on lap seven, it looked as if the 500 would again be a Dodge and Fomoco show. But that's not how things turned out. At 192 laps into the race, new Petty protege, Pete Hamilton, slipped past David Pearson's H&M Talladega to claim the lead for Superbird. For the next seven laps he held off all challenges from Pearson and when the flag fell, a

Superbird had won its first superspeedway event. It was but a hint of the winged car dominance that would characterize the 1970 season.

Richard Petty won the very next superspeedway event on the schedule at Rockingham to make it two for two: Superbird. Bobby Allison beat Cale Yarborough by a mere 50 feet to win the Atlanta 500 in his gold and red #22 Daytona, and

Opposite page
Pete Hamilton's win in the 1970 Daytona 500 (among others) was made possible by the homologation run of street legal Superbirds required by the NASCAR rules book. Street 'Birds today remind Plymouth fans of the days when the factory spared no expense in achieving Grand National glory.

The 1970 Daytona 500 was the first time that all four of the special aero-cars developed by Fomoco and Chryco (the Talladega, the Spoiler II, the Daytona and the Superbird) went head to head in superspeedway trim. Pete Hamilton's #40 Superbird carried the day and won that new winged car's first competitive outing. Author collection

when the tour rolled around to Talladega, it was Pete Hamilton who proved his Daytona win was no fluke by trouncing the field in the first "legitimate" (read: non-boycotted) Grand National contest at A.I.M.S. Bobby Isaac came home second in the Alabama 500, more than a lap ahead of the closest Talladega driver, David Pearson.

Pearson scored the first long track win for Ford in the Rebel 400 at Darlington, and Donnie Allison proved there was still some life left in the beleaguered Fomoco forces by winning the World 600 in a Banjo Matthews prepped Talladega two weeks later. Cale Yarborough won again for Mercury at Michigan in the Motor State 400 on June 7th. Donnie Allison won the Firecracker 400 for Fomoco, too, but after that

Plymouth's intermediate body style was even worse aerodynamically than its Dodge stablemates in 1968. As a result, fastback Ford and Mercury drivers won most of the high profile superspeedway events that year. Richard Petty's boxy Satellite featured a novel vinyl roof in the 1968 Daytona 500. Though rumored to be an aerodynamic secret weapon, it didn't help much during the race. Daytona Speedway Archives

win, the rains came for Ford and Mercury drivers as Daytona and Superbird drivers won the next 19 straight events. In that number were long track wins at Dover, Atlanta and Trenton for Richard Petty; Talladega (again) for Pete Hamilton; and Darlington for Buddy Baker (in the prestigious Southern 500).

LeeRoy Yarbrough rallied for Mercury with a mile-or-more win in the National 500 at Charlotte and Cale Yarborough made it two superspeedway wins in a row for Spoiler IIs with a triumph at Rockingham in the American 500.

When the season ended, Daytona and Superbird drivers had won 38 of 47 races they contested.

Mercury's aerowarrior was the Cyclone Spoiler II. Like the Talladega it featured an extended nose. And like the Talladega it was fast—even without a soaring rear deck wing. All told, Spoiler IIs (like LeeRoy Yarbrough's #98 car) and Talladegas (like Richard Petty's #43 car) won 23 superspeedway events in 1969 and 1970 compared to just 13 for Chryco aero-cars. Author collection

Bobby Isaac came out on top in the season points chase and his 11 wins and 32 top five finishes earned his K&K Daytona team $199,600 and the Grand National title. It had been an incredible season of triumph for Chryco's winged warriors. Unfortunately, it was also to be the last full season for winged cars and their long-nosed Fomoco rivals. Though work was still under way at Chryco's Special Vehicles division on a second generation of aerowarriors, Big Bill France brought a halt to that endeavor when he announced that any special aerobodied car that chose to compete on the Grand National series in 1971 would be limited to no more than 305 cubic inches.

Dodge engineers smoothed out some of the Charger's wrinkles for 1969 by moving the grille forward to a flush position and filling in the recessed backlight tunnel. They called the resulting new car the Charger 500 for obvious reasons. Here 500 pilot Bobby Isaac (#71) leads Charlie Glotzbach (#6) (also in a Charger 500) at Daytona in the second of the 1969 Twin Qualifiers for the 500. Isaac went on to win that race—the only superspeedway victory scored by a Charger 500 that year. Daytona Speedway Archives

With the stroke of a pen, the factory-backed aerowars were over. The final tally of superspeedway wins reads as follows: 14 for Talladega; eight for Spoiler II; seven for Superbird; six for Daytona and one for Charger 500. Though the winged Dodges and Plymouths fell short of their Ford and Mercury counterparts in the total number of mile-or-more wins raked up during the two-year factory-backed aerowars, they (and their street-going stablemates) are by far the most fondly remembered Grand National cars of the era.

The Charger 500 project began with pencil sketches that were then recreated in 3/8ths scale for wind tunnel testing. Author collection

Fomoco fired the first shots of the aerowars in 1968 when it introduced two all-new fastback rooflined intermediates. When those two new models ran off and left the equally new for 1968 Charger, the Charger 500 was born. Author collection

CHAPTER FOUR

1971: BIG BILL FRANCE PLUCKS THE WINGED CARS' FEATHERS

The significantly increased speeds made possible by the factory-built aerowarriors produced during the 1969 and 1970 seasons had caused NASCAR officials more than a few sleepless nights. While qualifying speed in the 200 mile per hour range and headline stealing hot laps like Buddy Baker's March 24, 1970, circuit of Talladega at 200.096 miles per hour were great for gate receipts, they raised significant concerns about safety at NASCAR's highest levels. Tech inspectors first addressed those concerns in August of 1970 with the introduction of flow restricting, horsepower robbing restrictor plates that were designed to trim top speeds. While that first ever use of those flow inhibitors had reined in superspeedway velocities somewhat, the NASCAR dons were not satisfied with the result. Something more would have to be done. For 1971 NASCAR officials decided to get even more serious about speed reduction by limiting all special aerobody cars to no more than 305 cubic inches.

Though Chryco's wing cars automatically became obsolete (with one notable exception),

The 1971 Charger turned out to be quite a successful race car. It also made a handsome street mount. Sometimes referred to as a coke bottle bodied car, the Charger was sleek and stylish.

Dodge and Plymouth drivers' collective fortunes were still improved for the upcoming season by the November 1970 announcement that Ford Motor Company was getting out of racing all together.

With the flow of factory dollars stopped, it was a sure bet that Fomoco drivers would be much less of an impediment to Chryco Grand National wins. As a result, Dodge and Plymouth drivers could hardly be blamed for expecting great things from the 1971 season.

With the winged cars that had so dominated the series in 1970 now (for the most part) sitting on the sidelines, most Chryco drivers elected to field more or less stock bodied Chargers and Satellites for 1971. Ray Elder, for example, scored first blood for Chrysler with a win at the season opener at Riverside earned in a stock bodied 1970 Charger.

Pete Hamilton made the new for 1971 Satellite body a winner with a twin qualifier victory at Daytona the Thursday before the 500. Buddy Baker came close to earning that same honor for the new coke bottle bodied 1971 Charger with a close second place (to David Pearson's Holman & Moody Mercury) finish in the second traditional speedweeks 125 miler. A.J. Foyt claimed the pole position for the 500 in the #21 Wood brothers

273

Mercury, but Bobby Isaac was just a heartbeat slower and his performance earned the #71 K&K 1971 Charger the outside pole on race day.

As mentioned, NASCAR rules for 1971 limited winged cars to just 305 cubic inches of displacement. As a result, most Chryco drivers opted to go wingless for the 1971 500—but not all. The lone exception was the Mario Rossi prepped Dodge Daytona that showed up at Daytona with a race-ready small block under its stretched bonnet. Driver Dick Brooks qualified the lone wing car a very respectable eighth on the field. When the green flag fell, the first 60 laps or so were dominated by big block powered cars as expect-

ed. But on lap 60, Brooks made fans in the stands rise to their feet and cheer when he pulled his #22 Daytona out in front to take the lead. He led again on lap 64 and yet another time on lap 98. Unfortunately, shortly after that last stint at the front, Brooks became involved in a fender bending shunt that upset his Daytona's aerodynamics and never led again. He still turned in a very respectable seventh place finish. That impressive run turned out to be the last competitive laps turned in by a Chryco winged car on the NASCAR tour.

Richard Petty earned his third Daytona 500 win that February day in 1971, and he did it in a conventionally configured 1971 Satellite race car.

Street Chargers continued to pack a Hemi punch into the seventies and the regular production status of that engine helped keep 426s legal in the NASCAR garage area. This particular car is the last Hemi Charger ever built. It belongs to Alabama's Doug Wellborn.

That triumph turned out to be the first of 21 Grand National wins scored for Plymouth by Petty that year. Along the way to the end of the 47 event 1971 season, Petty made visits to victory lanes at Richmond, Rockingham, North Wilkesboro, Martinsville, Atlanta, Richmond and Dover. When not in the lead that year, Petty wasn't very far off the pace as he finished in the top five fully 38 times. Petty's performance earned him more than $351,000 and his third Grand National driving title. Dodge drivers Bobby Isaac, Buddy Baker (in the Petty Enterprises Charger) and Bobby Allison added eight more wins to the Mopar total for 1971.

Though Ford and Mercury drivers claimed high profile superspeedway wins in the Atlanta 500, the Winston 500, the World 600, the Motor State 400, the Mason Dixon 500, the Talladega 500, the National 500 and the Southern 500, 1971 was still an exceptional year on the NASCAR circuit for Dodge and Plymouth drivers.

Petty's office during his Charger days was anything but plush. A single bucket seat kept him in place in the twisties and within easy reach of the Hurst shifter and steering wheel. Note how much less complex the 1970's style roll cage was than the safety assembly found on a modern cup car.

Richard Petty switched to Dodge late in the 1972 season not long after picking up STP as his primary sponsor. For the next five seasons his STP Chargers were the class of the field.

Though limited to a minuscule (by Daytona standards) 2-inch rear deck spoiler, Petty's Charger was plenty aerodynamic.

Unfortunately, it was the last year of Chrysler factory sponsored stock car competition.

1972
The Second Last Season for Plymouth Wins

1971 had seen the beginning of a move away from the 426 Hemi engine that had won so much glory for Dodge and Plymouth drivers since 1964. It was not a step that most teams took voluntarily. On the contrary, their collective decisions to eschew Hemi-headed big blocks in favor of conventional wedge-headed 426s was a

move that had been coerced by the official NASCAR rules book. More specifically, by the late season rules change that saddled Hemi-headed engines with carburetors carrying throttle bores far smaller than the fuel mixers permitted for use on top of wedge-headed power plants. That same trend away from Hemi power continued into the 1972 season. All too soon, the low bellow of a full race 426 Hemi would be stilled forever.

Richard Petty and his Mopar compatriots went to war in 1972 at the helm of essentially the

Richard Petty recently called the Charger he raced from 1972 to 1977 his all-time favorite race car. And that should not come as a big surprise since they helped him win 37 Grand National events and two NASCAR championships. Author collection

same Satellites and Chargers they'd campaigned the year before. Like virtually every Dodge and Plymouth stocker built since 1964, those cars were built around unit body chassis and featured HD torsion bar suspension components at the bow and a leaf spring corporate 8 3/4-inch differential at the rear. Drum brakes were still part of the program in 1972 (though disc brakes would soon begin to show up in the Grand National garage area). Still incredibly stock by modern standards, the Mopar stock cars that qualified for competition in 1972 no longer carried full side glass or door trim like their sixties progenitors had. Treaded racing tires and production based rims had also become a thing of the past by 1972. And, as mentioned, big block

Richard Petty's last Mopar race car was this 1978 Dodge Magnum. Unfortunately it was an unlovely car with all of the aerodynamic aplomb of a brick. Petty never won a race in the car and in 1978 he decided to switch to GM. It was the end of an era for Mopar fans on the tour. Daytona Speedway Archives

By 1978 Dodge drivers like Robbins and Petty had switched to small block engines for power. Though Chryco racers had once relied on thunder Hemi engines for NASCAR work, by the late seventies, small block engines had made big inchers as extinct as the dodo bird.

Previous pages
Country and Western star Marty Robbins was one of several Dodge drivers who tried to make the Magnum body style work in stock car competition. Unfortunately he had no more success than the others. Mike Slade

racing engines were on the verge of extinction in both wedge and Hemi configuration.

As per usual, the 1972 season began with the road course Winston 500 at Riverside. Richard Petty captured that challenging event in convincing fashion in his still, all Petty Blue #43 Road Runner. A broken valve in the Daytona 500 one month later kept Petty from victory lane and mechanical gremlins also undid Dodge driver Bobby Isaac's pole winning performance during the race. A.J. Foyt's Wood brothers Cyclone was top dog at Daytona in 1972 and the best a Mopar driver could manage was the one lap down second place berth turned in by Charlie Glotzbach in a Cotton Owens built Charger.

Petty was back in victory lane one race later at Richmond, however, and Bobby Isaac scored the first 1972 win for Dodge at Rockingham in the Carolina 500 less than a month after that. Buddy Baker made superspeedway headlines at Charlotte in the World 600 where he led the last 30 laps of that grueling event in a Petty prepped #11 Dodge before taking the checkered flag

A number of Mopar stalwarts like Buddy Arrington continued to campaign Chryco race cars into the eighties. One of the last Mopar race cars to take to the high banks was this Chrysler Imperial that Arrington drove during the 1985 season. Mike Slade

In the late 1980s, a number of ARCA teams built and campaigned a gaggle of specially lengthened Chrysler LeBaron stock cars.

By the late eighties, NASCAR stock cars had lost all touch with their "stock" origins. Arrington's car carried a fabricated bucket seat, for example, and lacked just about any factory original "ergonomic" equipment.

When NASCAR officials scuttled plans for a winged version of the 1971 Road Runner, Richard Petty was forced to campaign a stock (more or less) bodied version of the car. Even so, he had a good season. Daytona Speedway Archives

Though the LeBarons were fast and showed promise, NASCAR officials refused to allow the cars to compete on the Winston Cup circuit.

first. Team owner Petty scored yet another superspeedway win in the Lone Star 500 at Texas World Speedway in June. Petty scored that win at the helm of a 1972 Plymouth, but his Mayflower division days had nearly come to an end. He'd shown up at Talladega in May with a Petty blue (and STP red) Dodge Charger. He'd also campaigned that same car in the World 600, the Mason Dixon 500 and the Motor State 400 before hopping back in his Plymouth. Petty was back in his Dodge for the Firecracker 400 and then switched back to the Road Runner at Bristol. He continued to alternate between the two marques for most of the rest of the season scoring Plymouth wins at Richmond, Martinsville and North Wilkesboro

and Dodge seconds at Daytona and Atlanta. In 1973 Petty switched exclusively to Dodge and his Plymouth days were over for good. Buddy Baker finished the season on a high note for Dodge fans by winning the season-closing Texas 500 in the K&K Charger.

Petty's eight Plymouth wins and 25 Plymouth and Dodge top five finishes earned him the 1972 Grand National crown. It turned out to be the last NASCAR championship ever won by a Plymouth driver. Sadly, there was to be but one more Plymouth Grand National victory—that being the win Dick Brooks scored in the 1973 Talladega 500. After that triumph, the light went out for Plymouth drivers on the Grand National (now Winston Cup) tour.

Richard Petty switched to Dodge Charger race cars late in 1972. He continued to campaign coke bottle bodied Dodges for the next five seasons. Today Petty remembers the cars as his favorite Grand National stock cars. Mike Slade

1973 Petty Does Dodge

In 1973 Petty shifted his automotive allegiance to Dodge full-time. That proved to be a wise move as over the next five seasons Petty used a series of sleek 426 wedge and 366ci small block motorvated coke bottle bodied Chargers to win 37 Grand National/Winston Cup events (including back-to-back Daytona 500s in 1973 & 1974) and two more national driving championships in 1974 and 1975.

When recently asked to name his all-time favorite NASCAR stock car, Petty quickly chose the Dodge Chargers he campaigned from 1972 to 1977. And it is easy to see why—they were incredible competition machines and they returned a series of legendary performances. In that number was the unforgettable 1976 Daytona finish that saw Petty and arch Fomoco rival David (the Silver Fox) Pearson hammer their way around the track on the last lap of the race, only

Dodge and Plymouth race cars continued to roll on torsion bar front suspension into the seventies. This is the setup used under Richard Petty's 1974 Charger, for example. Note the fabricated control arms and the drum brakes. Also note the wedge-headed 426 engine that Petty switched to when NASCAR's restrictor plate rule choked the life out of the 426 Hemi.

to crash within sight of the checkered flag. While Pearson claimed the win by limping his battered Wood brothers Mercury across the line ahead of Petty's equally savaged Charger, that finish still stands out in Mopar fans' memories today.

Though few realized it at the time, Neil Bonnet scored the final Dodge victory in NASCAR history in the last race of the 1977 season. The event in question was the then season-ending Los Angeles Times 500 held at the now defunct Ontario Motor Speedway (which, by the way, had been built as an exact replica of the Indianapolis Motor Speedway). After that victory, there was to be only darkness for Dodge drivers in stock car competition. Mopar partisans like Petty and Buddy Arrington tried to make a go of the Dodge Magnum body style that had to be used starting with the 1978 season, but that unlovely car was nothing less than an aerodynamic disaster. Another problem confronted by Mopar racers in the late seventies was the increasing difficulty they had finding suitable high-performance engine parts. Dodge and Plymouth had been out of the racing business for most of a decade by that time and the Chevrolet small block dominated aftermarket parts industry simply had not stepped in to fill the high performance void.

In 1978, Petty made one last attempt to build a competitive Mopar-based NASCAR car out of a Mirada body. But when testing proved that car to be no better than the bulky and unwieldy Magnum, Petty bit the bullet and switched to Chevrolet. When Petty roared beneath the green flag at the Champion Spark Plug 400 at Michigan on August 20, 1978, he was at the wheel of a Petty Blue Monte Carlo.

It was the end of an era. Though feisty independents like Buddy Arrington and Frank Warren would soldier on with Dodge and Chrysler based stockers into the eighties, the glory days of Mopar stock car racing were well and truly in the past. The official NASCAR records book today lists 190 all-time stock car wins for Plymouth drivers, 162 for the Dodge counterparts and 59 for Chrysler drivers.

Though the later eighties saw a number of ARCA teams build and campaign a handful of stretch bodied Chrysler Lebaron stock cars, NASCAR officials did not allow those cars to run in the Winston Cup series. Until and unless Chrysler once again builds a chassis that is adaptable to the modern Winston Cup rules book, there will be no more Mopar victories added to the impressive total scored between 1949 and 1977. And that is very sad indeed.

The ARCA LeBarons were all powered by high horsepower evolutions of the 360 small block engine. Note the restrictor plate that teams had to carry at Daytona.

Index